THE HISTORY OF THE ORDER OF THE BATH

Her Majesty The Queen
Sovereign of the Most Honourable Order of the Bath
wearing the Mantle and Insignia.

The History of
The Order of the Bath

and its Insignia

JAMES C. RISK

By appointment
to Her Majesty The Queen
Medallists

By appointment
to H.R.H. The Duke of Edinburgh
Medallists

Published by Spink & Son Ltd
King Street St James's London SW1
1972

Printed in England by Robert Stockwell Ltd London SE1 1YP

In Memory of
Gerald
7th Duke of Wellington K.G.,
1885—1972

CONTENTS

FOREWORD

by Sir Anthony Wagner, KCVO, D LITT

To those who know, or know of Mr Risk as a widely recognized authority on the insignia of Orders of Chivalry it will be no surprise that he, though a citizen of the United States, has been chosen to write about this Most Honourable Order. Even they, however, will, I think, be surprised at the depth and breadth of his approach to the general history of the Order, which contains lightness of touch with keen historical insight.

Few countries in the world today, from the monarchical to the communist, find it possible to do without Orders of Chivalry to reward outstanding services. In the development of the modern orders of merit from the military orders of the middle ages the Order of the Bath holds a key position and constitutes in its evolution a link between the oldest and the newest forms and attitudes. For this reason, among others, Mr Risk's exposition, clearer and more complete than previous accounts, of what took place in 1725, in 1815 and thereafter, has a general value going well beyond his special subject.

At the other pole from this institutional aspect is the intensely human side, to which Mr Risk does full justice, whether he is quoting Hornblower, 'Pinafore', or more prosaic sources. To me it is, therefore, a special pleasure, as Genealogist of the Order, and as successor to John Anstis, but for whom it would not exist, to commend his work to a far wider public than would probably expect to find interest in the subject.

Anthony Wagner

Garter King of Arms and
Genealogist of the Order of the Bath

College of Arms
Queen Victoria Street
London
1972

PREFACE

The casual acceptance of tradition as an important force in British life has frequently aroused the puzzled admiration of foreigners. While the realities behind the colourful forms that still cloak the functioning of many aspects of the modern welfare state may be hidden from most overseas visitors, they flock to these islands sure of being able to find some slight relief from the mundane drabness characterizing a large part of an overcrowded world. The way in which ancient usages have been modified to meet the present needs of society, however, is often as much of a mystery to the Queen's subjects as to their guests. The purpose of this monograph is to explain the historic origins and development of the Order of the Bath, one of the oldest, yet one of the most important modern honours available to the Crown for the reward of distinguished public service.

There is good ground for the conjecture that the name of the institution, the Bath, is perhaps better known abroad than at home. The full style and title of the Order does not translate easily. The foreigner finds difficulty in not associating it with some form of personal ablutions. Oddly enough, in the historical context, he is unwittingly not far wrong. The designation, 'Companion of the Bath', has been known to arouse broad humour of a kind unacceptable in Victorian England. When moved to consider the matter the Victorians reserved their strictures for other things. Writing in 1842, that distinguished historian, Sir Nicholas Harris Nicolas, asserted that 'the ancient Rites' from which its title was taken, were wholly inconsistent with the feelings and usages of the eighteenth century.

These objections are interesting because they do not seem to have occurred to anyone in the eighteenth century. On the contrary, 'the ancient Rites' to which he refers attracted no significant objections. By 1847, however, the observances and ceremonies enjoined by the original regulations governing the Order had certainly become unsuitable to the nineteenth century. They were abolished in new Statutes issued in that year. For a long time thereafter the Bath, the only general Order of merit in Britain, was used by the Crown to reward a wide variety of military and civil achievements. At the end of Queen Victoria's reign, and in her successors', after a number of other awards were established, the

Bath became increasingly restricted to a select group of high officials who served the Crown. As a result it has become much less familiar to the public than a century ago. The development leaves much to be desired because the Order of the Bath, a living record of the nation's historic past, deserves wider publicity than it has received in recent years.

ACKNOWLEDGEMENTS

Strictly speaking the genesis of this book can be traced back to the author's father who remained an unabashed Victorian all his life and a British Subject for most of it. Quite innocently he exposed his son to the same course of reading he had found so satisfactory as a boy, beginning with G. A. Henty and Captain Marryat, and leading to all of Sir Walter Scott, complete and undiluted. It is not surprising that a keen interest in history as a form of intellectual recreation developed very early. With Queen Victoria and Lord Roberts, closely followed by Nelson and Wellington, as the household gods, curiosity about the British Orders of Knighthood followed naturally. In a very real sense, then, the author can credit his father for having made the book possible.

That it has finally appeared must be laid to a more contemporary set of circumstances. Late in 1969 an in-depth search for early records of the Order came to the attention of Major General Peter B. Gillett, C.B., O.B.E., Secretary of the Central Chancery of the Orders of Knighthood and Deputy Secretary of the Bath. General Gillett, after consultation with the other officers of the Order, came forward with the suggestion that it might be possible to prepare a history, and the author committed himself to do so. What had long been a nebulous idea then received the encouragement required if it was to take a concrete form.

Only those who have written can understand the effort needed to bridge the gap between a plan and actually putting pen to paper. The author must confess that for many months he stared at the yawning chasm and could not bring himself to bridge it. He only plucked up courage enough to try after the subtly increasing pressure exerted by his friend Mr David Spink became too painful to bear any longer. Mr Spink was in a strong position because he had played an important part in the archeological aspects of the author's attempts to discover something about the Order's insignia. Here it should be explained that there was no general accumulation of Bath insignia in public or private hands available for reference. While fairly modern pieces are sufficiently familiar, it was first necessary to gather together enough of the older versions to enable much of the evidence presented by documents, memoirs and paintings to be read. In this field of endeavour Mr Spink extended a cooperation over a period of more than twenty years for which the author is grateful.

While Sir Anthony Wagner, K.C.V.O., Garter Principal King of Arms and Genealogist of the Bath, was kind enough to read and approve the manuscript, the opinions expressed are the author's own. He is further indebted to Sir Anthony for having pointed the way to the solution of several problems that had long puzzled him. Particular thanks must also be given to Professor John Hurd, of Dartmouth College, Hanover, New Hampshire, for many valuable suggestions and improvements. As the author's former tutor he has had more than sufficient experience with his old pupil's too original habits in the spelling and use of the English language.

Her Majesty the Queen has graciously permitted objects in her collection to be illustrated on Plates III, VII, X, XI, and XII. The author is also obligated to Her Majesty for having allowed him to quote relevant passages from documents in the Royal Archives at Windsor. Other persons and institutions providing illustrations of material in their possession are: The College of Arms, Plate I; The National Army Museum, Plate II; Lloyds of London, Plate VIII; the Central Chancery of the Orders of Knighthood, Plates IX, XX and XXVIII; and Mrs Leonard Boden, the Frontispiece. Their cooperation is deeply appreciated.

Acknowledgement is also made to the authors, publishers and copyright holders for permission to quote passages from the following books: Dr J. M. Beattie. *The English Court in the Reign of George I*. Cambridge, 1967; John Murray, publisher of *The Letters of Queen Victoria* and Lord Hardinge of Penshurst's, *Old Diplomacy*; The Macmillan Co., publishers of Anthony Brett-James', *General Graham-Lord Lynedoch* and Arthur Ponsonby's *Henry Ponsonby, Queen Victoria's Private Secretary*; Little, Brown and Co., American publisher of, *Lord Hornblower*; H.M.S.O., publishers of Sir Anthony Wagner's, *The Heralds of England*; and Hutchinson & Co., publishers of Sir Ronald Wingate's, *Lord Ismay—A Biography*.

The author is also greatly indebted to Mr R. C. Mackworth-Young, C.V.O., the Librarian at Windsor Castle, and Miss Jane Langton, M.V.O., of his staff, for many courtesies he has experienced at their hands over the years. Thanks are also due to H.M.S.O. for permission to use documents in the Public Record Office, to the staffs of the latter institution and the British Museum for their help.

No words are really adequate to express his indebtedness to the officials of the Central Chancery during the past decade. The late Brigadier Sir Ivan De la Bere, K.C.V.O., C.B., C.B.E., and Major General Sir Cyril Colquhoun, K.C.V.O., C.B., O.B.E., made every facility available. The pattern thus established has been continued by their successor, Major General Gillett and his staff, among whom Mr G. A. Harris, M.V.O., M.B.E. and Mr D. Morrison, M.V.O. have gone out of their way to respond to inquiries on many occasions. Major J. M. A. Tamplin, T.D. of The Army Museums Ogilby Trust, a well known authority on

Decorations and war medals, has also cheerfully given of his time to verify details which, although small in themselves, must always be correct.

No one can possibly prepare a manuscript for the press without substantial feminine support. The author counts himself fortunate in having been able to call on the editorial talents and technical skills of Mrs Emmeline Body, his former secretary and old friend, and Miss Carol Genser, his present secretary. Without their support, this book could never have been finished.

J. C. RISK

American Club,
London

LIST OF PLATES

CHAPTER I

Mr Walpole and Mr Anstis

On 11 May 1725, Letters Patent were passed under the Great Seal creating a new order of knighthood. In the formal phraseology characteristic of a legal document King George I made his purpose clear: 'Whereas Our Royal Predecessors . . . have, on occasion of certain august Solemnities, conferred, with great State . . . That Degree of Knighthood which hath been denominated The Knighthood of the Bath; We . . . hereby declare Our Royal Intention . . . to erect the same into a regular Military Order: And . . . by these Our Letters Patents do institute . . . a Military Order of Knighthood to be . . . called by the Name and Title of The Order of the Bath.'[1] The formality of the language, awkward to the twentieth century ear, cannot obscure the meaning. Nevertheless, the machinery of State as represented by the Great Seal is seldom put into motion, unless there are powerful forces at work behind the scenes. These forces must be sought in the motives and needs of men who exercised power at the end of the reign of George I. Fortunately in this instance the choice can easily be narrowed down to two. They were Robert Walpole, the Prime Minister, and John Anstis, Garter King of Arms.

Horace Walpole, that unrivalled observer of his times, has put posterity in his debt because he knew everybody, was gifted with a sardonic eye, and was careful to see that few secrets died with him. In his 'Reminiscences,' written in 1788, he said, 'The Revival of the Order of the Bath was a measure of Sir Robert Walpole, and was an artful bank of thirty-six Ribbands to supply a fund of favours in lieu of places. He meant to stave off the demands for Garters, and intended that the Red should be a step to the Blue; and accordingly took one of the former for himself.'[2] The comment has a sound of devastating frankness that was missing in the eighteenth century. The thought of anyone 'demanding' the Garter, or any other Honour, today is distasteful to say the least, and the reception such a demand would be likely to receive, frightening. The calmness with which the son lays bare his father's intentions is an excellent indication of how different the standards of Walpole's time were from our own. The difference must be placed in context if the motives which led to the founding of the Order of the Bath are to be understood.

In Constitutional terms, Robert Walpole was the first Prime Minister as the existence of the office within the framework of Cabinet government is now understood. When he entered politics, Ministers regarded themselves as personal servants of the Sovereign and each became a competitor for a share of the Royal favour on which the success of their careers depended. If one was able to monopolize a greater part of the King's confidence, the others devoted themselves to intriguing against him. This arrangement made for Ministerial instability and dangerous internal jealousies. Walpole's invention was a Ministry jointly responsible for a common policy and represented in communications with the Sovereign only by its head, the Prime Minister. Collective responsibility was guaranteed by a common party connection that, in the nature of things, had largely to be consistent.

One of the results of the new Walpole pattern was a change in the location of ultimate power from the Lords to the Commons. With this change came the development of Parliamentary management as an important technique if the Government were to maintain a working majority in the House. Here it can be pointed out that even though party membership was important, the Members still had personal interest which the Prime Minister had to take into consideration if he were to be sure of their support. According to Chesterfield, Walpole was the greatest master of the art of Parliamentary management who ever lived. Lord Hervey said that he knew the strengths and weaknesses of everybody he had to deal with. Even though the centre of gravity may have shifted to the Commons, the Lords were far from a negligible quantity in Walpole's day and for a long time thereafter. Many of the Peers controlled the choice of Members of the House who, often enough, were their heirs or close connections of their families. Parliamentary management was not required for the Commons alone.

In spite of these changes the Sovereign still exercised a power to be reckoned with in the eighteenth century. The Court remained the centre of the political world. The King was limited in that he had to choose Ministers who could command a majority in Parliament, but the choice remained his. Early in Walpole's career, the Ministers also had to be courtiers. The leader of an administration still had to command the King's personal confidence and approval. A strong following in Parliament depended on being able to supply places, pensions, and other marks of Royal favour to the government's supporters. In the judgment of one scholar, 'It was essential to the ministers not only to influence the King's will in order to make supporters happy; it was perhaps even more important that they make their influence visible—ministers who wanted to dominate and lead a stable administration had to make the attractive powers of government work in their favor.'[3]

These powers manifested themselves in various forms. Many Court posts, but not all, had salaries attached and the money, as well as the honour of being near the Royal person, made them sought after. Peerages and the Garter were the ultimate rewards but with only a limited availability. There was, in fact, a distinct shortage of both paying jobs and socially valuable favours just at the time when Walpole's new system made the demands heavier than ever before. It was this that his son Horace had in mind when he referred to the Bath as, 'an artful bank of thirty-six Ribbands to supply a fund of favours in lieu of places.' Here it is important to grasp one vitally important fact about the eighteenth-century world. There was nothing in the least reprehensible about the universal scramble for rewards made available by the attractive powers of government. It was a normal way of life for those who were, or could put themselves, within reach of those prizes. Every man had his price, but also he was convinced that he had a perfectly clear right to it. It is the form, not the substance, that we find astonishing and slightly unpalatable today. The same process in different ways and in different areas of endeavour still goes on.

While Walpole was achieving and consolidating his power politically, an equally shrewd and hard-driving man was engaged in an entirely different sphere of activity.[4] In 1718 John Anstis was finally appointed Garter King of Arms after almost twenty years of hard work, clever manoeuvering, and setbacks that might have discouraged anyone less determined. He almost lost out to Sir John Vanbrugh, whose talents are better displayed at Castle Howard and Blenheim than they would have been as Garter. Born in 1669 of a good Cornish family, Anstis went up to Oxford in 1685, was admitted to the Inner Temple in 1688, and in 1702 entered Parliament. During these years he became a close friend of the Earl Marshal and was able to render him a number of useful services.

Anstis' training and background eminently qualified him for the appointment as Garter King of Arms. His experience in Parliament gave him an intimate familiarity with the rules of the game as played in Westminster and St James's. He also became acquainted with many leading personalities. A man of great learning with a marked capacity for hard work, he had in addition a natural antiquarian bent that was to stand him in good stead. The post of Garter offered many opportunities, and he was determined to make the most of them. As soon as his position was secure, he set about making himself indispensable to Walpole and the Whig Ministry. His first move was to establish in the right quarters his reputation as a scholar. A petition to the King resulted in a warrant stating that, by the advice of the Knights of the Garter, His Majesty commanded John Anstis to publish the Register of the Order (called The Black Book) associated with a series of biographies of the Knights. This work occupied him for several years. When it finally appeared in two folio volumes published in 1724 at his own expense, it was received with acclaim. The original Latin text was reproduced, meticulously translated, and accompanied by a highly informed commentary that showed the author's mastery of the medieval records. There now could be no question about his scholarship or his authority. But success in any field of endeavour must be accompanied by a certain element of good luck. Anstis had been most fortunate in the timing of his two volumes.

In these same years Walpole reached the pinnacle of his earliest success. In 1721 he had been appointed First Lord of the Treasury and Chancellor of the Exchequer. His most dangerous political opponent, Carteret, banished to Ireland as Lord Lieutenant, could no longer cause him trouble. By 1725 Walpole was at last master of England's government and England was at peace. The country was prosperous and contented. The Prime Minister also basked in Royal favour. At last he had the time to pay attention to those domestic matters which included the ways and means of satisfying his supporters.

At a propitious moment Anstis took the second step in his campaign to strengthen his own position. He suggested the creation of a new Order based on the medieval Knighthood of the Bath, a ceremonial custom not practised since the Coronation of King Charles II sixty-four years earlier. Walpole welcomed the idea with enthusiasm. In the words of Sir Anthony Wagner, 'Its attraction for Walpole was the same which its dozens of successors, in the eighteenth, nineteenth, and twentieth centuries have since had for every government in the world, theocratic, imperial, monarchical, republican and revolutionary, that it enabled him to gratify valued adherents at no cost to himself.'[5] Appropriately enough, Garter King of Arms was instructed to draft the Statutes.

The entire career of John Anstis shows that he seldom made a significant move without adequate preparation in advance. His book on the Garter was swiftly followed by another he modestly called, 'Observations Introductory to an Historical Essay upon the Knighthood of the Bath', which appeared in 1725. The small octavo volume must have been ready for publication at the psychological moment. The book contained just about everything historical research has been able to discover about the medieval background of the subject. There was nothing slipshod about it. He evidently wrote with a purpose. Nevertheless he was careful to disguise his own part in the proceedings which already had, or were about to take place. Knowing as we do that the whole idea of the new institution was entirely his own, the opening words of the 'Historical Essay' have a subtle humour. He wrote, 'On occasion of a late report, that a new creation of Knights of the Bath, is intended, questions have been proposed to me from several persons, both in private conversation, and by letters, as well concerning the origin, the antiquity, the dignity of their degree, as concerning the ancient and solemn rites of conferring it.' He then goes on to say that inasmuch as, 'the nature of my office hath obliged me to make some curious and particular researches into the different ranks and distinctions of men in civil office'[6] he will undertake to satisfy his inquirers. The news was out, and Anstis wished to lay a sturdy foundation of facts that would permit him to counter certain criticisms he may well have expected. He conceived the best way to meet the objections of the ill disposed was to emphasize the traditional and antiquarian elements used to shape the framework within which he fitted the Order of the Bath.

It is curious that, in spite of the wealth of information available, the history of the Order has been the subject of an almost continual series of inaccuracies, particularly in recent times. The record is plain enough. It was founded by King George I on the advice of his Prime Minister. Yet even today we find the editors of a revered quasi-official publication supporting the myth that, 'The Order of the Bath was founded in 1399. After the time of Charles II it fell into decay, and remained obsolete until it was revived by George I in 1725.' They also perpetuate another strange error by attaching the post nominal letters K.B. to the names of those who received their Knighthood by the Bath before the existence of the Order. And they are not alone in a simple misunderstanding of the historical record, in spite of Ashmole having dealt with it briefly but explicitly in his history of the Garter, published in 1672. Anstis was no less explicit if not so brief. It is necessary, therefore, to make another attempt to lay the ghost of a medieval order that never existed, as well as throw some light on the background of the institution Anstis played such an important part in establishing.

The source of much of the basic error can be traced to an almost total failure to comprehend the meaning of the word 'Order'. In the nineteenth century the custom of referring to a man 'Wearing his Orders' showed a complete mis-understanding of the difference between the decorations being worn and the Order itself. In the United States where these matters will not be clear for perfectly understandable historical reasons, the situation is further confused by the employment of 'medal' to mean any form of decoration. Not many years ago a photograph of General Eisenhower displaying the insignia of the Orders conferred upon him by the Sovereigns of Great Britain and Denmark was cap-tioned, 'Eisenhower wearing his medals'. In essence an Order is not a physical object but a brotherhood of knights whose organization is regulated by specific Statutes, administered by designated officers, and continued by a regular system of appointment or election of new members who are provided with distinguish-ing insignia to wear as outward symbols of their fraternal association.

The great increase in the number of Orders in the twentieth century has created another semantic trap into which too many have fallen too easily. For centuries 'Order' was generally used to mean a rank or class in society, as the medieval records show beyond any chance of contradiction. For example, at Christmas in 1383, John de Holt and William de Burgh, Justices of the Common Pleas, were, 'received into the Order of Knighthood after the manner of Bannerets'.[7] Slightly more than one hundred years later on the eve of his Coronation, King Henry VIII, 'appointed twenty-six of the most able persons and of honourable blood—being no knights of this Realm, to take the Order of Knighthood and to repair unto the Tower—to be made Knights of the Bath.' In

1553 Queen Mary called certain of her subjects, 'to take the Order of Knight-hood'. In our day the word is seldom given its broader social significance. When encountered in the documentary sources, it is not familiar to the modern reader who promptly gives it a meaning it did not have.[8]

The ancient chivalric associations of the Bath are much older than the name. There is evidence that the custom of conferring knighthood with distinctive ceremonies can be traced back to Saxon times. These ceremonies slowly evolved, becoming partly secular and partly religious. The religious aspects were regarded as a fitting preparation for the candidates before they received the accolade. At least by the reign of King Edward III the ceremonies included bathing as symbolic of spiritual purification. It is not improbable that the religious connotations associated with the act of bathing had their remote origins in the sacrament of baptism administered in early Christian times by total immersion. The bath was followed by a vigil before the altar bearing the candidate's sword as an act of dedication to the ideals of chivalry. In addition, candidates were provided by the Sovereign with gifts of robes, bathing vessels and materials to cover them, beds and bedding. These practices were followed for many years without the knights so created being called Knights of the Bath. During this same period the rank of Knight Bachelor was conferred by means of a simple stroke of the sword unaccompanied by any special ceremonial forms. The difference seems to have been that the candidates who received their honours with the more solemn ritual were the sons of substantial families summoned for the occasion by writs to Sheriffs in much the same way these Crown officials were required to arrange for the election of members of Parliament.

We have to thank the French historian Froissart for the detailed description of making forty-six Knights at the coronation of King Henry IV in 1399. From this year those who received the honour with the full ceremonial began to be called Knights of the Bath. Ashmole explained, 'If the ceremonies and circumstances of their creation be well considered, it will appear that this King did not institute, but rather restored the ancient manner of making knights; and, consequently, that the Knights of the Bath are in truth no other than Knights Bachelors, that is to say such as are created with those ceremonies wherewith Knights Bachelors were formerly created by ecclesiastics; but some of them having been for a long time laid aside with us, were then brought again into use, and made peculiar to the Knights of the Bath.'[9] Froissart has been frequently given as the main source for the foundation of the Order by Henry IV, but Anstis says that his description of the events surrounding the Coronation proves nothing of the kind, and he is strongly supported by Ashmole. In the latter's words, 'At first view, this Degree looks like a peculiar and distinct Order of Knighthood . . . But it cannot be properly and justly so accounted, if we consider, that they have not either Statutes or Laws assigned to them nor are they in the case of vacancy supplied; (which are the essentials of distinct Orders) nor do they wear their robes beyond the time of that occasion upon which they were created—whereto also is to be considered that their number hath been uncertain and always at the pleasure of the king.'[10]

The year 1599 is important, however, because it marks the beginning of the practice of restricting this form of conferring the honour to Coronations and other great State, or Court, occasions. The candidates were all chosen from what is now frequently called the 'Establishment'. Anstis points out that the distinction was highly regarded because, 'The quality and dignity of the person to be distinguished is demonstrated from the different habit appropriated to him.'[11] In other words, part of the appeal lay in the handsome robes given by the Crown to the new Knights. There was also another factor important in medieval times as it still is in our own. 'Where the Sovereign—appears—in all the splendour and majesty of the State Royal—though all honour is derived from him—yet every dignity—receives additional lustre, as it is more expressive of royal favour from the circumstances of conferring it.'[12] The rituals associated with the degree of Knighthood of the Bath enhanced the attractions of the honour. Anstis the antiquarian valued these old customs and made a point of incorporating many of them into the Statutes he was empowered to draw in 1725. In short, 'He had the happy inspiration of reviving this ancient name and chivalric associations, but attaching it, as it never had been before, to an Order or company of Knights.'[13]

Any view of Anstis as a dry-as-dust scholar interested only in old parchments for their own sake would do him a gross injustice. He was an intensely alert and practical man of the world. For this reason reference must be made to another thread running through his 'Historical Essay' because it foreshadowed a controversy that was to bedevil the Order of the Bath well into Queen Victoria's reign. The question was simply one of money, and it may well have been his principal reason in the first place for publishing the book. After describing the creation of Knights at the Coronation of Henry IV, he introduces an aside about the fees they were obliged to pay to the Heralds. These he calls 'legal and customary'. He is quick to add that the King also ordered a sum of money to be distributed to the Heralds for their attendance 'at the solemnity of creating these Knights' and claims that his successors continued the practice.[14] By the time of the Coronation of Henry VI, a court official called the Sergeant of the Ewery, who also exercised the office of a Barber at the gate of the palace, was granted a Patent confirming his right to certain fees, including those that had to be paid him by new Knights of the Bath. In time the Knights were charged fees by the Heralds 'according to the precedence due their birth'. In a document describing the creation of Knights on 20 February 1546, the day King Edward VI was crowned, it was explained, 'Then because they were nominate of the Bath, and made with so great Royalty, they were commanded to pay the duties of money, every of them after their degrees and estates, double the sum of other knights.'[15] His survey of the source material bearing on the history of the Bath finally led Anstis to the categorical statement that payments of fees to the Heralds, and certain other officers, by newly appointed Knights, 'are grounded on immemorial usage, and as such, confirmed expressly by the Statute-Law of this realm, and frequently recited in the records, and by our historians'.[16] Not for nothing had he been admitted to the Inner Temple. When it is remembered that in his world the rewards of public life were distributed somewhat differently than they now are, his emphasis on the traditional legality of these fees takes on a new significance. It is not difficult to believe that he had prepared his defenses in advance against an anticipated attack.

CHAPTER II

Mr Anstis' New Order

The last creation of Knights of the Bath according to the old formulas took place at the Coronation of King Charles II in April 1661. In the typically Victorian view of Sir Nicholas Harris Nicolas, the institution was allowed to lapse because the ceremonies were not consistent with what he regarded as modern usages. Sir Nicolas may have been partly right. As early as January, 1604, just before Prince Charles (later Charles I) was made Duke of York one writer commented, 'The interim was entertained by making Knights of the Bath, which was three days work.'[1] In 1661, it was said of the Knights candidates that, 'each bathed himself, more or less, as he saw fit'.[2] The attitudes implied were a far cry from what might have been expected in the fourteenth century and before. Nevertheless, what amounts to a sudden discontinuance of an old and respected custom cannot be so easily explained. There was more to it than a disenchantment with formal bathing.

Even before 1399 the degree of Knighthood by the Bath, as it was often called, was only conferred on special occasions, and in times of peace and stability. Of these, the Coronation was the most important. Beginning with the reign of Henry VII, the succession to the Crown was a relatively stable process, even allowing for a slight disturbance after the death of Edward VI. When Charles II came into his own, the public mood, released from the oppressions of the Puritan interregnum, was positively ecstatic. The people were eager for the pageantry of Monarchy once again. But the years following the King's death ushered in a time of troubles. The early months of James II's reign were marred by the serious rebellions of Argyll in Scotland and Monmouth in England, followed by Lord Jeffreys' 'Bloody Assizes'. Public opinion turned against the King and his Coronation was not a joyful national occasion. The accession of William and Mary in 1688 was uneasy, to say the least of it. When Queen Anne succeeded William III in 1702, her attitude toward the Old Pretender was, and remained, ambivalent, as was that of many of her subjects. George I knew that many of the leading men who greeted his arrival in London in 1714 were secretly in correspondence with Jacobites in France. In 1715 he had to put down a French-supported invasion by the Pretender in Scotland. In short, for five successions in a row no man was sure who his master might be, and even the occupants of the throne did not always find their eminence comfortable, or certain. It was only by 1725 that the Hanoverian dynasty at last seemed firm, with the administration in Walpole's hands. In summary, the circumstances of the country and Crown after the death of Charles II did not make the employment of the stately rituals associated with the Bath seem appropriate or possible. Conversely, the stability and peace of the last years of George I made their reappearance on the national scene in a new guise all the more fitting.

The Statutes of the Most Honourable Military Order of the Bath, as it was now to be called, were dated 25 January 1725. There is some evidence that such was Walpole's anxiety to draw on his 'artful bank', that they were written quickly. In a letter to the Dean of Westminster in 1731, Anstis confessed. 'These Statutes were drawn with much hurry, and formed mostly upon the practise and plan of the Garter.'[3] With the Garter supplying the form, it was only necessary to introduce the ritual elements characteristic of the old Knighthood of the Bath. Anstis was ready. He simply adopted those used in 1413 at the Coronation of King Henry V. After describing them in his 'Historical Essay', he added, 'Every one of the particular rites here expressed perfectly agrees with the ceremonial now in use.'[4] The full medieval panoply was laid out. The candidates had to appear in the Prince's Chamber within the Palace of Westminster accompanied by two Esquires Governors, who had to be gentlemen, 'of blood and bearing coat Arms,' chosen with the Great Master's approval. There he was to take his bath, after which he was to be put to bed to prepare him for a long night's vigil in the chapel of Henry VII. Before proceeding there, he was to be clothed with a robe of russet. Immediately after his arrival in the sacred precincts he was fortified with wine and spices. The vigils were followed by a short nap from which he was awakened by the sounds of music. He was then clothed in the crimson robes of the Order. Proceeding into the presence of the Sovereign, the gilt spurs were fixed on his heels, he received the accolade and was invested with the badge. He was then ready for the Installation, again held in the Chapel of Henry VII. After he had taken a mighty oath to honour God, love the King, and defend widows and orphans, before he was seated in his stall the gold collar of the Order was to be put around his neck. The moment was solemnly impressive. Even though most of this ritual was never intended to be performed, it remained part of the Statutes until 1847. Only the form of Installation was practised until 1812, when it too was allowed to disappear for a century before being revived and slightly modified for use in our own day. How Anstis managed this little bit of legerdemain will shortly be made clear.[5]

The parts of the first Statutes most nearly resembling those of the Garter dealt with the arrangement of the Stalls, the number, precedence and Arms of the Knights, and their qualifications. They were officially Knights Companions and authorized to use the letters K.B. after their names. Modern writers quite often fall into the error of describing them as K.C.B.s. This form was first introduced in 1815 and refers only to the Knights Commanders made since that date. The robes, and the insignia which the Companions were enjoined constantly to wear, were furnished at the Sovereign's expense and will be dealt with in a later chapter. It will suffice to say here that the Collar was substantially the same as it is today, and that the Badge and Star bore a close resemblance to those now worn by the Civil Knights Grand Cross. The motto assigned, TRIA JUNCTA IN UNO, dates back no further than the reign of King James I and, with evident reference to the crowns at the centres of the last two devices, is probably symbolic of the union of the three crowns of England, France and Scotland in the person of that monarch.[6] The Esquires were also given a special rank and costume of their own. On the anniversary of the Coronation of George I, 20 October, the Companions were required to foregather in the Prince's Chamber, Westminster, and proceed from there, robed to the Chapel of Henry VII to hold Divine Service. Article XIX declared that the King would have a special regard for the Knights of the Bath, 'in preferring, advancing, and presenting them to be Companions of the Most Noble Order of the Garter'. Article XX about whether a Knight would resign the Bath upon receiving the Garter was entirely equivocal. He could resign, but if he did not wish to do so was directed to 'make the Protestations usual in cases of acceptance of another Order'.[7]

Throughout the eighteenth century the holding of more than one Order was most exceptional. It became the almost invariable practice for the members of the Thistle, the Bath, and later the St Patrick, to resign those Orders upon promotion to the Garter. In fact, the Red Ribband never was regarded as a 'step to the Blue', as Horace Walpole would have it. The case of his father must be regarded as a special one rather than the rule. The Prime Minister became Sir Robert Walpole K.B. in the original list of the new Knights but resigned to accept the Garter a year later in 1726. Between 1725 and 1815 a total of only eight Knights were promoted to the Garter, two of whom were Princes, the Dukes of Cumberland and York, the Uncle and second son of King George III. All resigned the Bath with the exception of the Royal Dukes. Degradation, or expulsion, from the order is also provided for when a Knight has been convicted of Heresy, High Treason, or had fled from the field of battle. The only two cases of expulsion took place in 1814 and 1816 and will be referred to later.

In the arrangements for the internal government of the Order Anstis demonstrated the potential cash value of his historical researches. The membership was to be restricted to thirty-six Knights Companions, presided over by a Great Master, who was a Knight Companion, and administered to by no less than seven Officers. These were the Dean of Westminster for the time being, as Dean of the Order, a Genealogist, King of Arms, Registrar, Secretary, Usher and Messenger, none of whom were members of the Order. All these gentlemen were to receive fees because it was intended that they should be supported by the Knights. The original Letters Patent stated that the amounts were to be established by the Statutes, under the Seal of the Order which would have the same force and effect as if they had been specified by the Letters under the Great Seal. Inasmuch as the problem of fees was to become controversial by the end of the century, and well into the next, it might be worth while to see just what it cost to be a Knight of the Bath in 1725. Upon his nomination each paid:

	£	s	d
To the Great Master	138	0	0
To the Dean	22	6	8
To the Genealogist	22	0	0
To the King of Arms	22	0	0
To the Registrar	22	0	0
To the Secretary	22	0	0
To the Usher	22	0	0
To the Messenger	18	13	4
For his Dispensation from the Ancient Rituals	26	13	4
For a Copy of the Statutes, and Seal thereto, 10s 6d (To the King of Arms)	7	3	10
For a Notice of his Election. (To the Secretary)	6	13	4

To this total must be added £16 17s 6d to the Secretary of State's Office and £148 16s 6d to the Officers of the Royal Household, included among whom was the Barber, singled out by Anstis in his 'Historical Essay' as having a traditional right to the perquisite. The total, then, came to £494 17s 10d. But this was not all. In Article XVIII of the Statutes annual payments for the support of the officers were expressed in marks and nobles, the medieval money of account and gold coinage. Translating these monetary terms into the more familiar sterling, the annual cost of the Officers to the Knights was:

	£	s	d			£	s	d
To the Genealogist	4	0	0			148	0	0
To the King of Arms	2	13	4			98	13	4
To the Registrar	2	13	4	× by 37 =		98	13	4
To the Secretary	2	13	4			98	13	4
To the Usher	2	13	4			98	13	4
To the Messenger	1	6	8			49	6	8

By each Knight Companion, per Annum £16 0 0

By all the Knights Companions per Annum £592 0 0

The additional £16 ran the initial price of the Red Ribband to £510 17s 10d, a very considerable sum when we remember that the purchasing power of the Pound in those days was infinitely greater than it now is.[8]

According to Nicolas, the Officers' takings were probably increased by annual contributions from the Sovereign. If so, the Genealogist received an additional £4, the next four in precedence £2 13s 4d and the lowly Usher £1 6s 8d, the same amounts contributed by the Knights. Thus the regular income for the group of six (the Dean was not included) came to a not uncomfortable £608 in addition to what they received upon each new appointment to the Order. It is estimated that John Duke of Montagu, the first Great Master, received £9,500 in the years between his appointment in 1725 and his death in 1749. This was a convenient sum in extras to help even a Duke live comfortably during the first half of the eighteenth century.[9] In short, Anstis made the new Order a sound investment. Montagu, a Knight of the Garter and firm supporter of Sir Robert's, was also Captain of the Band of Gentlemen Pensioners, a para-military organization useful for keeping the crowds who thronged to Court on Sundays under control. His annual salary was £1,000. As Master of the Great Wardrobe for life, he gained another £2,000.[10] Such a powerful man had his own dependents to placate. It was to this end that the Great Master of the Bath was empowered to name the Officers of the Order, except the Dean. Without attempting an exhaustive analysis of his appointments a brief reference to some of them will establish the pattern. Edward Montagu, a near relation, was made Secretary. Grey Longueville, a connection of the Earl of Sussex and his Secretary as Deputy Earl Marshal, became the first Bath King of Arms. But the highest paying and ranking post after the Dean, that of Genealogist, went to John Anstis, Jr, the seventeen-year-old son of the man who had drawn the Statutes. These arrangements were recognized as a legitimate part of the system of patronage that helped keep the machinery of government in operation. Anyone misguided enough to question them would have had to face the powerful opposition of the elder Anstis, the man who had made himself useful to Sir Robert Walpole.

Montagu's responsibilities as Great Master went far beyond the appointment of Officers. He was the first official of this rank to be attached to a British Order and was endowed with extensive powers by the Statutes. Primarily he was to serve as the Sovereign's deputy. In this capacity he could preside over all Chapters and ceremonies, confer Knighthood, invest and install the new Knights, and otherwise arrange for their reception into the Order. He prepared warrants for the issue of robes and insignia to the Companions, held the seal and was empowered to affix it to all relevant documents. In short, the post was no sinecure. As active manager of the Bath's affairs, John Duke of Montagu earned his fees. Article VI of the Statutes, in which the duties of the Great Master are laid down, contains a clause revealing the subtle hand of Anstis, and goes far to nullify many of the criticisms levelled at him a century and a half later. First it declares that Montagu was knighted by the Sovereign with the Sword of State and invested with the insignia. On the face of it, this would appear to indicate that he may have been one of the few men who received a double accolade inasmuch as he had been admitted to the Garter in 1718. At the same time he was not required to undergo the formal rites of preparation specified for the Knights Companions. Then, 'since it may be found necessary by reason of un-foreseen accidents, to Dispense with some of the particulars in the ancient ceremonials of it, We do hereby empower and authorize the Great Master to grant such dispensations.'[11] Montagu dispensed all the original Knights from the Medieval ceremonial, except that of Installation, and the precedent was followed as long as the original Statutes remained unmodified. Anstis never had the slightest intention that they should be performed. They were introduced into the Statutes as a pleasant reminder of traditional customs in ages past and never were allowed to inconvenience anyone.

The duties of the remaining Officers were, in some ways, nebulous because they had been designed to be sinecures. The Dean, of course, served as Prelate of the Order without that title. As the principal ecclesiastical official, he solemnized Divine Service within the Chapel of Henry VII and administered the oaths to the Companions upon their installations. He was the only person, not a Knight, who wore the same mantle as the Companions. In the absence of the Great Master he was empowered to summon the members to a Chapter for the transacting of the Order's business. The most important of the other officials soon found themselves at odds with the College of Heralds, of which Anstis, as Garter King of Arms, was the head. The Genealogist was required to keep a record of the Knights' and Esquires' pedigrees and Arms. When John Antis Jr eventually succeeded his father, the office was merged with that of Garter. The Heralds insisted that his duties infringed on their rights with the result that no attempt was made to carry out the provisions until many years later when the Heralds' claims were upheld.

There was only one flaw in this comfortable arrangement, and it worried Anstis. What His Grace of Montagu had given, His Grace could take away. In short, the Officers had no security of tenure and depended on the personal whim of the Great Master. Anstis' popularity with the Prime Minister soon enabled him to render the situation more stable. By a special addition to the Statutes dated 14 January 1726, the three most important of the patronage appointees were declared Heralds. The Genealogist became Blanc Coursier and Herald of Arms attached to the young Prince William, the principal Knight Companion. Bath King of Arms was given the additional dignity of Gloucester King of Arms, 'Principal Herald of the Parts of Wales', and precedence over all other Provincial Kings of Arms. The Usher, whose duty was to guard the Chapter Room when the Knights were sitting as a body, was made Brunswick Herald with all the rights and immunities of a Herald in England. These dignities had the added convenience of the usual small salary paid by the Treasury to the other Heralds. The attractiveness of the appointments lay neither in the added money nor in their decorative nature. The offices of King of Arms and Heralds were granted under the Great Seal. The incumbents had life tenure, their situations safe from the passing whims of any man.[12]

The Registrar was required to keep the records of the Order and transactions of the Chapters, although he does not ever appear to have done so. About 1750 this office was united with that of the Secretary and both conferred on the same person. In any case, the Secretary was required only to prepare draughts of all official documents passed under the Order's seal. The Messenger was charged with conveying the commands of the Great Master and other information to the Knights. More important, it was his responsibility to collect the payments made by each Knight for the support of the Officers. Each of them was supplied with a mantle, surcoat, and particular badge to be described later. This large corps of Officers, most of whom were underemployed, provides an excellent illustration of the patronage system as it existed in the eighteenth century. Like most other human institutions, however, it underwent signal changes over the years until finally Prince Albert adapted it to the needs of the nineteenth and twentieth century Order.[13]

The Letters Patent declared it to be the King's intention to create a 'Military Order of Knighthood'. It might, therefore, be of interest to consider whether the character of the original group of Knights qualified the Bath to be called a Military Order at this time. The Letters and the Statutes differ slightly in describing the composition of the membership. The former document specified the Sovereign, Great Master, and 36 Knights, and in the latter we find the body is to be composed of the Sovereign, a Prince of the Blood Royal, Great Master, and 35 Knights. In the event 35 Knights were appointed in addition to the infant Prince William, later Duke of Cumberland of Culloden fame, and Montagu. The name of a (generally) senior member of the Royal Family has adorned the Order as Principal Knight from the beginning and the custom is still maintained. Nicolas points out that of the original 35 Knights, 14 were Peers, 3 were Peers' heirs and 5 younger sons. Of the whole group no fewer than 30 were members of the existing Parliament, including the Speaker. Beyond this his figures are slightly suspect. A scrutiny of the entire list discloses even more information about its makeup. Here it must be remembered that some of the Companions can be classified under several different headings so that a breakdown of their activities seems to show more than 35 which was not the case. With this in mind, the following table is revealing:

House of Commons	14
The Walpole Family, including the Prime Minister	3
Royal Household or holding sinecures	11
Diplomats	4

Naval and Military, including the Colonel of the 2nd Foot Guards	3
Irish Peers	2
Country Gentlemen with Court Appointments	2

No matter how the original Knights are classified, however, it is clear that the Order as it finally emerged was far from being a military organization. Sir Robert Walpole used it almost solely for his political purposes, as has been indicated earlier. With the passage of time the pattern was to change radically. Nevertheless, the Order did unexpectedly acquire a military facade in these years and one potentially involving a further call on the Knights' purses. An additional Statute dated 20 April 1727, declared that if a European war denuded the country of troops and the homeland was threatened by foreign invasion or domestic rebellion, each Knight would be required to provide, equip, and pay 4 men-at-arms for a period of not more than 42 days in any one year. The body could be required to serve in any part of the Kingdom and was to be captained by the Great Master. How much this regulation was inspired by alarms and excursions abroad and how much by the Duke of Montagu's well known overwhelming passion for any kind of a military command that would entitle him to wear a handsome uniform is open to question. In the event, the Knights were never called upon to supply the men-at-arms.

On 27 May twenty-eight of the newly appointed Companions were knighted by the King and invested with their ribbands and badges, in the Royal Closet at St. James's. Of the absentees, the Duke of Richmond was recovering from smallpox and Lord Glenorchy was abroad. The two Irish Peers, the Earl of Inchiquin and Viscount Tyrconnel, refused to attend because of a dispute about their precedence with the other Peers. They were received by the King and knighted the next day. The occasion was the cause of a domestic disturbance with the College of Heralds concerning the division of some of the fees. The Heralds finally concluded that their presence at the ceremony should be regarded as a personal service to the Knights and that only those who actually had been in attendance were entitled to a share of the money.[14]

The first Installation was held with great splendour in Henry VII's Chapel on Thursday, 17 June, following. The Great Master officiated, conducting each Companion to his stall where he put the Collar over his shoulders and handed him a copy of the Statutes. When all was over and the Knights were filing out the great West Door of the Abbey, they encountered the Sovereign's Master Cook, a burly aproned man armed with a massive chopping knife, who solemnly warned them that if they betrayed their oath, it would be his duty to hack off their spurs. The antiquarian touch was certainly dear to Anstis' heart. Fortunately for posterity when Canaletto was at work in England a few years later he recorded the procession in a fine painting, which now hangs in the Dean's residence within the Abbey precincts.

After a short respite the entire company then repaired to the Court of Requests in the Palace of Westminster where they were served a sumptuous meal. In the eighteenth century, it should be remembered, dinner was usually taken in the middle of the afternoon, a barbarous custom in what was otherwise an age of elegance. The Dean sat next to the junior Knight, the Officers at a table facing the Knights, but the Officers of Arms were relegated to the passage leading from the House of Lords to the Jerusalem Chamber. The Esquires were provided for in the Painted Chamber. In 1730 John Pine published a handsome folio volume celebrating the occasion with a verbal description of the great day, illustrated with a splendid series of engraved plates taken from watercolour drawings prepared for the purpose by Joseph Highmore. The originals are now in the Anglesey Abbey collection of the late Lord Fairhaven. He also gives us the details of the dinner menu. Many of the dishes have a somewhat modern sound. The Knights had an ample choice of lobsters, salmon, crawfish, turkey, chicken, wild fowl, veal cutlets, lamb, Westphalia ham, salad, fruit, lemonade and ice cream. They could also partake of dishes less familiar to our ears like patty of pigeons, veal papiettes, turkey pouts, potage craviz and compotes of green gooseberries or green apricots. What liquid refreshment was provided besides lemonade is, unfortunately, not recorded. At nine o'clock the same night everyone went to the Opera House in the Haymarket for a 'splendid collation'. Afterwards over seven hundred of the 'Nobility and Gentry of both sexes' were entertained with a Ball. Pine assures us that, 'the whole was conducted with such regularity and magnificence that it may be justly esteemed for its elegance and grandeur, the politest entertainment hitherto known.'[14] It should be added that all the eating, drinking, and polite entertainment was paid for by the Knights, and a pretty penny it cost them. But the Order of the Bath was fairly launched on what was to be a distinguished career.

CHAPTER III

The Order in the Eighteenth Century

From the circumstances attending its creation the Bath, as conceived by Anstis and used by Sir Robert Walpole, had little in common with what it has since become. Nevertheless, the institution quite naturally conformed to the customs of an age when the honours of the Crown were dispensed according to principles different from those now prevailing. The exercise of political and administrative power on all levels was largely confined to men of property. The heads of the great landed families monopolized the more important or decorative posts in the State and parcelled out the lesser ones among their relations, friends or dependents. Honours flowed to men because of who they were rather than because of what they had done. The now familiar concept of a reward for individual achievement evolved very slowly and did not reach full growth for a century. But, in spite of having begun as another manifestation of the age of privilege, the Bath belied its origins and evolved into something different with surprising speed. It became, in fact, the first British award for merit before the century was out.

The Order does not seem to have been afflicted with any of those growing pains familiar to later periods. The breezes of public opinion did not blow strongly in 1725 and there was no popular press. Some thanks are probably due to Anstis for giving the new brotherhood of Knights a facade of antiquity and thus circumventing the native dislike of anything new. There were, of course, some who were not enthusiastic for a variety of not very important reasons. One of these was Philip Dormer, Lord Stanhope, soon to be fourth Earl of Chesterfield, a member of Walpole's team. He found it difficult to run easily in harness with the Prime Minister on the box. Hopefully Sir Robert offered him one of the new ribbands, only to be rebuffed. Then he offered it to William, Stanhope's younger brother, who cheerfully accepted, much to his Lordship's disgust. About this time a massive Welsh Baronet, Sir William Morgan of Tredegar, also one of the original K.B.s, suffered a humiliating experience. While engaged in his lawful activities about London, he was rudely deprived of his Badge. An agile thief simply pulled it off the sash which, as was then the custom, he wore daily. The world was not yet familiar with the pen Stanhope was later to wield as Lord Chesterfield. On a level somewhat below his best he produced a set of doggerel verses using Sir William's mishap as an excuse to satirize both the Bath and Walpole. The following selection provides a sufficient illustration:

> Hear, all you friends to knighthood,
> A tale will raise your wonder,
>   How caitiff vile
>   By basest wile
> An hardy knight did plunder.
>
> Oh! had you seen our hero!
> No knight could e'er look bigger,
>   Unless his size
>   My song belies,
> Than Morgan of Tredegar.
>
> A ribbon graced his shoulder,
> A star shone on his breast, sir,
>   With smart toupee,
>   *Fort bien poudrè,*
> And cockade on his crest, sir.
>
> This ribbon held a bauble,
> Which his kind stars decreed him,
>   With which he'd play
>   Both night and day—
> 'Twould do you good to see him.
>
> Tho' I a bauble call it,
> It must not thus be slighted;
>   'Twas one of the toys
>   Bob gave his boys
> When first the chits were knighted.
>
> Learn hence, ye courtly lordlings,
> Who hear this fatal story,
>   On how slight strings
>   Depend those things
> Whereon ye hang your glory.[1]

The Prime Minister was incensed, particularly by the reference to, 'one of the toys Bob gave his boys', and deprived the author of his well paid post as Captain of the Gentlemen Pensioners. Stanhope affected to be relieved by no longer having to attend the House. It took him a number of years and much hard labour before he was readmitted to official grace and emerged as an Ambassador and Knight of the Garter. When he left the Government his brother, William Stanhope, went with him. Horace Walpole wrote, 'Sir William, going afterwards into opposition, affected to lay aside his ribband, as despising it, but hearing the other knights would resent that contempt, re-assumed it.'[2] This comment is most instructive on several grounds. It shows how political the Order was considered during the first years. Sir William's response to the pressure of his brother Knights indicates that, nevertheless, the honour was highly respected by the members. The reference to his reassuming the insignia is another reminder that it was usual in those days for the Star and Badge to be worn as part of the daily apparel.

The Sovereign Founder, George I, died in 1727, and was succeeded by his son as King George II. The Coronation the next year was distinguished by an odd contretemps in the Abbey. Stephan Martin Leake, then Lancaster Herald and later to be Garter King of Arms, recorded the event. The Royal Procession was already in motion with the King about to make his entrance when, 'The Judges refused to take the places assigned to them, because the Knights of the Bath were to sit above them, though the Order in Council had done it with a Salve Jure to their rights; It was done they said by Anstis in favour of his darling Order; but when I urged the Order in Council to them, and that whilst they were disputing his Majesty and all the Procession were stopt, they sat down grumbling.'[3] One would gather from this that the Judges were not happy about the Knights of the Bath. It is certain that Anstis enjoyed something less than the full approval of the members of the College of Heralds who were still smarting under heraldic privileges granted to the Officers of the Order.

No Knights were made for the Coronation although two vacancies existed by the promotion of the Prime Minister and the Duke of Richmond to the Garter. Sir Robert was either not in a hurry to fill the vacancies, or may have had difficulty in finding suitable candidates when accepting the Bath involved the appointees in such heavy personal expenses. It was not until January 1732 that four of the places were filled, all of them by Members of Parliament. No additions were made for another decade until 1742 when Thomas Robinson, later Lord Grantham, was nominated for his diplomatic success in arranging peace between Hungary and Prussia. Then in 1743 the signs of an entirely different pattern began to emerge. On 12 June of that year the victory of Dettingen took place, the last occasion when a British King appeared on the field of battle. This success was commemorated by Handel with a stirring military *Te Deum*, and by the appointment of one General and three Lieutenant Generals to the Order. One of the three was to become Field Marshal Lord Ligonier and live to a ripe old age. Although an Irish Peer and four more M.P.s were admitted the next year, the Order more and more frequently began to be restricted to men noted for their naval, military, or diplomatic achievements rather than political services rendered to the Government. With the accession of King George III in 1760 the process of change was speeded up.

In the course of these years several new practices slowly became commonplace in the administration of the Bath. The customary accolade and Investiture at the hands of the Sovereign or the Great Master had to be modified for various reasons. For one thing, John Duke of Montagu died in 1749, and his post as chief executive officer and Sovereign's Deputy for the affairs of the Bath was not filled, largely because there was no subject mighty enough to justify the perquisites and patronage he had enjoyed. The Governments of the time preferred to benefit from whatever these might have been worth themselves without such a Ducal intermediary. The Officers were chosen from among their own supporters and appointed by Treasury Warrant. In 1767, Prince Frederick, the second son of George III, was made a K.B. at the early age of four. He also had the interesting position and emoluments of Bishop of Osnabruck in Hanover until as late as 1803, although he is better known as Duke of York, the title he received in 1784. This Prince officiated at four Installations of the Bath and has generally been considered Acting Great Master until his death in 1827. But an Acting Great Master was a poor substitute for the powerful office once filled by Montagu, and some arrangements had to be made for investing the new Knights. The trouble was that many of the candidates were not within easy reach of St. James's. The problem was solved by authorizing an appropriate official or foreign Sovereign to confer the Order on the King's behalf, often with curious results.

Among the more remarkable of these deputies was the Nabob of the Carnatic, who invested Rear Admiral John Lindsay near Madras in 1771. The spectacle of a Moslem Prince bestowing so obviously Christian an honour surprised many people. Under less exotic conditions, Major General Jeffrey Amherst, Commander-in-Chief in North America, had been invested on Staten Island by the Governor of New York ten years before. This was the first, but not the last time that the ensigns of the Bath were delivered in America. Sir William Howe, then in command of the British forces, also received them in New York in 1777 from his brother, Admiral Lord Howe. The ceremonies accompanying these affairs presumably added distinction to each occasion, as was only suitable. But Sir Guy Carleton, commanding in Canada, was particularly unfortunate in this respect. He was sent the ornaments of the Bath in a plain packet, accompanied by a Royal Warrant authorizing him to invest himself. Such a prosaic document must have made receiving the Order almost indistinguishable from a regular morning's routine of dressing for the day. Others were luckier. In contrast, Robert Gunning, Esq, Envoy to Russia, was given it by Catherine the Great in St. Petersburg on 9 July 1773. After dubbing him with a handsome diamond-hilted sword the Empress put the ribband and badge over his right shoulder. Then she, 'took the sword from the table and delivering it to Sir Robert Gunning, Her Imperial Majesty most graciously condescended to do him the honour of desiring him to wear the sword with which he had been Knighted'.[4]

It was the Installation that was by far the most splendid ritual. In accordance with the precedent established by the Garter, a Stall was made available to each Knight in Henry VII's Chapel, above which his banner, helmet, crest, and sword were to be suspended. Until he took formal possession of it he was not authorized to wear the Collar or the Star, and was not qualified to attend Chapters. Throughout the century these regulations were regarded very seriously. Unless dispensed from participating in the ceremony by Royal Warrant signed by the Sovereign, he was not considered to be properly a member of the Order. In cases of unavoidable absence overseas, it was customary for a Knight-elect to designate a Proxy to take his place. In all, eleven Installations were held between 1725 and 1812. They were conducted with great solemnity. An open procession of the Knights from the Palace of Westminster to the Abbey and back gave the public a much greater opportunity to enjoy such spectacles than in the twentieth century when they are largely celebrated within the Abbey itself. In fact, apart from a Coronation, the Bath Installations were among the few Royal occasions to take place in London during these years. Each one, attended by the Royal Family and the Diplomatic Corps, gave Londoners a chance to participate in that pageantry of the monarchy they have always appreciated. The custom lapsed for a century for reasons that will be discussed in the next chapter.

The external manifestations of membership were certainly impressive and must have added to each Knight's consequence. Now that the Order approaches its two hundred and fiftieth year in a world that questions most values except the material, it may be appropriate to ask whether such rites could have had any real meaning for the participants. The answer, bound to be subjective to some extent, is not easy to frame. Oddly enough, there is a detail in a modern 'Biographical Study' of a well known British naval figure that does seem to catch the essence of the matter. For this reason it will be introduced into the narrative. Presumably the Installation of 1812 provides the setting. 'The chapel stall of carved oak on which Sir Horatio Hornblower was sitting was most uncomfortable, and the sermon which the Dean of Westminster was preaching was deadly dull. . . . This was the price he had to pay for having a ribbon and star to wear, for being a Knight of the Most Honourable Order of the Bath; as he was known to be on sick-leave in England—and fully convalescent—he could not possibly evade attendance at this, the most important ceremonial of the Order. Certainly the chapel looked effective enough, the dull sunshine which made its way through the windows being reflected and multiplied into a soul-stirring glow by the Knights' crimson mantles and flashing orders. There was at least this to be said for the pomp and vanity: it was certainly beautiful in a strange effective way, even without regard to the historical associations. Maybe the stall on which he sat had in earlier years caused the same discomfort to Hawke or Anson. . . . The important-looking person over there, with a silver-gilt crown on his head and velvet tabard embroidered in the royal arms, was merely Bath King-at-Arms—some well connected fellow who had this well paid sinecure . . . And there were soldiers, generals and colonels, with whose faces he was unfamiliar. But elsewhere in the chapel there were men with whom he was proud to share the brotherhood of the Order—Lord St. Vincent, huge and grim, the man who took his fleet down into the heart of a Spanish squadron twice its strength; Duncan who had destroyed the Dutch navy at Camperdown. . . . There was something pleasant and heartwarming in being the member of the same chivalrous Order as men like these—ridiculous but true . . . Hornblower felt a surge of patriotic emotion within him; his spirit soared, and then he incontinently began to analyse this wave of emotion and to wonder how much of it was due to the romantic beauty of his surroundings.'[5] The reader should recognize that Hornblower's fears about the validity of his feelings are reflections of our own age, not his. His response to the environment is, nevertheless, one that many members of the Order, irrespective of their grade, who have attended a similar service during the present reign may very well have experienced privately although they might be uncomfortable if called upon to admit it.

The passing reference to Bath King of Arms in the previous quotation is accurate because the Officers of the Order, even though no longer appointed by a Great Master, were still placidly collecting their fees, but not giving much in return for the money by modern standards at least. It should not be overlooked that being decorative on ceremonial occasions was part of their duty. Because the work was pleasant does not mean that it was less useful within its limitations. In 1794, however, there was a sudden eruption of activity on the part of one of them. The Heralds had always objected to that Statute which empowered the Genealogist to enter pedigrees and coats of arms in the books of the Order on the grounds that their rights would be infringed by the process. Actually they never were faced with a direct challenge on the issue until George Nayler became York Herald and Genealogist in 1794. Nayler was another of the Anstis breed and not the man to overlook what could be a fair opportunity. He claimed his rights from Garter King of Arms according to the eighteenth clause of the Statutes, provided a set of handsome books of his own to enter the pedigrees, and then intercepted each new K.B. before he could reach his colleagues in the College of Arms. In 1795 he obtained a Warrant from the Duke of York listing the fees he could claim for this service, and in 1799 asked the Secretary of State for the Home Department to authorize him to make entries of pedigrees and Arms for all members of the Order from 1725. The College was aroused to defend its rights. After the matter was referred to the law officers of the Crown, the difference was settled by a devious compromise in an additional Statute made in 1804. The rights of the Heralds were confirmed. The Genealogist was empowered to keep a record of the members' achievements in a special register and to collect the fees allowed him by the Duke of York in 1795, but only if he received the heraldic evidence through the College.[6] There the matter rested for the time being. The Knights, as usual, had to bear the expense of the operation.

During the last quarter of the century there was a remarkable exhibition of the working of the Constitution on the highest level, in which the Bath played a conspicuous role. After the fall of Lord North's Ministry in 1782 the Whigs enjoyed a short spell of power. Charles James Fox went to the Foreign Office. The news of the death of General Sir Eyre Coote, K.B., in India reached London in 1783. Fox wished to give the vacant ribband to Mr Beilby Thompson, a Yorkshire magnate who was his close friend and an M.P. of influence who supported the Government. After consulting two of his colleagues, Fox went to the King to inform him it was the Ministry's wish that Thompson take Sir Eyre's place in the Order. King George III seems to have said very little about the matter but to have left the Foreign Secretary under the impression that he approved the selection. The ensuing embarrassments are best described in the words of a contemporary observer.

"Without waiting, therefore, for any more implicit declaration from the King on the subject, as prudence seemed to dictate, Fox informed Mr Thompson of his having received the Royal assent; and added, that the Investiture would take place at the next Levee. Directions were accordingly issued to Norroy King of Arms and the proper Officers belonging to the Heralds' College, to attend at St. James's for the purpose. The circumstance being publicly known, Mr Thompson was felicitated by anticipation, on the Honour destined for him; but the sequel proved that Fox had either miscalculated or misunderstood the whole transaction. On the day fixed His Majesty went to St. James's at the usual hour, to prepare for the Levee. After he had finished dressing, he sent out the Groom of the Bedchamber in waiting, as was his frequent custom, to bring him information relative to the number of persons who were arrived. The Gentleman returning, acquainted the King, that besides a great crowd come to attend the Levee, the Officers of the Bath stood without, ready for the Investiture. With some surprise marked in his countenance, the King asked, what Investiture he meant. To this question he replied, not without hesitation, that he understood it was intended to confer the Order of the Bath on Mr Beilby Thompson, who was attending there in person for that express purpose. His Majesty made no answer; and immediately afterwards, the Duke of Portland entering, went into the Closet. In the course of his audience, the King observed to him, that no official account having as yet been received from India of Sir Eyre Coote's death, however authentic the information of that event transmitted from Madras might prove; and his Ribband, together with the other Insignia of the Order, not having been hitherto delivered back to himself, he apprehended it was informal to fill up the vacancy till those points were previously ascertained and executed. The Duke, taken by surprise, after attempting respectfully to bring His Majesty to another way of thinking, withdrew; and finding Mr Fox in the next room, communicated to him this most unexpected and mortifying piece of information. The Secretary, equally astonished as well as chagrined, instantly went in, when a long conversation took place between him and the Sovereign. In its progress, Fox stated, that having some days preceding laid the business before His Majesty, and conceiving that he had obtained his Royal approbation and consent to confer on Mr Thompson the vacant Red Ribband, it had been so signified to that Gentleman, who, together with the proper Officers, were then waiting without in readiness for the Ceremony. He added, that in point of fact, no possible doubt could be entertained of Sir Eyre Coote's death; and that a disappointment, after the preparations and publicity of the affair, could not fail to be attended with very unpleasant consequences to the Administration, in the general opinion. To all these arguments and expostulations the King, after alleging his own reasons, remained inflexible. Fox, therefore, quitting the Closet, returned to his Colleagues, various of whom, assembled in the outer room, were waiting under considerable anxiety, and imparted to them the unsuccessful result of his audience. No little confusion ensued among them. Mr Thompson, apprised of the mortifying fact, returned home. The Officers of the Bath, ordered to withdraw, were acquainted that the Ceremony expected would not take place that day. Every person present formed his own comments or conjectures respecting the scene which had just passed under his eyes, and the old Courtiers did not fail to draw inference from it highly adverse to the duration of the Ministers. It was obvious that the King, who felt no disposition to oblige them, had got possession of the advantage ground in the contest; whereas Fox had acted with some degree of precipitation, in presuming upon an assent, rather implied or assumed than unequivocally expressed.[7]"

This example of how a Ministry could not control the prerogatives of the Crown in face of the Sovereign's opposition makes interesting reading today. The incident also marked one of the last times that the Bath in its original form was used in a purely partisan context. Merit was waiting off-stage for a cue that would not be long in coming.

The transformation of the Order that began in the 1740's was not caused by a deliberate change of policy on the part of the Governments of the day. The Statutes remained the same, apart from a few minor additions to take care of particular cases. It came about as a result of the pressure of international events. Beginning with the American War in the 1770's, Britain was to have few intervals of peace until 1815. The rising generation of leaders in war and diplomacy deserved recognition for their achievements that submerged the claims of party loyalty and the requirements of Parliamentary management. Probably one of the most historically significant appointments ever to be made was that of Captain John Jervis in 1782. Commanding H.M.S. *Foudroyant*, he took a French ship of the line in a hotly contested action. Here was a clear case of merit that combined great professional ability and personal valour. Jervis' later career did not belie the early promise. He became the formidable Earl of St. Vincent, a great leader of fleets, and one of the principal architects of the naval strategy that made such a large contribution to the defeat of Bonaparte. He lived long enough to earn an unusual distinction. St. Vincent was one of the five Admirals of the Fleet ever to receive a Baton, like that of a Field Marshal but bound in blue. Another was the Duke of Clarence, later King William IV. Both Batons can be seen in Greenwich. When George Augustus Eliott, afterwards Lord Heathfield, was given the Bath the next year it was an open recognition that he alone prevented the capture of Gibraltar in spite of a gruelling siege that had lasted three and a half years. Before 1790 a total of seventy-four civilians were admitted to the Order. After that year up to 1814 there were only nine additional appointments, six of whom were diplomats.

It would not be correct, however, to assume that the Order was suddenly converted into the type of Honour it has become in our time. Hereditary rank was still regarded as being of paramount importance. It was not customary to confer the Bath on any officer whose personal rank was already higher than that which membership in the Order would give him. Admiral Earl Howe was promised the first vacant Garter after his great victory on the Glorious First of June 1794, and had to wait three years before he received it. Admiral Lord Collingwood was never given the Bath at all because he reached a rank which precluded him from it and did not live to receive a G.C.B. in 1815. After a successful Fleet action it was the practice ot reward the Commander-in-Chief with a Peerage, the senior Admirals with Irish Peerages and the junior Flag Officers with Baronetcies. This did not mean that the K.B. had become a secondary distinction for secondary achievement, as the story of its award to one of the greatest names ever to be included within its ranks will show. On 15 February 1797, Commodore Nelson sought out his friend Sir Gilbert Elliot, who had been somewhat inadvertently present at the Battle of St Vincent the day before aboard a small vessel. Elliot had gone off to congratulate Admiral Sir John Jervis, and Nelson found himself discussing the battle with a Colonel Drinkwater. In due course the Colonel speculated on the nature of the Honours to be given for the great victory and suggested that the Commodore could count on a Baronetcy. The idea was rejected with feeling. When Drinkwater then suggested that he must want the Bath the Commodore replied, 'Yes, if my services have been of any value, let them be noticed in a way that the public may know me, or them.'[8] A day later Nelson wrote Elliot explaining that he did not wish an hereditary honour, and asked him to urge that Lord Spencer, then First Lord of the Admiralty, advise the Crown to give him one of those 'other Honours, which die with the Possessor, and I should be proud to accept, if my efforts are thought worthy by my King'.[9]

Nelson got his K.B. and Lord St Vincent was empowered to invest him. Before the instructions arrived in the Mediterranean, Nelson lost his arm in a minor action and returned home to convalesce. This accident had one good result because he was able to attend a levee at St James's on September 27, 1797, and receive the insignia from King George III. He was installed by proxy in May 1803 and his plate can now be seen under the seat of the fourth stall on the right of the altar in Henry VII's Chapel. In June he had received a letter from George Nayler relative to the fees due and promptly answered, 'As the Government have always, I believe, on occasions like the present, paid all the Fees of Office, Installation, etc., I expect they will do it on the present occasion, for I cannot think of being at one sixpence expence.' Nelson's brisk reply to the alert Genealogist is another indication of the way the wind was blowing. The original members of the Order could afford to pay what were then regarded as properly traditional costs. The men who were now earning it defending their country could not, or would not, and the Crown had to step in and relieve them of the embarrassment. Nelson's bill amounted to £428 7s 5d.[10]

The Order played a curious role in the great sailor's life. His relationship with Lady Hamilton had already begun and was to ripen quickly after his return to the Mediterranean. Her husband, Sir William, an Ambassador to the Court of Naples, had possessed the Bath since 1772. Making an interesting use of the motto, she described the triangular Nelson-Hamilton household as, TRIA JUNCTA IN UNO. When Lord Nelson's Ribband became vacant after Trafalgar his successor was none other than Sir Arthur Wellesley, whose recent Indian exploits caused him to be called the Sepoy General. Circumstances made the future Duke of Wellington another victim of one of those pedestrian Investitures without benefit of ceremony, relieved in his case by a touch of schoolboy humour. The insignia arrived in Madras early in March, 1805, where he was awaiting transportation home. The recently appointed Governor, his old friend Sir John Cradock, somehow got hold of the Star and had it put on Wellesley's coat while he was still asleep. But the case containing the Collar was left neglected or ignored in several places for the next two weeks before it was delivered. There is no record that it fell to the lot of any other members of the Order to wake up in the morning and find themselves equipped with a Star they had not had the night before.[11]

If the Navy dominated the scene during the years between 1794 and 1808, the

Army's turn was not long in coming. The Peninsular campaign between 1809 and 1814 produced a number of distinguished candidates for the Bath, in fact almost too many. The original Statutes had limited the membership to thirty-five. From time to time extra Knights had been made when there were no vacancies available, with the proviso that they should succeed to the first vacancy that occurred. The exigencies of the war now made it clear that this arrangement was not satisfactory. Accordingly, an additional Statute was issued on 8 May 1812, removing all limitations on the number who could be admitted to the Order. The extra Knights were to succeed to stalls when vacant, by seniority. At the same time it was confirmed that the fees of the Knights nominated for extraordinary military services should be paid by the Treasury, as had in fact been done for several years. On 1 June 1812 what turned out to be the last Installation for a century was held with the usual splendour except that the Ball was cancelled. At the suggestion of Admiral Lord Northesk, each of the newly installed Knights contributed the handsome sum of £350 to charity.[12]

It fell to the lot of Lord Wellington to invest the General Officers who had received the Order under his command in Portugal and Spain. He quickly became something of an expert on how to handle matters of this kind with efficiency and style. In his usual dry way he wrote his brother, Sir Henry Welles-ley, in Cadiz, on 6 April 1812, 'I congratulate you on being made a Knight of the Bath. You must be introduced by a Knight of some Order to the person who is to Invest you, carrying in your hand the insignia of the Order. The authority to Invest you is read; and the person who is to Invest you must Knight you by passing his sword over your shoulder. He then puts the ribbon over your right shoulder, and the Star on your left breast. The ceremony here generally ends in eating and drinking.'[13] This matter of fact comment was not a fair statement of his own views about how to do it. Wellington was a great believer in the familiar adage about all work and no play. He went out of his way to relieve the tedium of war whenever he could. To this end he kept a pack of hounds and an ample supply of drinkable claret, and he took every opportunity to organize a party.

There was no better excuse for one of these social affairs than a Bath Investi-ture. One example will suffice. In March 1813 Sir Thomas Graham returned to the Peninsula bearing gifts. These took the form of the Garter for Lord Welling-ton and the Bath for General Sir Galbraith Lowry Cole, a very capable Divisional Commander and much liked in Spain. The Peer wrote from Frenada on the seventh to Cole's headquarters in Ciudad Rodrigo, seventeen miles away, congratulated him, and expressed the intention of presenting him with the insignia. It was finally decided to hold the affair in Ciudad Rodrigo because there was more room available there. Considerable organization was required. About one-hundred-fifty gentlemen and forty ladies were invited. The food was half cooked at Frenada and, with the wines and silver, conveyed to Ciudad

Rodrigo. Glassware and crockery came from Almeida. The Ball was held in a room with shell holes in the roof and a crater in the floor decorously covered with a mat. Sentries were posted to keep dancers from falling in. All guests enjoyed themselves hugely, none more than the Commander of the Forces who did not leave until 3.30 a.m. on his long ride back to Frenada. According to a now untraceable source, he had given Cole his own K.B. Star at the Investiture, realizing that it would now be replaced by that of the Garter.[14]

Honours for services in the Peninsula were not limited to the Bath alone, but included the much esteemed gold medals and crosses given by the Crown to officers of Field rank and above. It was in connection with those awarded for his own victory at Barrosa that Graham sounded a warning note that eventually led to consequences later in the century. He wrote the Prime Minister about military distinctions in general, pointing out that the Austrian Order of Maria Theresa was one of the most prized in Europe because it was open to officers of every rank. Then with reference to the British Peninsular gold medals, he added, 'I own it is impossible for me to understand on what principle (generally speaking) all officers of a particular description and rank should be entitled to a reward of this kind, while none of an inferior rank can be admitted for the most transcendant merit.' Within three years the same criticism was to be directed at the Bath. The problem was not to be solved until well into Queen Victoria's reign.[15]

The last glorious years of the old Order were marked by two sorry examples of limited official and political vision. When Sir Thomas Graham delivered the Garter insignia to Wellington, it was accompanied by a letter from Lord Liverpool, the Prime Minister, informing him that it was expected he would resign the Bath. Wellington promptly wrote George Nayler that he was returning the Collar and Badge, and instructed Lady Wellington to deliver them. But the Officers under his command, who had received the Order at his hands, strongly protested. In consequence he reluctantly brought the matter to the attention of the Prime Minister. In his letter he pointed out an earlier precedent and noted that since the Statute of 1812, his resignation did not create a vacancy. Making his own position clear, he said, 'God knows I have plenty of Orders, and I consider myself to have been most handsomely treated by the Prince Regent and his Government, and shall not consider myself the less so, if you should not think it proper that I should retain the Order of the Bath.'[16] Lord Liverpool frostily replied that it was not considered advisable to submit his wish to the Prince Regent and there the matter rested, although not for long.

Whatever the reasoning behind the Government's refusal to accede to Wellington's request, it must be remembered that while commanding in Spain he was not popular at the Horse Guards. The legend of the infallible Iron Duke had yet to be born. He was subjected to a whole series of harassments from home, most of which he blandly ignored. If Captain Lord Cochrane, R.N., had been blessed with the same equanimity, he would have saved himself a great deal of trouble, and the Bath a disgraceful spectacle of an unmerited expulsion of one of the Knights. Cochrane's exploits have seldom been equalled in the annals of the Royal Navy. It is sufficient to say here that he came home in April 1809 to deliver dispatches and receive a K.B., in a flaming temper. He had been let down in the face of the enemy at Basque Roads by his commander-in-chief, Admiral Lord Gambier. The Admiral, a leaden-footed plodder hardly qualified for a command on the Serpentine, was unfavourably known throughout the fleet as 'Dismal Jimmy'. Like many other officers of the day, Cochrane had a seat in the House. The Government made plans for a vote of thanks to Gambier for the engagement, and Cochrane declared he would oppose it. He did, but managed the matter so badly that his naval career was ruined. During the next few years he became a persistent thorn in the side of authority and attacked the Admiralty in Parliament on every possible occasion. As a result he found himself with nothing but enemies in high places. When he was accused of being party to a fraudulent Stock Exchange manipulation in 1813, the ambiguities of the law were turned against him. Although innocent, he was sentenced to a year in prison and a fine of £1000. The judgement provided the excuse for a piece of arrogant political revenge. The Ministry expelled Cochrane from the House, and from the Bath in plain defiance of the Statutes.

The only grounds for Degradation listed in Article III of the Statutes are heresy, high treason, or cowardice. Lord Cochrane was not convicted of any of these crimes. In addition, Degradation could not be carried out until the accusation had been considered by the Knights Companions sitting in Chapter. Cochrane's case was handled by addressing a Royal Warrant to the Dean of Westminster, signed by the Prince Regent and countersigned by Lord Sidmouth, the reactionary Home Secretary. Afterwards Bath King of Arms was directed to remove his Banner, Achievements and stall plate. The Banner was ignominiously kicked out the Abbey door. The entire incident reflects little credit on anyone concerned and was essentially an open affront to the whole body of Knights Companions. Cochrane was a great fighting sailor, although a tiresome person in some respects. Fortunately he lived long enough to see himself vindicated. The Prince Consort eventually became interested in his case and re-admitted the 10th Earl of Dundonald, as he became, to the ranks of the Order. General Sir Eyre Coote, similarly Degraded and expelled for equally transient political reasons in 1816, did not live long enough to see himself rehabilitated.

The last K.B. appointed was the Prince of Orange, later King William II of Holland, who was invested in Brussels on 22 August 1814. With Bonaparte safely established on the Island of Elba, the minds of Europe's statesmen could turn to straightening out the confusion left by twenty years of almost continuous war. At home one piece of tidying up took the form of changing the Bath into an institution that bore little resemblance to what it had once been.

Drastic as these modifications were to be, in retrospect we can now see that they permitted the Order to evolve and adapt itself to the still greater social upheavals that have characterized our own times.

CHAPTER IV

The Great Upheaval of 1815

The cessation of hostilities in 1814 found Britain an entirely different place than it had been 20 years before. The prolonged period of total war made the transition to peace doubly difficult. New problems had to be faced and solved at once with little or no experience to serve as a reliable guide. What to do about appropriate awards for distinguished military service was hardly the greatest problem that faced the nation's leaders, but it was a very real one. The body of men who deserved some token of recognition from their country looked embarrassingly large. Exactly what course to take was not clear to those who had to make the executive decisions, particularly when there was so much else of urgent importance to attend to. At this juncture it is unfortunate that more attention was not paid to the views of the Duke of Wellington, who was certainly better qualified to have an opinion than anyone else. That astute and experienced soldier was gifted with a devastating common sense not yet fully appreciated. After Waterloo the position was different but by then much had been done that could not gracefully be undone even if it had been wise to try.

The basic problem was simple. It had never been a generally accepted British custom to make serious awards outside the limited confines of one of the few Orders of Knighthood. Across the Channel Bonaparte's Legion of Honour, itself an extension of Louis XIV's Order of St. Louis, hardly provided an example likely to commend itself to London in 1814. Naval and military gold medals established during the late war for Field Officers and above were really only substitutes for some of the Military Orders available to the Sovereigns of Austria and Russia, Britain's Allies. Although appreciated by the recipients, they were much too limited in scope and application, as Lord Lynedoch had pointed out. The whole picture looked extremely foggy to the War Office. In the end the solution hit upon was fully in accord with the national genius. That is to say, a compromise was triumphantly adopted. It was decided entirely to revise the Order of the Bath and suspend the issue of gold medals in the future.

The advantages were obvious. A large number of officers could be taken care of within an old established Order. The limitation of the various new grades of the Order to the same ranks upon whom the medals had been conferred looked neat and tidy. The nominal responsibility was Lord Bathurst's, then Secretary of State for War and the Colonies. The real authors of the measure seem never to have received their due credit, an oversight for which they later had reason to be thankful. There were two, Sir Henry Edward Bunbury, Bart., one of the Under Secretaries in Lord Bathurst's Department, and Major General Henry Torrens, Secretary to the Duke of York, then Commander-in-Chief.[1] Who played the creative role is not known, but the dual cooperation produced a document, published in the *London Gazette* on Tuesday, 3 January 1815, that virtually re-founded the Order of the Bath and made it substantially what it is today.

Contrary to usual practice, the document that found its way into the *Gazette* was not an addition to the Statutes, but a Warrant under the Royal Sign Manual dated 2 January. It gave every outward indication of having been drawn with little consideration of the difficulties involved and suffered a great deal of criticism at the time and later. For this the authors should not be too severely blamed. They had to work with speed to meet the urgent demands of a Minister in a hurry. The conditions under which Anstis had written the original Statutes were virtually duplicated, but with modern complexities. Bunbury and Torrens were also required to prepare the lists of new recipients, work they were certainly qualified to do. Through no fault of their own, they were not so well qualified to draw up provisions changing the entire nature of the Order, and Lord Bathurst was no fit judge of the results. If Sir George Nayler, the Genealogist who later became Garter, had been given the responsibility, the outcome might have been more satisfactory. Called upon to act only as advisor, he was unable to control the operation.

The Warrant opened with an expression of faultless intent. The Prince Regent acting on behalf of His Majesty, the Sovereign of the Order, was, 'desirous of commemorating the auspicious termination of the long and arduous Contests in which this Empire has been engaged, and of marking in an especial manner His gracious sense of the valour, perseverance and devotion manifested by the Officers of His Majesty's Forces by sea and land'.[3] To achieve this desirable end the Order was to be composed of three classes, 'differing in their ranks and degrees of dignity'. The members of the first two classes, called Knights Grand Cross and Knights Commanders, were to consist of 72 and 180 members respectively. In the event of special acts of distinction, or future wars, the number of K.C.B.s could be increased. The number assigned the First Class included all K.B.s and new appointees. Exceptions were the Sovereign and Royal Princes who would be considered as extra Knights. The civil appointments within the total were limited to 12. The First Class could only be given to officers holding the ranks of Rear Admiral and Major General, or above, while the qualifications for the Second Class were restricted to Post-Captains and Colonels or above. The number of K.C.B.s was exclusive of 10 places reserved for foreign officers holding

British commissions. Future promotions to the First Class were only to be made from the body of K.C.B.s. No numerical limitations were placed on the Third Class, called Companions, except that implied in the regulation that it could be given only to those officers who held a 'Medal, or other Badge of Honour'. Subsequent appointments could be made only from among those officers whose names have appeared in *The London Gazette* as having distinguished themselves in combat.

The G.C.B.s were to be governed by the old Statutes, but the lower grades were to be regulated by special provisions not mentioned. The insignia of the First Class were loosely described, but the devices to be worn by the lower class were simply referred to as 'appropriate' Badges, and an equally appropriate Star for the K.C.B.s. The K.C.B.s ranked before all Knights Bachelors. The Companions, not to be knighted, had precedence before Esquires. Nayler's delicate touch appears in the final Article. Two new Officers were created. Sir George Nayler in his triple capacity of Genealogist, Blanc Coursier and York Herald was endowed with a plural personality and became 'Officers of Arms Attendant Upon the Knights Commanders and Companions', who were instructed to furnish him with a verified statement of their military careers to be entered into the 'appropriate' record books. Nothing was said about a fee for this service, but Sir George did not overlook the matter. William Woods was made Secretary to the same members of the Order, and eventually had a most distinguished career with the College of Arms.

Evidence of the haste in which the document had been prepared was provided when three days later, on 6 January, a series of additions and corrections were inserted into the *Gazette*. The most important of these was a provision making 15 K.C.B.s available for officers of the East India Company's service above the original 180. An unspecified number of C.B.s were also to be given to 'certain' of the Company's officers. The validity of the Warrant was based on the Royal Prerogative and 'the powers reserved to the Sovereign in the Statutes of the said Most Honourable Order'. The vast changes it introduced were regarded as advancing the splendour and extending its limits so that officers who had distinguished themselves in the late war, 'may share in the Honours of the said Order and that their names may be delivered down to remote posterity accompanied by the marks of Distinction they have so nobly gained'.

Given the conditions under which it had been produced, the Warrant nevertheless seems on the whole to have been justifiable as a general measure. The criticism often heard that it would have been better to create an entirely new Order doesn't take into account the circumstances of the time and bears all the earmarks of brilliant hindsight on the part of those not faced with the immediate responsibility of coping with post-war problems. The desire to adopt the familiar to suit new conditions without destroying the apparent facade is fundamental in the British character. Of course, the results of the effort as it stood in this instance were not perfect. There were limits to the adaptability of the institution. It can perhaps be argued that the effect was not to extend the Bath but to shatter it, and that most of the members of the Second and Third Classes did not feel that they shared in, 'the Honours of the said Order', because they were unable to recognize it in its new form. If this were true in certain instances, the reaction was neither prolonged nor lasting.

One grave objection to the provisions of the Warrant voiced at the time, however, has great interest today. The conditions regulating the award of the Third Class were most peculiarly phrased. By limiting it to those who had received one of the gold medals, the C.B. was effectively reserved for Field Officers. At the same time the qualifications were extended to include those whose names had been published in the *Gazette* for 'valour in action against His Majesty's enemies, since the commencement of the War in 1803, or shall hereafter be named in despatches published in *The London Gazette*, as having distinguished himself'.[4] Here one senses an element of confusion. A man could be given a C.B. because he had collected a medal not awarded for valour in action. On the other hand, if he had distinguished himself, he could also receive it, but only if he had the medal. The terms cancel themselves out. The Duke of Wellington pinpointed part of the problem in a letter to the Commander-in-Chief after Waterloo. He wrote, 'I confess that I do not concur in the limitation of the Order to Field Officers. Many Captains in the Army conduct themselves in a very meritorious manner and deserve it; and I never could see the reason for excluding them either from the Order or the Medal.'[5]

The real question lay in just what function the Bath was supposed to fulfill. It had been the British custom to give Orders only to those in positions requiring varying degrees of command responsibility. The idea of using an Order as a combat decoration was alien to the system but understood by those soldiers who had recently witnessed the award of the Austrian and Russian Orders of Maria Theresa and the St. George to junior officers only for action before the enemy. The conflict of function was never explicitly resolved within the Bath; it just slowly ceased to exist. The Order continued in the British tradition. Officers below Field grade substantially had to wait seventy-two years for the creation of the D.S.O. before their services would be recognized within the terms of reference used by the Duke of Wellington.

When all these allowances have been made, however, the measure emerges as a very bad one, not so much for what it was but for what it became. Perhaps there might have been something to recommend it as a brief outline of modifications later to be worked out in greater detail. In fact, the Warrant became virtually the sole working constitution of the drastically modified Order for the next thirty-seven years, a role it could not possibly fulfill given the sketchy terms in which it had been drawn. Why this happened is hard to understand. The initial responsibility must be laid at the door of Lord Bathurst, and that perpetual Prime Minister, Lord Liverpool. Perhaps they had been too long in power and rejected the thought of a new set of Statutes that would inevitably have limited their freedom of action with regard to the Order. Possibly no one was in a position to give them advice they would listen to. Not even Wellington showed any desire to come to grips with the problem during his term of office as head of the Government. Although King George IV was not happy, it seems evident that the two successive Acting Great Masters, the Dukes of York and Clarence, were oddly satisfied with arrangements. The latter, as King William IV, eventually resisted attempts to end a chaotic state of affairs. in effect, the Bath was without consistent executive control. The anomalies that developed make an interesting study.

Some of these peculiarities are obvious at a first reading of the *Gazette* of 3 January. The Order was now military in function and composed of three classes This being the case, what was the position of the Civil G.C.B.s? Didn't their existence imply four classes rather than three? Were they not in the peculiar position of being Civil Knights Grand Cross of the Military Order of the Bath, a contradiction in terms? The number of K.C.B.s after being specifically limited for the moment were immediately increased by the addition of the East India Company's officers and ten places set aside for foreign officers holding British commissions. Were these latter Honorary K.C.B.s? Was there any plan in mind to award the Order to foreign officers in the same way that so many British officers had recently been given foreign Orders by the Allied Sovereigns? The articles in the *Gazette* were silent on these points. Apart from indicating that the insignia of the Military G.C.B.s was to be differentiated by the addition of a laurel wreath to the Star and Badge, nothing was said about the devices to be worn by the two lower classes although entirely different insignia were quickly adopted for the First Class from that described in the Warrant and the lower classes were given decorations similar in most respects but smaller in size. These matters will be treated in more detail in Chapter XI. Given the precision with which the Statutes of 1725 laid down the fees to be paid to the Order's Officers, it is strange to find that there is no mention of fees for the new officials assigned to the Knights Commanders and Companions. It was all very well solemnly to declare that the Banners and plates of Arms of the K.C.B.s were to be affixed within the Cathedral Church of St Peter, Westminster, but no attempt seems to have been made to find out where. That edifice was already fairly cluttered with assorted monuments and the Chapel of Henry VII no longer had room for the G.C.B.s Banners. Every one of these points required that specific steps be taken to cope with them. Nothing was done. Things just happened.

The fundamental question of picking the candidates was not well handled by Bunbury and Torrens. In considering their efforts, one must remember that after a century and a half it is easy for us to see where they went wrong. Nevertheless we can understand how they must have been much harried men frantically in search of a formula that would both work and make some kind of sense. If no one made any rules, nothing could have been done. On the highest level they were not entirely their own masters. Some of the appointments of the new G.C.B.s were influenced by forces brought to bear from the Cabinet level. There was more freedom in dealing with the K.C.B.s. Here the fixation about using the Peninsular gold medals as a qualification bedeviled them. It was decided that only officers with the Peninsular Gold Cross and two bars should be eligible for the Second Class of the Bath. Bathurst and Wellington both understood the hardship that such restriction would cause. It excluded such fighting soldiers as Colonel James Campbell who had only one clasp to his Cross, but it did include many officers who had been present but not much engaged in some of the battles in Spain. On 15 February Bathurst proposed that five hard cases be given the K.C.B., only to find his suggestion vetoed by the Horse Guards.[6]

All this was bad enough, but the Admiralty introduced a distinctive twist of its own. Only those officers in possession of a Gold Medal were to be eligible for the Second Class. A letter dated 3 January, was sent to each Naval K.C.B. informing him of his honour and telling him that he was not to wear the Insignia of the Order until he had received, 'further and sufficient authority to do so'. Inasmuch as no one yet knew what these devices were and it is questionable if they had yet been determined, this instruction can be considered over-cautious. The letter then concluded with the altogether surprising statement, 'And when you shall receive the Insignia, you will return to me the Naval Medal heretofore conferred upon you, which is considered as superseded by the decorations of the Bath. I am, Sir, Your most obedient humble servant, J. W. Croker.'[7] The Admirals and Captains who received this communication had won their Gold Medals commanding ships or fleets in direct combat with the enemy, but some Army awards had been given to men barely within sound of the firing and only technically engaged in battle. The Admirals and Captains were not pleased at being deprived of these honours, particularly when Army officers were allowed to keep theirs. They expressed themselves on the subject to their 'most obedient and humble servant', the Secretary of the Board of Admiralty, with such force and unanimity that the absurd requirement was dropped. There is no better example of the difficulties that grew out of different authorities, each interpreting the Warrant of 2 January without reference to what the other might be doing. In this instance what should have been a combined operation was badly mismanaged, just as too many similar efforts had been during the war.

The seriousness of the problems created by these haphazard decisions was even commented upon by the Regent himself. Writing to Lord Bathurst on 7 December 1819, he said, 'With respect to the modern Rules and Regulations that I was, in the hurry of the whole proceeding, induced to adopt in the year 1815, they formed a severity of code, that did not leave me the power of alteration in any of its principles; yet, I had scarcely sanctioned those positive Enactments before I was desired to dispense with them in favour of cases for whose merits I nevertheless entertained an high consideration, and which dispensation I most willingly granted. I cannot however avoid observing that these Enactments have since proved to be both embarrassing and objectionable.'[8] So even the initial appointments to the Order created as much heartburning among those who did not receive one, as pleasure among those who did. It was not a satisfactory state of affairs even though it was one bound to ameliorate itself in due course. In view of the Regent's understanding of the problem, it is doubly astonishing that nothing was done to correct such obvious inequalities.

There was also confused thinking in another area. The War Office and the Horse Guards should have realized that something would have to be done for senior foreign officers of Allied nations in accordance with accepted international procedure. Bunbury and Torrens were well aware of the protocol in this area, and it is difficult to grasp why, even under pressure, they neglected to make some provisions for Honorary Members of the Bath. In the event, no provisions were made, but Honorary Members were. Sir Benjamin Bloomfield, acting as the Prince Regent's Private Secretary, took the G.C.B. insignia to Paris, and on 18 August 1815, the Duke of Wellington invested five Austrian, Russian and German senior commanders. The Duke then entertained them with a banquet in his accustomed style. Their names were not published in the *Gazette* until 9 September following.[9] In due course several foreign officers not holding British commissions also were given the K.C.B. and C.B.

A particularly astonishing *faux pas* soon took place. In the original complement of 108 K.C.B.s, 58 were Flag Officers and 46 General Officers. Of the remaining number, 19 were naval Post-Captains, 22 Colonels and 35 Lieutenant Colonels. At the first Investiture held in Carlton House 12 April 1815, the Flag and General Officers present were knighted, if they had not received the accolade before, and all were properly invested with their decorations by the Prince Regent. The officers of lower rank able to attend were instructed to appear wearing their Badges. When the investment of the senior officers was completed, the Regent went to the levee room and simply knighted the others without investing them. A 'Memorandum' published in the *Gazette* of 18 April 1815, stated that it was the Regent's pleasure that those K.C.B.s 'as shall not have undergone the due Ceremonial of Investiture, shall wear the appropriate Ribband and Badge only, and shall not wear the Star of the Second Class, until they shall have been so invested'. In this way the Order was given a fourth military class not envisaged by the terms of the original *Gazette*. This was the result of the seniors complaining about junior officers having the right to wear the same decorations they themselves did. The members of the unexpected and unofficial group of second class K.C.B.s had to wait for promotion before becoming fully qualified Knights Commanders. Several never did reach a higher rank. Those surviving in 1837 were finally allowed to have Stars by William IV.[10]

This will explain why some of the portraits at Greenwich show their subjects wearing a K.C.B. Badge without the Star. If the terms of the *Gazette* had been embodied in carefully written Statutes, this indirect method of creating a fourth class could have been either officially recognized or not recognized at all, in which case an unfortunate and embarrassing situation would never have arisen. The fact that a personal intervention of this kind caused so basic a violation of the terms of the Royal Warrant is the most amazing aspect of the proceedings. The senior officers had not only overplayed their hand but were successful in the attempt. It was later decided that the K.C.B. should be reserved for Flag and General Officers in the future.

There seemed to be no end to the spur-of-the-moment decisions to which the 3 January *Gazette* gave rise. The salaries of the seven original officials of the Order were by this time being paid by the Crown. No provision was made to pay anything to the two new ones appointed for the benefit of the Knights Commanders and Companions, a state of affairs alien to the thinking of Sir George Nayler. Although salaries were never attached to these appointments, Nayler was successful in persuading Lord Bathurst to fix fees payable by the members of the Second and Third Classes for services to be rendered by the two Officers. Accordingly, letters were sent out on 9 January, to each K.C.B. In one, Nayler asked for a family pedigree and a copy of the recipient's Arms to permit the preparation of a Banner and armorial plate for display in the Abbey. In the other, Woods delivered a bill of particulars and costs. After noting that the regular fees were to be paid by the Crown, the only payment required was one to the Officer of Arms attendant, 'agreeably to the Rules and Ordinances appertaining to the Knights Commanders', apportioned in the following manner:

	£	s	d
For the Escocheon, or Plate of your Armorial Ensigns to be affixed in Westminster Abbey	8	0	0
For the Banner of your Arms emblazoned on silk to be placed over the said Eschocheon or Plate	5	10	0
For recording the Pedigree of your Family, your Coat Armour, and statement of Military Services, in the Books appropriated to the Knights Commanders	7	8	0
For copy of the Rules and Ordinances	1	1	0
	21	19	0

On the face of it, the demand was not unreasonable and some of the K.C.B.s paid. So did the C.B.s who were charged £6 17s 8d for a plate, the recording of their services and a copy of the Rules. What they got for their money was something else again. Their Banners, plates, and the C.B. plates were never prepared and never appeared in the Abbey. The College of Heralds next entered the lists and prepared to do battle. Nayler's original attempt to usurp their privileges twenty-five years before had been defeated when the Statute of 1804 specifically declared that he could only receive evidence of pedigrees for Bath Record Books through the College. The Heralds publicly accused Nayler and Woods of violating their privileges and breaching the Statute of 1804. Faced with such a vigorous opposition, apparently these gentlemen quietly dropped the whole issue and decided to forgo their profits. In the end, the 'Rules and Ordinances appertaining to the Knights Commanders', and Companions, were never drawn up until they appeared in the Statutes of 1847.[11] For this Nayler could not be blamed. He did his best, but his efforts came to nothing, thanks to the opposition of that somewhat difficult officer, Sir George Murray, at the Horse Guards.[11]

Strange as these proceedings now look, it should not be assumed that such distinguished Heralds as Sir George Nayler and William Woods had knowingly engaged in a plot to squeeze the already thin purses of the K.C.B.s by a subterfuge of obvious illegality. Before they tried to implement one of the few specific provisions of the Warrant, however, the Dean and Chapter of Westminster should have been consulted as the authorities responsible for the already overcrowded Abbey. The increase in the number of G.C.B.s had made the furniture in Henry VII's Chapel inadequate. Without some modification of the stalls the Chapel could no longer be used for an Installation. This problem was not overlooked by the Duke of York, who, as Acting Great Master, inspected the Chapel in 1827 with a view to having the necessary alterations made, but nothing was done.

In 1832 King William IV raised the question again. Dr John Ireland, then Dean of Westminster and the Bath, looked into the problem in the company of Sir Willoughby Gordon and Sir William Woods. He concluded that arrangements could be made to accommodate the G.C.B.s. It would only be necessary, 'to suspend the new Flags a little above, or a little below the present Flags in the intermediate spaces. The Chapel also presents sufficient room for a second row of Knights' seats, by lessening the depth of the present single row, and throwing out another row in front of it towards the area of the Chapel, still leaving 21 or 22 feet on the floor of the Chapel for the display of ceremonies practised at the Installation.'[12] This suggestion had to wait almost a century before being adopted. Dean Ireland then went on to say that placing the K.C.B. Banners above the choir stalls was not practicable because a large part of the choir enclosures had to be removed at every coronation. He thought these Banners just could be suspended from the iron rods extending from the columns near the east end of Edward the Confessor's Chapel if the K.C.B.s had them, but inasmuch as they didn't the issue was not pressing. He gave only grudging approval to putting up Brass armorial plates for the Second Class. These comments show that the idea of hanging the K.C.B. flags had already been abandoned and explains why the whole plan of commemorating the members of the Second Class of the Order within the Abbey eventually had to be dropped. But as it took some years to reach this decision, it may be presumed that Nayler and Woods retained the money they had received for services they were never able to carry out through no direct fault of their own.

The confusion that marked the steps taken to enlarge the Order, though generally familiar only to those most intimately connected with the measures, did not escape more public attention. With that willingness to consider subjects not entirely familiar to the speakers, for which the Mother of Parliaments is so justly famous, the Bath was discussed in the House. In February and March 1815 a question was raised about expenses the extension might entail. The Chancellor of the Exchequer denied that any significant increase in expense would take place. One member objected, with more relevance, to the almost total exclusion of 'the civil classes of Society from participating in the Honours of this Order'. He was a generation ahead of his time. The ghosts of 1688 jogged the elbows of others who wondered if a new military Order was not a disguised attempt to convert the country into a military despotism. The same group protested that the fact that the number of Army officers among the recipients was greater than those of the Navy and had to be put in their places by the production of the relevant statistics. Predictably one sturdy country gentleman, 'objected to the measure as an imitation of Foreign manners, and of Foreign frippery and frivolity'. One member wanted to know by what means the changes had been carried out and observed, 'he could see that no change had been effected in that Order, except through the instrumentality of the Great Seal'. This was a telling point. With a calm disregard for the facts the Government replied that, 'the Order had been regulated as usual by Patent'. It had not been, and would not be so regulated for another thirty years. The real cause of all the trouble was that it was hardly being regulated by a recognizably rational system at all.[13] Unfortunately, after this flurry the House forgot about the whole matter and devoted itself to other things, more pressing or more interesting.

CHAPTER V

Transition and Attempts at Reform

Any analysis of the chaotic state of the Order immediately after the great reformation of 1815, unless hedged about with a number of qualifications, must be accepted with a certain reserve. The too critical observer is like a man who, after examining a grain of sand through a microscope, believes that he has just seen a mountain top. Nothing is ever so bad in Britain as it sometimes appears. In spite of confusion behind the scenes, the general purpose expressed in the preamble to the Royal Warrant was largely fulfilled. The Crown did find itself provided with an instrument that permitted past and future distinguished military services to be recognized. Time would permit the rough edges to be given a final polish. After the initial shock the drastically revised Order of the Bath gave general satisfaction. Fitted within a traditional framework, it was largely successful in overcoming the national dislike of anything new. As a pragmatic fact, the Bath was made to do the job for which it had been designed. An excellent example of how this came about can be found in the award of a G.C.B. to General Sir David Ochterlony of the East India Company's service in 1818. After he had been invested, Lord Hastings, the Governor General, remarked, 'You have obliterated a distinction painful for the officers of the Honourable Company, and you have opened the door for your brothers-in-arms to a reward which . . . could not be more deservedly extended to the officers of any army on earth.'[1]

In 1820 the pleasant old custom of creating Knights of the Bath preparatory to the Sovereign's Coronation was revived. A group of 17 G.C.B.s and 6 K.C.B.s was appointed as Extra Knights to rank within the Order according to the date of their appointments, but after their deaths no vacancy within the Order was to be considered to have taken place. A similar creation of 8 G.C.B.s, 26 K.C.B.s and 79 C.B.s was made immediately after the Coronation of King William IV in 1831. These additional members were also considered as extra to the established complement. The large number of G.C.B.s made for George IV's Coronation included most of those who had a valid claim to the Order but could not be given it in 1815 because their services had been performed before 1803. As the time for the Coronation approached, it was decided that the Knights should be represented as a body at the ceremony. Those of the First Class were still controlled by the provisions of the Statutes of 1725 stipulating they could not wear the Collar until installed. No one had yet faced up to the fact that with a greatly increased complement an Installation was out of the question because there simply would not be sufficient room in Henry VII's Chapel. To get around the difficulty, all 63 G.C.B.s were dispensed from the Installation on 6 July 1821, and allowed to wear their Mantles and Collars at the Coronation.[2] This practice was continued until 1913 when the Installations were once more resumed.

During these years some attention was devoted to the number of members and how they should be allocated between the services. In December 1823 the Duke of York (Acting Great Master) and Lords Bathurst and Melville (Secretary of State for War and First Lord of the Admiralty) allocated 42 places in the First Class to the Army and 18 to the Navy. In 1827 the Duke of Wellington decided that George IV's Coronation Knights would fall into the number of regular G.C.B.s and that no new ones should be made until the total had been reduced to the 60 fixed in 1815. At the same time the apportionment of the members of the First Class was made in 1823, the same authorities limited the eventual total of K.C.B.s to 112, a figure considerably lower than the original number. It is a curious fact that during the next thirty years the K.C.B.s were reduced at a much faster rate than the G.C.B.s, who by 1834 numbered 99. The official thinking about the matter was neatly summed up in a comment made by the Duke of Wellington in 1839 that makes amusing reading today. He wrote to the Permanent Under Secretary of State for War, '. . . after the year 1814–15 there were to be in the Army and Navy 240 Admirals and Generals decorated; that is to say 60 with Grand Crosses and 180 with Commander's Crosses. Such a notion is ridiculous; it is quite impossible that any war of which this country could bear the expense could produce 240 Admirals and Generals deserving such decorations.' The Iron Duke was a shrewd observer of contemporary events and people but apparently gifted with no better foresight than anyone else. The number of C.B.s in this period was allowed to float. Although no limits had been set, Sir George Nayler was informed in August 1823 that the figures were to be fixed at 250 for the Army and 50 for the East India Company's service. The number of Naval appointments was never settled. By 1834 the C.B.s totalled 487, with those allocated to the Navy being just below half the Army allotment.[3]

Appointments to the Order were handled through two channels. Recommendations for the Civil G.C.B. were dealt with by the Home Secretary, who advised the Sovereign, largely because he had formerly been responsible for the K.B.s. The custom became established that this division was granted to a very limited group of persons; namely, Ambassadors, Cabinet Ministers, the Sovereign's Private Secretary, and to the Speaker, generally on his retirement. Naturally there were exceptions to the rule from time to time, and the custom was modified in some respects later in the century. The first Civil G.C.B. was awarded on

1 April 1815 to the second Earl of Clancarty in Ireland, then serving as British Plenipotentiary at the Congress of Vienna. Sir Benjamin Bloomfield, who was Private Secretary to the Prince Regent and George IV, without the office having that title, received it on 1 April 1822. Among the Cabinet Ministers who accepted the G.C.B. during these years, the name of the third Viscount Palmerston, Secretary of State for Foreign Affairs, can be mentioned as among the most familiar.

All the military appointments, including those for the Navy, were dealt with by the Secretary of State for War and the Colonies. Occasionally of course, there would be a slight contretemps. On 27 July 1835, the Secretary of the Board of Admiralty wrote the Secretary of State (Lord Glenelg) to inform him of the King's intention to give Admiral Lord Amelius Beauclerk the first available G.C.B. and of a vacancy caused by the death of Admiral, the Hon. Sir Thomas Pakenham. It was suggested that His Majesty's commands concerning the appointment be taken. Three days later another letter from the Admiralty was delivered to Downing Street with the chastened comment, 'I now have the honour to inform you that the statement of Sir Thomas Pakenham's decease is found to be incorrect, and I have therefore to request that your Lordship will take no steps in the matter.' What Sir Thomas thought about this premature attempt to dispose of his Grand Cross has not been disclosed.[4]

Throughout the reigns of King George IV and King William IV the Bath enjoyed possibly a greater prestige than it had during the eighteenth century, or after 1870. There are several reasons for this happy state of affairs. It was the country's only military Order of merit and was distributed on a wider scale than it had been before. Soldiers were popular in those days, and the public knew the names of many of the Knights. In short, the Bath benefited from a fairly wide publicity among the growing middle classes, many of whose sons were now able to look forward to a military career. The Duke of Clarence had been made Acting Great Master after the death of his brother, the Duke of York in 1827. When he ascended the throne in 1830, he continued to regard himself as Great Master and devoted marked attention to the Order. The Investiture of the Duke of Saxe Weimar in 1830 took place with great splendour in St George's Hall, Windsor Castle, and was followed by a dinner and a ball. On 12 April 1832, the King entertained the G.C.B.s and the Officers of the Order at a State Banquet at St James's Palace, a graceful gesture he was to repeat several times during his reign. The Duke of Wellington's practice of holding the famous annual Waterloo Banquet on the anniversary of the battle brought out his 'Old Comrades' in force, all wearing their decorations displayed on the increasingly magnificent full-dress uniforms of the era.

Nevertheless, beneath the comfortable facade all was not well with the fundamental administration of the institution. Most important, many of the recipients increasingly grumbled about the fees they were charged. For the G.C.B.s these were very nearly the same sums established by Anstis in 1725, although they were now somewhat reduced. The Knights of the First Class appointed in 1815 had them paid by the Crown for services in the field. When a K.C.B. was promoted after 1815, however, he had to face the full financial burden represented by bills from the Heralds and Officers of the Order. Many simply refused. It was not a happy state of affairs. Almost by coincidence the Knights found themselves provided with a champion in the person of Sir Nicholas Harris Nicolas K.C.M.G., who played a very important if unpublicized role in the history of the Bath. He was almost another Anstis, without enjoying Anstis' success, through certain defects in his personality.

Like Nelson, Nicolas came of a family with a strong clerical background. Born in 1799, he entered the Navy in 1808. By 1815 he had reached the rank of Lieutenant and was placed on half pay in 1816 during the great contraction of the Services after the wars. Casting about for something to do, he turned to the law and was called to the Bar at the Inner Temple in 1825. Nicolas never practised but confined himself to arguing the intricacies of Peerage cases before the House of Lords. In the course of time he found himself as much an antiquarian as a lawyer. The two strains ended by combining within him. On one hand, he became an active and productive historian. On the other, he lived in an age when reform was in the air, and Nicolas was emphatically a man of his times. Although he had no interest in politics, he directed fierce attacks on the abuses he encountered in the scholarly areas where his interest lay. His attempt to reform the Society of Antiquaries was defeated by the other officials of that organization. Nicolas then engaged them in an aggressive public controversy. He next attacked the practices of the Record Commission (in effect, the predecessor of what is now the Public Record Office) and was more fortunate. His efforts resulted in a select Parliamentary committee to look into the problem. He successfully struck down many of the outmoded regulations of the British Museum Reading Room, for which all subsequent scholars have had reason to thank him. He even advised the establishment of life Peerages.

In all these activities he was a stubborn and passionate advocate of his own point of view. He emerges as a curious amalgam of a medieval Crusader with the conscience of a late Victorian Non-Conformist. He viewed all opposition as automatically wrong and ill-motivated. The eye of his judgment never recognized the existence of pastel shades. Under the circumstances it is not surprising that he made more enemies than friends. His unfortunate habit of being in the right most of the time didn't help. When this man directed all his emotions and energies to reforming the Order of the Bath, only to fail when he appeared on the brink of success, the result is predictable. He became a vocal Cassandra forced to speak his lines from the wings because he never had a chance to take the stage. Nicolas is an excellent witness who deploys his facts with great skill, but he is a poor judge. Anyone reading Volume III of his monumental 'History of the Orders of Knighthood of the British Empire', cannot avoid the impression that the story of the Bath is one of unrelieved mismanagement from the date of its foundation. This view is nonsense, of course, and can only be explained by the author's frustrations. How and why he became so embittered is part of the history of the Order.

If Sir Harris Nicolas was a premature late Victorian, William IV remained a man of the Age of Reason. The King was simple, straightforward, with an uncomplicated view of life, people and problems. Like most monarchs, he resented petty interference and objected to arguments, particularly when the finer points eluded him. It is hard to imagine two more potentially incompatible characters than Harris Nicolas and his Sovereign. To use a figure coined by Sir Owen Morshead in another context, the two were not formed by nature for mutual admiration. By a combination of bad luck and bad management Nicolas became involved in a head-on collision with the King that had as much to do with his lack of success in reforming the Bath as anything else. Sir George Nayler's death in 1831 made the office of King of Arms of the Order of St Michael and St George available and Nicolas was successful in securing the appointment in March 1832. This position gave him a place in the Royal Household. Full of zeal he surveyed that Order and soon convinced Lord Goderich, who then headed the War and Colonial Department, that it was seriously in need of reform. By August he had produced an entirely new set of Statutes, and on the 16th of the month had the honour of reading them to the King who gave his approval.

Among other re-arrangements the Statutes provided for a Chancellor who should rank as senior G.C.M.G. or senior K.C.M.G., depending on which rank within the Order was conferred upon him. Nicolas was successful in suggesting his own appointment as Chancellor and was given the Second Class of the Order. This was no sooner done than Sir Frederick Hankey, who was actually the senior K.C.M.G., objected to being superseded by the Chancellor in that rank and brought his complaint to the King's attention. He received a sympathetic hearing. Meanwhile Nicolas persuaded the Secretary of State that his new office really required that he be a G.C.M.G. He was actually given the First Class much against William IV's wishes. After two months the appointment was cancelled, whereupon he wrote a long paper to prove that he had a legal right to his G.C.M.G. In the King's eyes an officer of his Household was trying to quote the law against his Sovereign. Thus the King developed a strong personal dislike for the Chancellor of St Michael and St George which time and further acquaintance could only exacerbate.[11]

Nayler's death also made vacant the position of King of Arms Attendant on the Knights Commanders and Companions of the Bath. Nicolas made a concerted effort to obtain this office, but it was given to Sir William Woods, the Secretary, who had by far the better claim. And so Nicolas had to be satisfied with being made Secretary to the Knights Commanders and Companions in place of Woods on 7 April 1832. This may have been the most junior post within the Order, but it was all that he needed. He had no trouble persuading Lord Goderich to authorize him to devote his considerable talents and great energy to an analysis of the present position of the Bath and to make recommendations for improvements.

The crux of the problem was uncomplicated. When the Order had been founded in 1725, it was placed on much the same footing as the Garter and Thistle. It was not viewed as an award for meritorious achievement but as an honour to be given to men of high position, both social and economic. The great revision of 1815 had, in fact, remade the Bath without introducing any of the necessary changes in administrative procedure required if it were to function successfully within the new frame of reference. In the years following the war the Tory Governments of Liverpool and Wellington refused to recognize what had happened, partly because they were desperately afraid of anything that could be called reform and partly because, as men of their times, they could not recognize that the Order was actually no longer what it had once been. By 1832, with the Whigs in and the Tories out, the opportunity for changes had arrived, or so it seemed. Nicolas set to work, first to demonstrate what was wrong and then to suggest what should be done about it.

His first step was to review the positions of the seven old Officers and of the two new ones attached to the Second and Third Classes and to summarize their functions and duties. He found that most of them were sinecure appointments with no duties worth mentioning, particularly now that the ceremony of Installation had, in practice, been allowed to lapse. The difficulty was that, according to the additional Statute of 31 July 1820, the G.C.B.s were held liable to pay all the original fees upon their appointment, with the exception of £138 to the Great Master. During the war these fees had been paid by the Crown, but as soon as promotions from the Second to the First Class began to take place, they became the personal responsibility of the Knights Grand Cross. At some indeterminate time during the previous century the Crown had undertaken to pay the Officers salaries. The total amounted nominally to £663 6s 8d and £478 16s 4d net after deductions. Between 1800 and 1832 the fees paid came to £7,913 1s 4d, or about £245 a year. As a result the Officers were costing the net sum of £723 a year, not counting the small sums only partially collected from the K.C.B.s and C.B.s. The real difficulty lay in the system of fees established when the Order had been founded, and continued now that it was no longer what it once had been. As Nicolas very cogently said, 'The objection to demanding fees on receiving an Honour in reward of Services must be sufficiently obvious; and the only apology for it is that the Officers of the Order would not otherwise be paid. To this it may be said that the Services required of the present Officers are amply paid for by their salaries, inasmuch as the situations of

Genealogist, Registrar, and Gentleman Usher are little more than sinecures, unless attendance at one or two Investitures in a year can be called *Services*. Contrary to the spirit and intentions of the Statutes, the Offices of Registrar and Secretary have long been united in the same person—and the present Secretary and Registrar performs his duties by deputy, which circumstances sufficiently prove the uselessness of the situation of Registrar, and the necessity of appointing some superior and responsible Officer to conduct the business of the Order.' After having exposed the outdated financial structure under which the members of the Order suffered, he went on to summarize the condition of the institution making many of the same points about the lack of organization we have noted earlier. He introduced the following two new criticisms, however, which were all his own:

1. The Original Statutes with all their anomalies and absurdities are still in force, though they in no way apply to the present Constitution of the Order.
2. No proper instrument for the enlargement of the Order in 1815 has even been executed, so that the Knights Commanders and Companions can scarcely be deemed to have a legal right to their Honours.

His objection to the 'absurdities' of the old Statutes is purely Victorian and has been commented upon earlier. It was to meet with opposition not entirely irrational. But when Harris Nicolas pointed out that the enlargement of the Order in 1815 had not been legally executed, even though his view was sound, it looked at first glance much as if he were questioning the Royal Prerogative. This was just the sort of thing calculated to provoke the explosive anger of King William IV and, at the same time, involved a legal point he could not easily grasp.

After his masterly attack on the irrationalities of the system under which the Bath was being administered, Nicolas then proceeded to advise what ought to be done to correct the faults. All fees should be abolished except for a token payment to the Dean of Westminster amounting to £8 10s from the three grades of members upon nomination. The only other expenses would be for the actual cost of Banners and armorial plates set up in the Abbey. The Officers were to be reduced from nine to three, Dean, King of Arms, and Secretary. Inasmuch as it would be difficult to decide about the relative importance of their positions and about the officer responsible for the affairs of the Order, Nicolas advanced a brilliant solution. What was required was a new and definitely superior Officer—a Chancellor of the Order of the Bath! 'His duties should be to keep the seal of, and countersign, all Instruments connected with the Order; to receive the commands of the Secretary of State and the Sovereign; to preserve and register all records; notify all appointments; and, in fact, to transact all the business of, and be responsible to, the Government for everything relating to the Order. As his time would be very much occupied, and as his situation would be one of some importance, his Salary ought not to be less than £300 a year, and, if possible, apartments should be assigned to him. . . . '

Practically speaking, the Chancellor would become the senior executive with all the authority and with more responsibilities than John, Duke of Montagu, had had when he was Great Master. There was much to be said for the idea except that the King was not enthusiastic about Chancellors. Considering the source the suggestion was certain to arouse the aging monarch but not bring on an attack of that ailment diagnosed by one observer as resulting from the suppression of bad language. With a statesman like Lord Althorp (later third Earl Spencer) who, although supposedly unduly attracted to the opposite sex, was really interested only in the finer points of livestock, the King was rendered costive. Like all the sons of George III, he knew a great deal about the opposite sex but nothing about farm animals. When it came to what he regarded as the transgressions of a member of his own Household, he felt able to indulge in that linguistic freedom the Royal Navy had raised to the status of a minor art form.

The reaction within the walls of St James's boded no good for the Order. Of this the enthusiastic reformer was blissfully unaware for some time. He went happily on. With a view to enhancing the dignity of the Chancellor, and in accordance with the practices in most foreign Orders, he should, by inference, be a G.C.B. The remaining Officers if they could not be induced to resign, ought to be appointed to some other situation of equal value and given their full nominal salaries, with Sir William Woods eventually promoted to be King of Arms, and his own post of Secretary to the Second and Third Classes abolished outright. The total cost of the Genealogist, Secretary, Registrar, King of Arms, Gentleman Usher and Messenger was £636 0s 8d, from which could be deducted the £245, the average annual fees still paid by the Crown for the fees of some of the Knights. The eventual extinction of these charges would more than cover the salaries suggested for the Chancellor, King of Arms and Secretary under the new arrangements. 'Nor would this be the only saving of expense which would arise from reducing the Officers of the Order, for about £120 are spent on each nomination of an officer for his Mantle, Chain, and Badge, and all officers now receive new Mantles and Badges at every Coronation, a custom which might with great propriety by discontinued.' According to Nicolas' calculations, the eventual total savings on the cost of administering the Order would be 'upwards of £400 per annum'. In these proposals, however, he attacked two of the great canons of William IV's eighteenth century world—the inviolability of vested interests and the principal of seniority.

This document was only the first of several the indefatigable Nicolas prepared for the information and edification of R. W. Hay, Permanent Under Secretary at the Colonial Office. He turned his analytical eye to a thorough consideration of the membership of the Order. Early in 1833 he found that the G.C.B.s numbered 99, compared with the total of 72 established by the terms of the Royal Warrant of 1815. It seemed to him that 80 would be a much better number and observed that a Coronation or Royal marriage, 'afford the only opportunities for the Sovereign to confer the Honour for personal considerations without reference to merit'. Like the Duke of Wellington, he was convinced that there never again would be a war equal in scope to the last one.

Here he made an interesting suggestion that showed how the Bath was then regarded as an award for combat services rather than for general merit in a military career. Writing to Hay he said, 'There will be a few officers, after a lapse of ten years, whose services will entitle them to a Grand Cross; and the principal claims will most likely be for services of a Civil description. For these reasons it does not seem wise to limit by Statute the number to which the different classes of the Knights Grand Cross shall be confined.' The K.C.B.s were reduced to 175 compared with the original limitation of 205. But the total of the C.B.s had risen to 525, a figure he recommended being cut back to 400. He thought that by confining the First and Second Classes of the Order to the same class of officers lessened the value of the K.C.B. This opinion was influenced by the slow promotion of officers during the years 1815 to 1854, when few reached a rank as high as Vice Admiral and Lieutenant General. In another paper he raised the question whether there ought to be a Great Master and suggested the creation of a Civil Class of K.C.B.s and C.B.s. Still later he drafted a new set of Statutes that covered 134 pages written in fine Spencerian script. Many of the provisions foreshadowed those that were eventually adopted.

At this stage in his campaign Nicolas had his only piece of good luck for a number of years. On 3 April 1833 the ineffectual 'Goody' Goderich was replaced in the Colonial Office by the Hon. Edward Stanley, later Lord Stanley, fourteenth Earl of Derby, K.G. and twice Prime Minister. Then the shining light of the Whig party, he had been a firm supporter of the Reform Bill of 1832. While in the Colonial Office it fell to his lot to carry the famous measure in the House that freed the West Indian slaves the next year. With the slavery question out of the way he turned to other Departmental matters and was much struck by the thick docket he found dealing with the Order of the Bath. No sooner had he mastered the papers and talked to Nicolas than he became his friend in the battle to be waged at St James's. As Cabinet Minister he was in a position to persuade the King that the Bath must be drastically reformed and revised in accordance with Nicolas' suggestions. The most important changes the Sovereign agreed to was the need for new Statutes properly executed, the abolition of fees, and the reduction in the number of Officers from 9 to 4. Stanley determined to do something Nicolas had not dared even to hint at: retire the superfluous Officers of the Order and compensate them for lost income. To this end he brought a message from the King to the House asking that the whole question be looked into and the necessary funds provided. The House resolved itself into Committee to consider the question.

In the ensuing debate the Colonial Secretary's presentation made use of all Nicolas' arguments. He concluded his remarks by offering the resolution: 'Thus it is the opinion of this Committee that the Lords Commissioners of the Treasury be authorized to make compensation out of the Consolidated Fund of the United Kingdom, to such Officers of the Most Honourable Military Order of the Bath, as shall be deprived of Salaries and Fees to which they are entitled under the existing regulations and Statutes.'[12] The discussion that followed was marked by the usual number of red herrings. Hume emphasized that England was a civil country with only military honours available to the Crown. He then lumped all the British Orders together as being solely military. Peel took exception to what he understood was Hume's suggestion that a new Order for rewarding scientists be created. He could not believe that it would raise the integrity of science to establish a new system of reward. He then went on to prove that he was no better a prophet than Wellington by saying, 'If this suggestion were attended to, in the same manner the Members of the House of Commons might look for the institution of Orders to reward their public services. The practice would not be correspondent with the simplicity of the English character. . . .'[13] It was fortunate that Sir Robert did not live into the twentieth century because he would have been due for a surprise.

Admiral Sir Edward Codrington was more to the point than most of the speakers because he was in a position to know something about the fees demanded of a G.C.B. He produced the bill he had received with charges coming to £386 7s 2d, which he had flatly refused to pay. He added, 'After a certain time, I was sent for by the First Lord of the Admiralty who told me I should hear no more of this claim. I said, 'If this distinction is conferred only upon the condition of paying for it, you may take it back again from me, for I would not have it on such terms;' and I do think, sir, that in acting as I did, I only performed my duty as well to the Order as to the Service; and I repeat that it is my conviction, that if every officer had acted as I did, The Order would be held in higher estimation than it is.'[14] On 21 April 1834, Stanley's motion was agreed to, and a bill was ordered to be brought before the House to implement it. Nicolas had a right to be pleased. It looked as if he had won and as if the Order would be reformed on the lines he advocated. What must have been a natural feeling of satisfaction was short lived. No bill came before the House. On 5 June Lord Stanley resigned as Colonial Secretary over a difference of opinion with his colleagues on a matter affecting the Irish Church. Nicolas had lost his only supporter at a very critical time. The whole question of reforming the Bath was allowed to drop.

During the hopeful days of April 1834 Nicolas wrote again to R. W. Hay in the Colonial Office. This time he discussed his own personal position. With the impending changes almost certain he recommended himself for the position of

Chancellor of the Bath. He felt he had proved his qualifications by the papers he had submitted. He was the only Officer of the Bath who had made the slightest effort to induce the Government to remove manifest abuses, and the contemplated changes would probably all be founded on his suggestions. He recollected Lord Stanley saying the King had once commented that on all matters relating to Orders Nicolas was very competent. If he were not made Chancellor, he would be forced to retire with no compensation for all his work. Referring to his mortification at having to resign the G.C.M.G. he believed that if he were not promoted in the Bath, he couldn't prove to the world that he hadn't been guilty of some offense which caused the King displeasure. It was all rather sad, and poor Nicolas, as usual, was right. He deserved a promotion if anyone did, but he wasn't going to get it. Across the back of his letter Hay wrote, 'I find from Mr Stanley that there is no chance the King will consent to any arrangement which included Sir H. Nicolas' appointment as an Officer of the Bath under the new arrangement. It will be as well to acquaint Sir H. at once that this is the case. It may be as well to give as the reason the priority of Sir W. Woods' claims.'[15] Not even Stanley could persuade the King to overlook his dislike for the worthy, if sometimes overzealous, servant.

Unfortunately for Nicolas his cup of sorrow was not yet full. Natural as it was to disguise the real reason why he was being refused the promotion he sought, the mention of Sir William Woods exacerbated him. He had always felt himself superior to Woods in all respects and greatly resented finding what he believed to be his own just claims rejected in favour of a man he regarded as incompetent. Aroused by this grievance, and unaware of the real source of the opposition to his advancement, he put the case to Sir Herbert Taylor on 1 May in a long letter. Taylor was Private Secretary to William IV, as he had been to George III in his last years. He certainly knew the King's mind and was not favourably disposed to Nicolas. His reply to the petition contained still another rejection.

It is apparent that Nicolas was no courtier and not sensitive enough to take the hint that he was in real trouble in the highest quarters. He demanded, and was granted, an interview on 10 May with Sir Herbert, conducted in the presence of Sir Henry Wheatly, another member of the Household. The result was extremely painful. Nicolas was accused of having induced the Government to employ him in reorganizing the Bath and having then taken the opportunity to propose the creation of a high office for himself at a salary double that of any then being paid. He had been guilty of trying to force the other Officers into retirement. Taylor observed, 'That it was natural His Majesty should desire to protect the Officers from such mortification, and from the supersession which must produce it.' If it could have been shown that his suggestions had been disinterested and considerate towards the feelings of others, he would have been entitled to credit and reward, but this was not the case. Then the whole question of the Chancellorship of St Michael and St George was gone into, details which had produced, 'a painful impression on the King's mind'. It was pointed out to Nicolas that he strongly urged the justice of his claims for a G.C.M.G. even after it had been objected to by the King. By extension, the arguments about his legal rights to the Grand Cross meant that if he were Chancellor of the Bath he would be entitled to claim a G.C.B. He was told that, 'Chancellorships are in general filled by Persons whose rank in the State would entitle them to the highest dignity in the Order, and who therefore would not have occasion to assert a legal claim to it in right of the office of Chancellor.'

With reference to the question of legality, Nicolas was told that he appeared not to give due consideration to the Sovereign's pleasure or authority in these matters. His statements that no legal instrument had ever been executed for the enlargement of the Bath in 1815 was particularly resented because, after all, the Knights had received the accolade from their Sovereign and no appointments to the Order had been made without the Royal approval. All this was a devastating accusation of conniving selfishness by Nicolas. It was also grossly unfair and almost a deliberate misinterpretation of some of his most carefully argued points in the papers he had submitted analysing the state of the Order. But the interview explains very clearly why nothing was done to put the Bath on a proper footing after Lord Stanley had given up his Secretaryship of War and the Colonies. Once William IV disliked someone, nothing could change his mind.

It is difficult not to think that Nicolas was the architect of his own downfall. With all his great talents he lacked a light touch and subtlety of understanding. Like all great reformers, past and present, he never realized that humourless diatribes seldom advance a cause, no matter how just. He emerges as a sympathetic figure, nevertheless, if only because he was so desperately sincere. Certainly he did everything he could to use the Order of the Bath for his own self-advancement. But in that field of endeavour, compared to those past masters, Anstis and Nayler, he was a naive amateur. There were other differences separating him from them. With private means permitting them to live comfortably regardless of what they did, they were able to attach themselves to powerful patrons. A poor man, Nicolas lived by his pen. Apart from the brief tenure of Lord Stanley in the Colonial Office, he had never known the support of anyone who could be called his patron. Happily married, he was the father of many children for whom he had to provide. Part of his eagerness for the Bath Chancellorship lay in the anticipated salary, a sum large enough in those days to take care of his immediate needs.

Anstis and Nayler were able to command 'Lady Luck', who conspicuously withheld her favours from Nicolas. It is pleasant to be able to record that eventually his efforts on behalf of the Bath were at least partially requited. When his great work on the British Orders was published in 1842, he deftly evened the score with Sir Herbert Taylor. He carefully noted, 'The next appointment to the

Order was attended with some anomalies. Lieutenant General Sir Herbert Taylor, Knight Grand Cross of the Order of the Guelphs, Private Secretary to the King, was nominated a Military Knight Grand Cross on the 16 April (1834); . . . But he had never been a Knight Commander, nor had he distinguished himself against the enemy as a General Officer; and no other deviation from the regulation of 1815 had occurred, except in the instance of the Marquess of Hastings, who was, however, Commander-in-Chief of an army, and had gained distinction in the field. It is obvious, therefore, that the precedent of Lord Bloomfield, in April 1822, should have been followed, by appointing Sir Herbert Taylor to the Civil Class, and which would have been only a just reward for his long service to his Sovereign and the Royal Family.'[16] In October 1840 Queen Victoria gave Nicolas back his coveted G.C.M.G. After his death in 1848, the Queen conferred a much needed Civil List pension on his wife. He had lived just long enough to see most of the necessary changes in the Bath he had so strongly urged introduced by Prince Albert, into whose capable hands the fortunes of the Order had been placed.

CHAPTER VI

Prince Albert Takes Charge

In the early hours of Tuesday, 20 June 1837 King William IV died quietly at Windsor. Almost immediately afterwards, Nathanial, second Marquess of Conyngham, K.P., Lord Chamberlain, Dr William Howley, Archbishop of Canterbury, and Sir Henry Halford, the late King's physician, entered a waiting carriage, and set off for Kensington Palace to take part in what is probably the best known accession scene in history. If Sir Henry was included in this select group because the gentlemen were afraid that a delicate girl would need his attention after the first shock of her uncle's death, they underestimated their new Sovereign. Queen Victoria, well prepared, astonished the veteran courtiers by her composure and maturity. She found the heavy burden of the crown extraordinarily light.

After the Accession Council and the funeral of the late King, she entered into the duties of her new position with youthful enthusiasm. Her first ceremonial function was to confer the G.C.B. on John George Lambton, Earl of Durham, at Kensington, on 27 June. The Sword of State was still being used for the accolade, and Queen Victoria found it too heavy to lift. The ensuing awkwardness was overcome when Lord Melbourne supported it, and the Queen recorded, 'I only inclined it.' When she undertook the same duty a month later in favour of the Austrian Ambassador, she wrote in her diary, 'Seated myself on the Throne. I then conferred the Order of the Bath (not sitting of course) upon Prince Esterhazy.'[1] Although the Red ribbon may have been the first Honour conferred in the reign, the Queen had some personal reservations about it. In these early sparkling days she recorded the following conversation with Lord Melbourne: 'I likewise told him that the Duke of Wellington has let me know that George IV and William IV always wore the Order of the Bath on Waterloo Day and on the Anniversary of the Battle of Trafalgar; and I asked Lord Melbourne if he thought I should do so or not. He said he thought I should. I observed that I didn't like giving up my Blue Ribbon, even for one night.'[2] The Duke himself always wore the Bath at the annual Waterloo Banquet as a tribute to the guests, most of whom had won admission to the Order under his command. It was a graceful gesture that might well be adopted once again by those Knights of the Garter who are also G.C.B.s.

The next step affecting the Bath was more practical than ceremonial. On 14 November 1827 as Duke of Clarence, King William IV had been appointed Acting Great Master and devoted considerable time to the management of the Order's affairs. After he acceded to the throne in 1830, he continued to regard himself as the principal Officer, although he naturally was unable to give as much attention to matters affecting the Order as he might have liked. The question of who should be the next Great Master now had to be considered. The appointment was both surprising and remarkably successful. On 15 December 1837, Augustus Frederick, Duke of Sussex, the Queen's uncle, was given the Civil G.C.B., and named Acting Great Master the next day. The Duke, the sixth son of King George III, was one of the most respectable and intelligent members of the old Royal Family. As a young man he suffered from asthma and had never been able to follow a military career. He developed into a student, a bibliophile of international repute, and never acquired the notorious Georgian habits which were among the least attractive characteristics of most of his brothers. He took his new responsibilities seriously and served the Order well. During the greater part of his term of office he had to work with two outstanding personalities in the War and Colonial Department, the first being Lord John Russell from 1839 to 1841. The second was Lord Stanley, the same Secretary of State who had supported Harris Nicolas' abortive attempts at reform. The approach adopted by both Secretaries of State was entirely different. Russell was a pragmatist, largely interested in making the system work efficiently. Stanley, although he had crossed the floor of the House to join the Conservatives, remained an innovator searching for improvements. The Duke of Sussex cultivated good relations with both statesmen, although it may be presumed that he was more in sympathy with Stanley.

It is curious that Lord John, while Colonial Secretary, showed so little interest in his predecessors' plans for introducing modifications in the structure of the Bath. He was not above interfering in the Order's administration and spent a great deal of time devising new ways to avoid the expense of purchasing additional insignia. It was recognized procedure for each new G.C.B. to ask the appropriate Minister to have the Sovereign graciously dispense him from the ceremony of Installation and direct that he be issued a Mantle and Collar. On one occasion Russell was asked to arrange for the issue of Collars to two Civil G.C.B.s. Across the back of the letter the Under Secretary wrote the tart comment, 'It has not been usual for the Secretary of State for War and the Colonies to meddle with the Civil Knights Grand Cross. It does happen, however, that Lord Gosford and Lord G. W. Russell were gazetted from this office on the occasion of the Coronation (of Queen Victoria) and that instance might be sufficient reason for moving Lord John Russell to act upon the Duke of Sussex's suggestion.'[3] The Secretary of State, a typical product of the old Whig ascendancy, never questioned his natural right to do more or less as he pleased while in Office.

Lord John was difficult about Collars, apparently with some reason. For almost two decades following 1825 there was a chronic shortage of Collars and C.B. Badges. Although the story of the insignia is considered at some length in Chapter XI, a word about the administrative aspects of the problem might not be out of place here. Part of the trouble can be explained by the inability of the authorities to estimate how many members might in the future be in the Third Class. The number of C.B. Crosses returned after the decease of the holders never kept pace with the new appointments. On one hand, Sir William Woods, the Officer responsible for receiving back the K.C.B. and C.B. Badges, told the Colonial Office in 1834 that he had found it impossible to secure the C.B. Badges of several officers killed in action or dying abroad.[4] On the other, the Treasury was slow to sanction the expense of additional Badges. The Duke of Wellington's firm opinion that there never would again be so many senior officers eligible for the first two classes of the Order led him to sanction a curious bit of economy in 1827. He ordered that some of the surplus Collars in store should be melted down to help defray the cost of making up a new lot of C.B.s.[4] This ill-advised decision was probably the basic cause of the shortage of Collars that later developed. At the same time it provided only a temporary increase in the total number of C.B.s required. Between 1837 and 1841, 29 officers were appointed to the Third Class, and none of them was issued his insignia. In the latter year there were only 15 damaged Crosses in store. Russell's solution was to have the damaged pieces repaired and given to the officers according to their seniority, with the others having to wait until a supply became available.[5] These few were comparatively fortunate. There were even cases of Companions waiting five and six years before they received the Badge of the Order.

The Treasury's professional interest in economy was not limited to such easy victims as the C.B.s. As early as 1830 the King proposed to confer the G.C.B. on his brother-in-law, the Duke of Saxe-Weimar. Nayler was instructed to procure the insignia and forward it to Windsor. He applied 'in the usual course' to the Home Department for them and had to report that his request was refused.[4] Presumably none of the ornaments was available. In 1834, Lord Ponsonby, who had received the Civil G.C.B. a month before, made his usual application to be dispensed from the Installation and requested that a Collar be issued to him. The dispensation was granted, but he didn't receive his Collar for another ten years. When Sir William Woods asked the Lord Chamberlain for the insignia to be used for the Investiture of the Prussian General Count Walmoden he was supplied with the Badge and told that there were no Collars available.[4]

By 1840 with few Collars in store, 10 G.C.B.s had not received one. In April Major General Sir Alexander Dickson applied in the usual way to be dispensed from the Installation and asked for his Collar. This request inspired Russell to meditations on the whole general subject. He wrote the Duke of Sussex on 15 April, 'I am well disposed to recommend to Her Majesty to comply with Sir A.

Dickson's application, but as there are other Knights Grand Cross of the Order of the Bath who may claim Her Majesty's Dispensation from the ceremony of Installation, and as Her Majesty's Government would be extremely unwilling to incur the expense of providing the Collars for a larger number of Knights Grand Cross than would be required under ordinary circumstances, I am of the opinion that the proper course to be pursued will be to grant such Dispensations at present to the extent of the number of Collars which may be now at the disposal of the Lord Chamberlain of Her Majesty's Household; and to continue to grant such Dispensations in future according to the number of Collars which may be disposable. . . . I have therefore to request that your Royal Highness will cause to be prepared and will transmit to me for Her Majesty's signature, Warrants of Dispensation from Installation in favour of the Knights Grand Cross who have not already been honoured with that mark of her Majesty's Royal Favour, it being understood that the number of Warrants is to be regulated by the number of Collars available for use; that the Collars be issued to the Knights Grand Cross in order of their nomination; and that preference be given to those who have been invested with their insignia over those who have not been invested.'[8] Nothing in the original Statutes, or in the practices of former Colonial Secretaries, provided any precedent for such a direct interference in a matter so closely affecting the Order. The spectacle of a Minister arbitrarily limiting and directing the distribution of the insignia of the Bath by his own individual fiat, without reference to the legal regulations under which the organization had functioned for well over a century, provides a remarkable example of early Victorian political self-assertiveness in what amounts to a usurpation of the Royal Prerogative. It also shows that the time was at hand when some steps were required to place the administration of the Order on a more rational footing.

In the Autumn of 1841 the Whig Government fell, and Lord Stanley returned to the Colonial Department in the administration of Sir Robert Peel. During the next year he was deep in correspondence with the Duke of Sussex about changes to be made in the structure of the Order of the Bath. The ambitious reorganization projected by Harris Nicolas was not again discussed in detail. The points covered seem to have been limited to removing the financial and other inequalities under which the members of the Second and Third Classes suffered and to considering the position of the Officers of the Order. It was agreed that all fees for the K.C.B.s and C.B.s should be abolished. They recognized that in all probability no room could be found in the Abbey for the K.C.B. Banners and that armorial plates, if erected at all should be provided at the personal expense of the members. The Duke pointed out that the fees for the G.C.B.s were excessive because there had been no Installation since 1812, but a decision about how to reduce them was not reached. With reference to the Officers attached to the lower grades he observed that the late Sir William Woods (who died as Garter King of Arms in 1842) had been most successful in recovering over 200 Badges and thus saved the cost of new ones. He felt that the whole question of returning the insignia needed looking into because on more than one occasion his legal claim to the Collars of deceased G.C.B.s had been questioned.

The most flagrant case of this kind occurred in the Spring of 1842 when he had had to write briskly to Count Kielmansegge, the Hanoverian Minister, to persuade the heirs of General Count Alten to restore his Collar. The heirs claimed the piece was a gift to the General. Lord Stanley's views about the Officer of Arms and Secretary of the K.C.B.s and C.B.s throws a most revealing light on the thought processes of the age. He agreed with Nicolas that the Warrant of 1815 was not a proper legal authority for any of the changes it had introduced but was unwilling to abolish the positions in question. It would be much better to let them fall vacant and then not make new appointments because, 'By that means Her Majesty's Government will be relieved from the disagreeable task of expressly discontinuing pecuniary demands which have never been duly authorized.' The correspondence proceeded most satisfactorily, although without reaching a stage of definitive action, until 21 April 1843, when the Duke of Sussex died at Kensington.[9] He was a splendid old gentleman, and by no means a fool, but it is doubtful whether he was really able to cope with two such successful and devious politicians as Russell and Stanley. His successor was a man of entirely different calibre.

Queen Victoria had married Prince Albert of Saxe-Coburg-Gotha on 10 February 1840. On 6 March, he was invested with the G.C.B. and dispensed from the Installation on 25 March. There was no question about the Prince being supplied with a Collar. The Lord Chamberlain provided it, along with a Mantle, promptly on 30 March. He was not only the logical choice to succeed the late Duke as Acting Great Master, but the only one, and was so appointed on 31 March 1843. The prince was a young man of exceptional toughness of mind and character. Throughout his career he never undertook any responsibility without at once setting about mastering the essential details. His probing intelligence, united with a passion for work, was now directed to the problems being presented by the Order. He was to be helped by an official who made his own far from negligible contributions to the history of the Bath. In 1827 Captain Michael Seymour, RN, later Rear Admiral and G.C.B., had been appointed Registrar and Secretary. As a serving naval officer he was unable to attend to duties associated with this office and appointed a Deputy, none other than Albert Woods, son of Harris Nicolas' old antagonist, Sir William Woods. In 1841, Woods, who had entered the College of Heralds as Portcullis Pursuivant, was promoted Lancaster Herald and combined this office with that of Deputy Registrar and Secretary. He did not succeed Sir Michael until 1859 but went on to become an Officer in most of the other Orders. He survived until 1904 when he died in his eighty-eighth year as Garter King of Arms, G.C.V.O., K.C.B. and K.C.M.G.

These high Honours were fairly earned. In 1842 in his father's place he took over the responsibility of handling the return and issue of the insignia of the then existing Orders on behalf of the Lord Chamberlain's Office. Industrious, more than a little pedantic, he was well equipped to carry out his duties to everyone's satisfaction, including his own. In addition he had that necessary faculty of permanence. Great Masters and Ministers of the Crown came and went but Albert Woods was always there. He formed a connecting link between what had been done and what was going to be done. He made himself not only useful but also essential. Under the circumstances it is not surprising that Prince Albert came to depend upon him for sound information about any problem concerning the Orders of Knighthood.

In a long letter dated 13 June 1843 Lord Stanley put the new Great Master in possession of the details of discussions between himself and the late Duke of Sussex. The Prince's reply a month later expressed a cautious agreement with the proposals to abolish all fees for the lower classes of the Order and to leave the matter of providing armorial plates to the members. He confined himself to urging that Woods be given the responsibility of recovering the insignia and that he should receive a small addition in salary to cover out-of-pocket expenses. Inasmuch as the time-consuming formality of recording the services and Arms of the K.C.B.s and C.B.s in a special book was to be abandoned, the Prince suggested that the recipients nevertheless prepare statements of their services and transmit them to Woods, who would deposit the accumulated total annually with the Horse Guards and Admiralty. Obviously he was feeling his way delicately. In the course of the next two years, however, both men came to dramatic conclusions. They agreed that little could be gained by any more tinkering. A complete revision of the Statutes was finally accepted as an absolute necessity. In view of Stanley's hesitant approach to this problem there can be no question that the idea was the Prince's. On 23 July 1845, the Secretary of State wrote formally to the Great Master that the Queen had decided the Order should be enlarged to permit it to be conferred for civil services to the Crown and he added, 'Her Majesty's Confidential Servants are of the opinion that the object so stated, may most conveniently be accomplished by opening the second and third Degrees of the Order to additional Classes and numbers of persons.'[10] He then went on to say that the proposed change would provide an opportunity to revise the Statutes and bring them up to date. The Prince was asked to prepare a draft of the changes to be suggested for the Queen's approval. Prince Albert promptly instructed Woods to draw up an entirely new set of Statutes for his consideration and to make whatever comments he felt necessary about any particular clauses.

The draft prepared by Woods was not to be adopted in its entirety later, but it provided the basic shape and form of the modern Order. Although the final high level decisions were taken by Stanley and the Prince, and although many details had been discussed during the previous two years, it was Albert Woods who reduced the volume of Harris Nicolas' suggestions to manageable proportions and made them acceptable to his superiors. His scheme, meticulously detailed, need not be examined at length, but a few comments about some of the proposed provisions may be useful. Prince Albert was to play an active and decisive role as Great Master rather than merely to be presented as a figure-head. All Anstis' historical protocol—the bathing, robing and the Installation itself—was eliminated. The only concession to ceremony was a formal investiture conducted in great State. Wearing the Mantle and Insignia the Sovereign, seated on the throne, would be attended by all the officers of the Order and to lend dignity to the occasion as many G.C.B.s in their Mantles 'as could be conveniently assembled'. This provision, adopted two years later, was rigorously enforced by Prince Albert throughout the rest of his life.

Even though one may regret that so colourful a function is no longer used, the Bath investiture was virtually the only one which could actually be performed. The order of St Michael and St George had a very limited distribution at this time, and the Knights of the Garter, Thistle and St Patrick received their insignia in private audience with a minimum of ceremony. The proliferation of Honours in the succeeding century and the desirability of having a great many persons receive their insignia from the Sovereign, has made it impossible for the Queen to confer the Bath in the style used by Queen Victoria during the first half of her long reign. The practice of having the K.C.B.s assume the appellation of knighthood upon their appointment was abandoned. A clause was inserted providing that the form could not be used until the candidate received the accolade from the Sovereign except when unavoidable absence made it necessary to dispense with the Investiture by Royal Warrant. Woods noted that it had been customary for Civil G.C.B.s to resign upon election to the Garter, although not required to do so by the Statutes of 1725. The ambiguity was removed by making the resignation a requirement. All the original seven Officers were continued at their same salaries, although the fees paid by the members were drastically reduced. Only the two Officers attendant on the lower grades were dropped.

By far the most important of the changes was a reconstruction of the membership, in accordance with the ideas contained in Lord Stanley's letter to the Prince of 23 July 1845. The Order was to be composed of three sub-divisions, Military, Civil and Honorary, with three grades of members assigned to the Civil branch paralleling those in the Military branch. The Honorary division regularized the practice of naming distinguished foreigners to all grades of the Order. They were not to be included within the maximum number of members of their respective classes. At this time there were 47 Military and 28 Civil G.C.B.s; 96 K.C.B.s and 514 C.B.s. Under the new scheme, Lord Stanley suggested the following distribution:

	G.C.B.	K.C.B.	C.B.
Army	42	56	250
Navy	18	42	100
Civil Service of the Crown } Diplomatic Service	20	20	30
Colonial Service	2	12	24
East India Company's Military Service	3	12	60
East India Company's Civil Service	2	8	18
	87	150	482

This numerical breakdown of the categories of members gives a good indication of how different the political, social, and economic position of Britain had become in the century and a quarter after 1725. Her contacts with a great variety of European States had multiplied, but, above all, she had expanded outside the narrow confines of Europe to become a vast and growing imperial power. A revision of the Bath would help lubricate the ordinary human machinery used to control the Empire and keep it in sound running condition.

The orderly progress of consultations between the Minister and the Prince was interrupted in December 1845 when Lord Stanley once more found himself at odds with his colleagues in the Cabinet on a question of principle and resigned. His place was taken by Gladstone who seems to have done nothing during the few months in office that remained to him. In 1846 Peel's Government fell, and the Liberals returned to power under Lord John Russell. Henry, third Earl Grey, was given the Colonial Department and lost no time in taking up the threads of Bath reform where Stanley had left them. In view of Lord John's record as Colonial Secretary it is interesting that it was he who urged Lord Grey to get on with the business.[11] There was apparently something about the Victorian Court that could even give some sense of direction to the wandering whims and fancies of a Russell. The Prime Minister was acting under direct instructions from the Queen, which meant, of course, that the Prince had jogged her elbow. Lord Grey reported Woods' draft of the Statutes was fairly satisfactory except for a strong legal objection. The original Statutes of 1725 had been established by Letters Patent under the Great Seal, and an instrument of this kind could not be revoked, or altered, by one of inferior authority. Required were new Letters Patent to revoke those of 1725 and sanction the modified Statutes. He went on to say, 'In 1815 when the Order was extended this course was not taken, and it is not a little extraordinary that for the extension at that time made, there exists, as I am informed, no proper authority of any kind, and that the whole arrangement rests upon a mere memorandum published in the *Gazette*. I beg leave to represent to Your Royal Highness that this was a very inconvenient course to adopt, and that in a matter of this sort it is of great importance strictly to adhere to those legal forms which have been established by prescript and ancient usage. . . .'

Lord Grey was obviously a master of the art of understatement. His was exactly Harris Nicolas' most important argument for reform and the one so indignantly rejected by Sir Herbert Taylor on behalf of William IV. The Prince agreed wholeheartedly. On September 14 Grey added that inasmuch as no one was in a position to question the nominations made since 1815, 'It will be enough to take care that in the intended extension of the Order now, a more regular course of proceeding is adopted.' He concluded by asking for the service of Albert Woods to help in preparing the final drafts. They were ready in December, and the number of members of the different grades had been taken directly from Lord Stanley's earlier memorandum. His last comments before Christmas were not without a note of asperity. Woods proposed clauses requiring the G.C.B.s and K.C.B.s to have their pedigrees recorded. Grey learned only later that a regulation of this kind would have increased the cost of accepting the Order because the Knights would be compelled to pay heavy fees to the Heralds' College. His Lordship was not pleased with Mr Woods who, it will be remembered, was also Lancaster Herald as well as Deputy Registrar and Secretary of the Bath. He struck out the offending clauses.

The Prince's response to the papers sent him by the Colonial Secretary was generally favourable, but at the same time he unerringly singled out the weaknesses in the proposals. He urged that the qualifications for the different grades be very carefully considered because, 'An Order of merit like the Bath is a great means of encouragement in the hands of the Crown, but its value depends solely upon the sparingness with which it is given.' He objected to the original Stanley group of Honorary members, suggesting they should simply form a subdivision of the Military and Civil branches, rather than a major category of their own. These observations are followed by a discussion of a problem that seems to have escaped everyone. What would happen if a military or naval officer holding the military division of the Bath were to win distinction in a civil capacity? Actually the potential difficulty had occurred before and called for specific regulations.

In 1840 Lieutenant General Howard Douglas, Lord High Commissioner of the Ionian Islands, was given a K.C.B. for purely military services. The next year he was awarded a Civil G.C.B. in recognition of his superior performance of duty as Lord High Commissioner. He wrote the Duke of Sussex asking that he be allowed to retain his K.C.B. in spite of having been promoted to the First Class in the civil branch of the Order. The Duke passed this request on to Lord Stanley with a strong recommendation that the Queen grant Sir Howard's wish. In a long reply Stanley refused to lay Douglas' letter before the Queen. He feared the creation of a precedent that would effectively divide the order into two distinct groups.[12] Now, five years later, the Bath was to be divided and enlarged just as Lord Stanley had feared. The Prince's solution to the problem was eminently logical. He concluded that there was no conflict involved in being a member of both divisions of the Order at the same time because each one would be granted for entirely different reasons. But when the numbers in a grade were limited for each class he suggested that a man who found himself a double recipient of a Knighthood in the Bath should become an Honorary Knight of the class in which he held the lower rank, be allowed to keep the Badge but not to wear the Star. In addition to Honorary Knights of this kind, the others would be foreigners and all others not holding Military or Civil office under the Crown. Eventually two of these categories were abandoned and the Honorary members were restricted to foreigners alone. Sir Howard Douglas who had been deprived of his K.C.B. was allowed to have it back again.

In later years holders of both Divisions, while not unknown, have always been rarities in the ranks of the Order. Of this limited group, there are two persons of great interest. By coincidence they were naval officers, and each had the unusual distinction of being a double G.C.B. The exploits of Edmund Lyons as a young officer during the French wars were almost on par with those of Lord Cochrane. From 1840 until 1853 employed on diplomatic service, he earned a Civil G.C.B. in 1844. When the Crimean War broke out he went afloat as second in command of the naval forces in the Black Sea, eventually to become Commander-in-Chief and Vice Admiral of the White. He was one of the few senior officers whose reputation was improved by service in the Crimean area. Awarded a Military G.C.B. in 1855, after the war he was elevated to the Peerage as the first Baron Lyons. Lord Lyons' efficiency was remarkable, and the characteristic appears to have been transmitted to his great-grandson, the present (1972) Duke of Norfolk.

The second of the two 'Double Firsts' was Admiral of the Fleet, the Marquess of Milford Haven. Known during most of his life as Prince Louis of Battenberg, he was First Sea Lord in 1914. Thanks to his foresight, the fleet was ready when war was declared on 4 August. He had already been given a Civil G.C.B. in 1887 on the occasion of the Golden Jubilee of Queen Victoria's reign and gained the Military G.C.B. in 1919. Prince Louis was an outstanding naval officer whose services were lost to the country exactly when they were most needed. Because of his German name, he fell victim to one of those spasms of intolerance that occasionally overwhelm the generally sensible British public. His second son is now Admiral of the Fleet, the Earl of Mountbatten of Burma, a Garter Knight and a Military G.C.B. The Father-and-son succession to the highest ranks in the Navy and the Order is unique.

The pace soon began to quicken. In January 1847 Sir Robert Peel was asked for his views about the proposed arrangements and promptly sounded like the voice of the future. He was afraid that the wording of the clauses describing the qualifications for admission to the Order would exclude distinguished scientific and literary men and wanted the term, 'or by great eminence in art, science or literature have deserved our Royal Favour', added to the appropriate section. This same point he had raised in the debate over Stanley's original motion in 1834. The suggestion was not taken. The Letters Patent passed the Great Seal on 30 April and shortly afterwards the Queen signed the new Statutes. At the last minute Lord Grey introduced a small technical modification of his own. The original Seal of the Order had been a double one, with a mounted Knight on the obverse and the Arms of the Order impaled with those of the Hanoverian Monarchs on the reverse. This device 'was attended with great inconvenience' when used for small documents and Grey had the new one made one sided. The impaled Arms of the Order and the Sovereign were encircled by the inscription, SIGILLUM HONORATISSIMI ORDINIS DE BALNEO. The omission of the word MILITARIS indicated that the change in the composition and function of the Order required that the title be modified accordingly. The Seal was ready on 21 May and on the 25th the Statutes were published in the London Gazette. Harris Nicolas was then spending the last months of his life in France for private financial reasons. If he read them, he would have found himself largely vindicated.

The basic framework established by the regulations of 1847 made the Order essentially what it has remained to this day and need not be discussed in any great detail. The new insignia for the Second and Third Classes of the Civil Division will be mentioned in Chapter XI. A few carry overs from the historic past, not all of them satisfactory, are worth mentioning. The numbers of ordinary members were assigned to the various classes in the following manner:

	G.C.B.	K.C.B.	C.B.
Military	50	102	525
Civil	25	50	200

The First Class was restricted to Flag and General officers as in 1815. The initial difficulty concerning the rank of officers eligible for the Second Class that resulted in a large number of the original appointees not being allowed to wear the Star was dealt with only tangentially. The Military K.C.B. could only be conferred upon persons actually holding a Commission of, or above, the rank of Captain in the Navy, or Colonel in the Army, Marines or East India Company's service. Very few, if any, officers of this rank ever received a K.C.B. but the clause permitted it to be given in special cases. The qualifications for the Civil K.C.B. were rendered especially stringent by limiting it to those eligible for a Civil G.C.B. The 'distinctive appellation of Knights Bachelor of these Realms' was not to be used until after the recipient had been properly invested with the insignia. After noting that the arrangements of 1815 were of doubtful validity, it was emphasized that the changes and appointments made in accordance with them should be considered as having the 'same force, virtue and effect' as if they had been duly made.

A compromise was reached with the Heralds, by permitting but not compelling members of all grades to have name plates erected in the Abbey by Bath King of Arms at their own expense. If Arms were used, the College had to be consulted and the usual fees paid. Each recipient had to sign a form arranging for the return of the insignia by his heirs or executors. Prince Albert was named Great Master and all the original seven Officers were to be continued, the positions to be held by their present possessors who were allowed their salaries and fees on an entirely new scale. Their duties were much the same, with the costs weighing most heavily on the G.C.B.s, who upon appointment were required to pay the Dean £22 6s 8d, the Genealogist, King of Arms, Registrar and Secretary £22 each, the Messenger £18 13s 4d, with an additional £6 3s 4d to Bath for the Statutes and the same amount to the Secretary who sent them their notice of nomination. The total of £129 was a good deal less than it had been in the past, but still formidable. Inasmuch as the offices of Registrar and Secretary were held by one man, he must have received a double fee. Part of his takings, however, had to be paid to Albert Woods. The K.C.B.s and C.B.s paid the nominal sums of £2 and £1, respectively, to the Secretary upon nomination and to Bath only if their plates were actually put up. The other changes made, 'in the constitution of the said Order, with a view to the adaptation thereof to the altered state and circumstances of society within the United Kingdom aforesaid, and our Dominions beyond the seas', also eliminated all Anstis' medieval panoply.[13]

By strange coincidence, at the same time the finishing touches were being put on this document, the Earl of Dundonald, formerly Lord Cochrane, was readmitted to the Order as a G.C.B. He had already been restored to his rank in the Navy, and the Prince felt strongly he should have his Red ribbon back. Although the proposal was Prince Albert's, Lord Grey played a graceful part in the restitution. On 21 May 1847, while asking for the date of an Investiture about to be held, he wrote, 'I may mention that if the investiture should be held before Thursday, Lord Dundonald would be enabled to wear the Order at the drawing room and also at the Official dinner at the Admiralty.'[14]

In the years immediately following the momentous reconstruction of the Bath, a period of quiet ensued. The institution, at last placed on a well organized footing, was sensibly and quietly administered according to a routine varied occasionally by the colourful formal Investitures. But in 1849 there occurred a contretemps of the sort familiar to all bureaucracies but seldom made public. Albert Woods was able to unravel the complicated twists and knots of red tape with consumate skill and to record his actions urbanely and ironically. The successful Punjab campaign in India was rewarded by a suitable shower of Baths. When 2 G.C.B.s, 5 K.C.B.s and 30 C.B.s were nominated and their names Gazetted on 7 June Woods picked up his pen, the most important tool of his trade, and went to work. He had to prepare a special addition to the Statutes for the admission of 21 of the C.B.s. A letter was then addressed to each recipient informing him of his good fortune and forwarding the Warrant of appointment. Lord Grey asked the Prince for a Warrant directing and empowering the Most Honourable, The Marquess of Dalhousie, K.T., Governor General of India, to knight and invest the G.C.B.s and K.C.B.s on the Queen's behalf. Woods prepared the three Warrants because one of the K.s was in the Civil Division. On 18 June and 19 June, the Prince directed that the Lord Chamberlain deliver the insignia to Woods, who prepared the requests. Woods then wrote three separate letters to the Governor General asking him to see that the three classes of recipients signed the forms promising to return their Badges. Inasmuch as the C.B.s were not to be invested, Woods wrote still another letter to the Governor General requesting that he forward their insignia to them. This vigorous epistolary activity consumed three weeks. Finally, on 30 June all was ready. The letters, the Warrants, and the insignia were packed up in a stout box for shipment to Calcutta.

Wood's peace of mind was not again disturbed for four months. At the end of October he received an unsettling communication dated 7 September from F. F. Courtney, Esq, Secretary to The Most Honourable, the Marquess of Dalhousie, K.T., Governor General of India. Mr Courtney informed Mr Woods that the parcel of insignia had arrived without the usual Warrants empowering the Governor General to invest the Knights and that his Excellency was puzzled about what to do. He also enclosed a letter from Lord Dalhousie to the Prince. His Lordship acknowledged the insignia but declared he didn't feel justified in proceeding with the Investiture without a Warrant. On the other hand, the recipients were scattered all over the sub continent on military duties and could not be spared from their commands. With respect, he suggested that a Dispensation from the Investiture be issued. This thunderbolt was at once sent to the Great Master and the wheels began to turn. Woods was first off the mark in a communication of his own to Mr Courtney. On 2 November he wrote with exquisite courtesy to that gentleman describing in detail what he had sent to India. He had packed everything in three parcels and 'then tied the letters and insignia together with red tape. I feel persuaded if you examine the packets you will find the documents. You may have possibly omitted to remove the tape. . . .'

Woods was informed, on 6 November, that Prince Albert agreed with the Governor General's suggestion and a new batch of Warrants and letters authorizing, cancelling and instructing were prepared. Of course each officer also had to have a letter enclosing the dispensation. When these were ready they were despatched. Some weeks afterwards a letter from, 'Camp, Loodianah' dated 7 November arrived from Mr Courtney. With commendable calm he confessed that indeed, he had neglected to open the packets so that the papers remained undiscovered. He enclosed an apology from Lord Dalhousie to the Prince for having bothered him in this matter. The end was not just yet. Woods replied post haste asking to have all the original Warrants returned to him immediately for cancellation. He didn't get them for several months because they were all in Courtney's office at Simla and could not be sent until the Governor General returned to that place at the beginning of the next hot weather. After this nothing was heard of Mr Courtney. Presumably his career did not prosper, and all because he failed to cut red tape. Woods' record of the incident takes up 150 foolscap pages written in a neat small hand.[15]

During the early years of Queen Victoria's reign the Royal Prerogative became more limited but at the same time began to be more sharply defined, largely because of the guidance given the Queen by Prince Albert. His well organized German mind and acute intelligence found the insouciant ways of unregenerate eighteenth-century Whig eccentrics like Palmerston and Russell positively offensive. The Queen was particularly sensitive about the Sovereign's position as Fountain of Honour, as the Ministers found to their cost on several occasions. All recommendations for appointments to the Orders had to be supported by chapter and verse in a manner no longer possible in our day. The Queen had no hesitation in enforcing her own views, sometimes regardless of precedent. When the fourth Earl of Clarendon was given the Garter in 1849, Queen Victoria told him he could keep the G.C.B. because he so fully merited both distinctions. This permission was easily granted, but created certain problems.

In 1851 Lord Grey called the Queen's attention to the fact that the promotion of Sir Henry Bulwer left no vacancy in the list of Civil G.C.B.s unless Lord Clarendon and the Marquess of Normanby, both K.G.s resigned theirs as had formerly been the custom. Although it very properly had not been followed in the cases of the Duke of Wellington and the Marquess of Anglesey, who were Military G.C.B.s for their distinguished services in the field, 'the same reason does not seem to apply to allowing the Civil Grand Cross to be retained with the Garter, and Lord Grey submits it as a point requiring Your Majesty's consideration whether as regards the Civil Grand Cross that wh (which) was the former practice though not enforced by any written rule ought not to be adhered to.'[16] The Queen agreed with her Minister's basic premise, but thought that the rule should not apply to Military G.C.B.s. She added, 'The Queen also wishes that those Civil G.C. who give it up on receiving the Garter shld. have permission to wear the Badge around the neck in order to show that they have had it.'[17] This proposal was similar to the Prince's of having Knights of both classes of the Bath wear the Badge of which ever division was the lower, without the Star. Nevertheless, it does not seem to have been put into effect, and Lords Clarendon and Normanby did not give up their Civil Grand Crosses. When Lord Palmerston was given the Garter 12 July 1856, he also retained his G.C.B.

The Crimean War (1853–1856), had a far reaching effect on the Bath. When the Queen received the final list of proposed nominations to the Order in 1856, she was startled by its length and promptly returned it to Lord Panmure, the Secretary of State for War with the observation, 'Before sanctioning it, she thinks it right to ask for an explanation of the services of the officers, and the reasons for which they were selected for the honour. She returns the list for that purpose to Lord Panmure who will perhaps cause a statement to be attached to each name.'[18] Although the increase in the membership could be expected, other side effects were not so easily predictable.

The public outcry against the mishandling of the military operations and the appalling medical conditions disclosed by Miss Florence Nightingale resulted in the creation of a Parliamentary Commission of Inquiry. The Commission's report minced no words about where, and upon whose shoulders, the responsibility for gross inefficiency lay. Inasmuch as many of those who had received the Bath were prominently mentioned, the Order once again became a subject of comment in the House. When it was moved that a complete report of all awards given since the war be furnished Parliament, Queen Victoria wrote tartly to Lord Palmerston on 14 February 1856, 'The Queen hopes the Government will not allow the House of Commons so much further to trespass upon the prerogatives of the Crown as virtually to take also control over the distribution of honours and rewards into their own hands.' The criticisms might have had a greater effect if those who voiced them paid more attention to the accuracy of their own facts. For example, the archeologist A. H. Layard, then a stormy political petrel, referred to a 'Dr Hall', who he averred had been strongly censored in the report, 'Yet, in defiance of all this, on 6 February, only three weeks ago, he was gazetted K.C.B.'[19] The trouble with this attack was that the only K.C.B. gazetted on the date mentioned had been given to Sir Benjamin Hawes, Deputy Secretary of State at War.

As usual, the political fracas soon died down. The war had, nevertheless, an important effect on everyone's thought patterns. For the first time the Order was wrenched free from a purely domestic context and compared to similar foreign institutions. In spite of the reforms of 1847, there were still obvious anomalies. The award of decorations for combat service to foreigners whose heirs were expected to return them suddenly appeared to be a poor exercise in international public relations. The use of tinsel-embroidered Stars reflected on the dignity of the Order and the nation. To tell distinguished French or Sardinian Generals that they would not be given a Collar because the Lords Commissioners of the Treasury refused to sanction the expense looked ridiculous. So the foreigners were provided with silver Stars and were not required to return the military insignia of the Bath, except for the Collars furnished the Honorary G.C.B.s. The Military Division of the Bath was still regarded as an award that could be earned only on active service against the enemy. If the privilege of keeping the insignia were granted the Honorary recipients, insistence that ordinary members promise to return theirs lacked an element of logic. The Officers of the Order supplied the stickiest problem, for all the reasons listed by Harris Nicolas. The Government now found itself paying their fees and salaries not only for the Honorary members but also for the ordinary ones who had earned the distinction during the late war. It was plainly time to solve these thorny questions.

Throughout 1856 and 1857 the problems were thoroughly canvassed and the difficult decision taken not to require that the insignia be returned, except for the Collar, and to issue silver Stars to all recipients. These matters will be discussed in more detail in a later chapter. The Officers' position was narrowly examined and the old system finally abandoned. With it went the last trace of the profitable internal administrative arrangements so carefully worked out by John Anstis in 1725. The positions of Genealogist and the Messenger were abolished and those of Registrar and Secretary permanently united. All fees were done away with and the holders of the various offices granted annual sums in compensation equal to two-thirds of their average income during the last ten years. The Dean was to have no compensation, but the seven Prebendaries of Westminster who had shared his fees were granted a stipend of £5 19s 2d each. Bath King of Arms was allowed £120, the Registrar and Secretary £260, and the Gentleman Usher £100 as annual salaries. If the same persons were re-appointed their salaries and compensation would not exceed those of the average annual income for the previous ten years. All of these matters were to be embodied in another set of Statutes shortly to be issued.[20] The new Statutes were dated 31 January 1859. Apart from the changes just mentioned the Military K.C.B.s and C.B.s were increased by 8 and 25 respectively. This represented no change over the small increase made in 1850 to take care of the Medical and Commissariat branches of the Navy, Army and East India Company's service. No fewer than sixteen Statutes were added during the rest of the reign, but they were generally limited to increasing the membership.

Shortly after the Statutes were issued, the Order began to feel the full impact of the Indian Mutiny. In the Spring of 1860 the Secretary of State for India, Sir Charles Wood, submitted a long list of awards to the Great Master for his consideration. The results of this submission may have surprised Sir Charles. What he received was a very smart rap over the knuckles of a kind present-day Ministers of the Crown would find startling. Mincing no words the Prince wrote, 'I cannot say that the perusal of so many distinct cases, without classification, has enabled me to form a satisfactory judgment, nor will it be easy for you to do so, unless a classified list be prepared according to some principles to be agreed upon, and some distinct principles to be settled with regard to these rewards, which should take the decision in each case out of the range of arbitrary favour or disfavour.' After pointing out the difficulties of deciding about the use of the Civil and Military divisions, and the promotions, if any, when rewards had already been fairly recently made for Indian service, he asked two very pertinent rhetorical questions. 'Should the Governor General alone be responsible for the recommendations, or should other bodies here in England make separate recommendations, distinct from and differing from his?' After saying that he considered the latter practice very dangerous, the Prince sharply pointed out that it was exactly the one Sir Charles had followed. The Council of India and a special Committee worked over the list of recommendations and promptly added the name of one of their own members to it for a K.C.B. He continued, 'I think that was very wrong and in bad taste. I feel certain united responsibility alone will save us from inconsistencies and arbitrary treatment of different cases, implying favouritism, or causing unjust suspicion of favouritism.' After delivering this chilling rebuke, the Prince then proceeded to teach the Secretary of State his business by explaining exactly how to prepare a classified list and recommending that the whole question be kept secret and out of the hands of his Council, 'who are not the advisors of the Crown.'[21] The sharpness of the reprimand and the knowledge of exactly what to do and how to do it are measures of the Prince Consort's (as Prince Albert became in 1857) complete competence. The incident also gives an insight into the practical constitutional value of the Crown because the same efficiency was at the service of the State in other more serious matters, as the next year was to show.

Handling large numbers of recommendations for the award of the Order presented special problems. It was frequently no easier to deal with individual cases. The Military division could almost take care of itself because the distribution was based on wartime service. Under normal circumstances the distribution of the Civil class could be a little complicated. Because of the Prince Consort's views, it is interesting to find his old antagonist, Lord Palmerston, inadvertently giving him support in a way that twenty years earlier would have suggested promotions to G.C.B., in a letter dated 15 October 1860, that is eminently worth quoting.[22] It is a fine example of the incisive Palmerstonian style and throws considerable light on the use of what was then the only award for civil merit available to the Crown. The Prime Minister wrote:

"I ought to have answered your views about the Grand Crosses of the Bath . . .

When Canning & the others who succeeded him, were at the For: Off:, it was usual to shower the Bath on Diplomatists without reference to personal merit, & merely because they were abroad.

When I came to the For: Off: I discontinued this practice which seemed to me founded on no great reason, but on the contrary liable to great objection, as diminishing the value of the decoration. At that time there was only one Class. Afterwards the Second and Third Classes were added to the Civil Order, but I still used it very sparingly, & confined it chiefly to Embassies, or to particular cases of Missions . . . Since my time the Order has been more easily given—I confess in some instances, in my opinion, without just grounds. The Order of the Bath is now available as a reward for civil service of all kinds, & I should say that there ought always to be kept one or two vacancies in the first & second Classes for distinguished merit requiring immediate or early acknowledgement. The Grand Cross has been given to some Cabinet Ministers who have, in difficult times, had to administer important Departments, but never as matter of course to a Cabinet Minister because of his merely having been such.

I see that . . . and . . . are both of them Knights Commander & I presume they were made so as an acknowledgement of their good services as Diplomatists. Now the question arises, what have they done since they were made Commanders to require that they should be made Grand Crosses? The Bath is not like the Brevet Establishment in the Army & Navy, in which men are entitled to expect promotion by mere lapse of time. My own impression is, though it may be founded in imperfect knowledge, that both might be satisfied with the Honours already conferred upon them.

Independent of the personal question there is the Question of the Establishment. I know that the list of Commanders is full & that no more can at present be appointed consistently with the Statutes of the Order.

I do not know how the list of Grand Crosses may stand, but even if the Establishment should not be full, it would, I should think, be better to keep a vacancy for an unforeseen case, rather than to fill it up, merely because it happens to exist."

The Prime Minister's comments certainly get to the heart of the problem of how to administer the Honours of the Crown. Within a year he was to have just the sort of example for which he felt it wise to be prepared. The last days of the Prince Consort's life in 1861 were bedevilled by the repercussions of an awkward diplomatic controversy between Great Britain and the United States. An American Naval vessel had stopped the Royal Mail Steamer *Trent* on the high seas and removed the Confederate envoys, Messrs. Mason and Slidell, who were being despatched to Europe by the Government of the Southern States. The situation could have resulted in war. The fact that it did not was, on the one hand, owing to the Prince's shrewd modification of the demands being sent to Washington, and, on the other, to the subtle handling of the crisis by the second Lord Lyons, the British Minister on the spot. Early in 1862 Lord Palmerston gave his strongest recommendation to the Queen for the appointment of Lord Lyons as a Civil G.C.B.

The role of the Prince Consort in reforming the Bath and making it a useful instrument in the hands of the Crown was of the greatest importance in the history of the Order. After his initial and laboriously careful reply to Lord Stanley's first letter of 13 June 1843, he quickly became the moving spirit behind all the subsequent modifications. Of course he was hardly able to move faster than the various Secretaries of State were prepared to go at a given moment, but he exercised persuasive powers of a high order. The final impression left by his letters to the Ministers is that of a carefully organized charade planned by the Prince. Many are simply formal acknowledgements of what had already been decided in conference. Through them all the Prince's guiding hand can be detected. Even when a Secretary of State presented a bright thought of his own, the Prince often offered suggestions for changes so subtly presented that the Minister accepted them as his own clever improvements. Naturally the Queen's ideas about the Bath were actually her husband's. That clever manipulator John Anstis would have recognized the Prince as a master of diplomatic procedures beyond the understanding of poor Harris Nicolas. The Order which Anstis had founded was given a Constitution by the Prince Consort enabling it to survive successfully in the troubled twentieth century. Shortly after this major achievement he died on 14 December 1861.

CHAPTER VII

The Late Victorian Age

Before 1861 the history of the Order of the Bath was one of internal modification, and sometimes upheaval, as the institution slowly was made to conform to the rapidly changing social patterns in Britain. Afterwards this process continued but in an entirely different fashion. The organization left by the Prince Consort was flexible and responsive to the needs of the Crown without further drastic alterations in structure. During the early years of the century the strains affecting the Order were often purely internal. In the heyday of the Victorian Age difficulties tended to be external. Nevertheless, one source of trouble with far-reaching effects came from within the Order itself. We have seen how the appraising eye of the Prince weighed all appointments in the hope of avoiding lax practices to which the Ministers were frequently prone. Once removed, his guiding hand was never replaced. As the Queen sank deeper into her self-appointed role of national Victorian widow, she found it more and more difficult to conceive of anyone filling the places in which her late husband had once been so active. The position of Great Master of the Bath was left vacant for thirty-five years. She was strongly urged to fill it by the last remaining person she recognized as having authority in her personal affairs. Leopold, King of the Belgians, came to London to support his niece in her hour of trial and remained several weeks. If the late Prince Consort could be said to resemble anyone, it was the sternly capable King Leopold, founder of the modern Belgian State. He had been a G.C.B. for forty-five years. As early as January 1862 he saw the need and urged that another Great Master be named. Queen Victoria refused to acquiesce.

The King changed his tactics and suggested that Field Marshal Viscount Combermere be made Deputy Acting Great Master. At the age of ninety, he was an amazing survival. As Wellington's commander of cavalry in the Peninsula, the last living member of the Bath who had received it as a K.B. he still had most of his wits about him. The Queen engaged in delaying tactics. The King then advised that George, second Duke of Cambridge, the Queen's cousin and Commander-in-Chief of the Army, be made Acting Great Master, to hold the office until Albert Edward, Prince of Wales, became of age. Sir Charles Phipps, Keeper of the Privy Purse, also acting as Private Secretary at the time, observed that 'to offer the Duke of Cambridge a temporary dignity, until somebody else could hold it, was no great compliment.'[1] The Duke was notified, nevertheless, that the Queen wished him to serve. He expressed his appreciation of the offer and willingness to accept it. The appointment, never formally announced, does not, in fact, appear to have been made.[2] Although the Prince of Wales became twenty-one in November 1862, he was not given the G.C.B. until 10 February 1865. The Queen kept him waiting for his father's place as principal Officer of the Order until it was time to celebrate the Diamond Jubilee of her reign. On 6 June 1865 the Prince was allowed to act as the Sovereign's Deputy at the first Investiture conducted according to the full ceremonial prescribed in the Statutes to be held since the Prince Consort's death. He invested 11 G.C.B.s and 27 K.C.B.s on that occasion. This was the closest association he was to have with the Order for a long time.

Given the inevitable erosion of the Prerogative, if the Prince Consort had survived into old age, it is questionable whether he could have continued to exert such a powerful influence on the affairs of the Bath as he had acquired. The sudden removal of all executive control at the top, however, was bound to have a number of results. The first of these was the most important. It will be remembered that the qualifications for members of the Military Division were keyed to rank in the armed forces of the Crown and to outstanding service against an enemy in the field. After 1815, with few exceptions, promotion within the Order had depended upon further distinguished active service. In the long interval of comparative peace following the French wars the total number of K.C.B.s fell below the full statutory number allowed. These regulations now began to be given a new interpretation. To complicate matters the practises of the Admiralty and the War Office varied in certain significant respects. With regard to the Military K.C.B., there was substantial agreement, at any rate on the surface. The Statutes restricted this grade of the Order to officers of, or above, the rank of Colonel and Captain, R.N. (Active or Retired) who held the C.B., had distinguished themselves before the enemy, or who had rendered good and efficient service as General or Flag Officers. The reference to 'Active or Retired' had curious implications presently to be made clear. It was in the application of the relevant clause restricting the award of the C.B. to Majors and Commanders that the two services found themselves at odds. The position was rendered more difficult by the fact that the First Lord was not a Secretary of State so that all his recommendations had to be submitted through the War Office.

In May 1873, Goschen at the Admiralty wrote Cardwell, the Secretary of State, and accused him of introducing a new principle in awarding the third Class of the Bath. The Army had been giving it to officers who, after rendering their qualifying services as Captains, were gazetted brevet-Major and C.B. on the same day. As Goschen said, 'The immemorial custom of the Navy has been not to give the C.B. for services rendered by an officer below the rank of

Commander.' Cardwell's reply to the complaint took the form of a memorandum, obviously prepared for him, in which he rather coldly said, 'The Army practise was acted on in the Army so far back as 1842; indeed there is nothing to show that it has not always prevailed.' This was not strictly true, either as a statement of fact or as a surmise, but it was a good military answer. George Duke of Cambridge, the Commander-in-Chief, made the apt comment that the Navy had adopted a self denying ordinance not required by the Statutes, and flatly refused to change the Army's customary method of awarding the Order. In the Admiralty their Lordships were equally sure of the wisdom of their own familiar habits.

The argument was continued sporadically for years. It was not finally settled until January 1895, when a joint Service Committee was convened at the War Office to see if the contending parties couldn't agree what to do and how to do it. Thanks to the fact that by this time the issue was really dead, the decision reached was a victory for Admiralty views. With great delicacy the Committee's report stated, 'It was finally agreed that endeavours should be made to assimilate the Army practise to that of the Navy, as soon as it could be conveniently done.' An easy agreement was rendered possible by the existence of the D.S.O., founded in 1886, which effectively did away with the need to use brevet promotions as rewards for service in the field, and the Third Class of the Bath as a combat decoration for junior officers rather than as a form of recognition for officers with command responsibility.

The question of promoting retired officers was something else and again the two Services followed quite different principles. Inasmuch as retired Army officers no longer held the Queen's Commission, it was the War Office view they were not eligible for appointment to, or promotion in, the Order of the Bath. Naval officers, on the other hand, continued to hold their commissions and were often promoted after retirement. Mr W. H. Smith, First Lord in 1879, observed, 'It must happen in time of peace that the most distinguished men are found among those who have been placed on the retired list by operation of the old age clauses.' The War Office objected as an officer on the Retired List could not possibly be eligible on the ground that, if his services had been sufficiently distinguished, he would have obtained the honour before retirement. Part of the difficulty stemmed from the differing personnel policies of the two services. Naval officers tended to be compulsorily retired at comparatively earlier ages than those in the Army, for reasons of health and as a result of the higher professional standards they were then required to meet. To encourage optional retirements the Navy made a distinct effort to assimilate the position of the Active and Retired lists as regards honours, pensions, and employment not of a Naval or Military kind. In spite of a vigorous exchange of views between successive First Lords and Secretaries of State for War from 1873 onwards the issue was not resolved during Queen Victoria's reign.[3]

In retrospect we can now see that these differences had a Gilbertian aspect fraught with consequence. The iron refusal to award the Bath to retired Army officers was subject to a curious qualification. The regulation was not applied to veterans of the Crimean War and the Mutiny. Almost every reasonably senior Army officer, therefore, was eligible for appointment to the Order. The Navy meanwhile continued to give promotions in retirement in addition to the Bath. As a result, the higher ranks of the Order began to be filled with superannuated officers whose campaigns were confined to their daily tottering walks along the sands of Brighton. A brief illustration will suffice to indicate the general pattern. After a distinguished, if somewhat irregular naval career, Captain Sir George Rose Sartorius came ashore in 1844 and never received another command afloat. He was then fifty-four years old. During practical retirement his promotions arrived with comforting regularity. He became Rear Admiral in 1849, Vice Admiral in 1856, Admiral in 1865, Admiral of the Fleet in 1869, and lived to enjoy his high rank until 1885 when he was in his ninety-fifth year. He had never been awarded a C.B. but he received a K.C.B. from the hands of the Prince of Wales at the 6 June Investiture in 1865 and the G.C.B. in 1880.

So ingrained did this system become that when Major General Sir Garnet Wolseley (afterwards Field Marshal Lord Wolseley, K.P.) was offered a G.C.B. in 1874 in recognition of his successful campaign against the Ashantees, he refused it. He was afraid that accepting the Bath when he was only a comparative stripling of forty-one would create jealousies which might blight his future career. He also declined a Baronetcy much as Nelson had. According to his biographers he is said to have told his friends that he did not care to share the honour with the Duke of Devonshire's gardener. This was somewhat arrogant even for Wolseley, who cultivated a disregard for everyone's dignity and position except his own. The 'gardener' to whom he referred, Sir Joseph Paxton, designer of the Crystal Palace, is likely to be remembered longer than the Field Marshal. Recognizing the force of Wolseley's argument, the Commander-in-Chief recommended him for the double honour of a G.C.M.G. and K.C.B. A Parliamentary grant of £25,000 must have gone far to soothe whatever longing he may have felt for the lost Grand Cross.[4] While the Bath was still to be given for combat services in Colonial Wars, the Boer War, and both World Wars, from this period it was also used to crown a successful military or naval career even though the highest ranks had been achieved in a comparatively peaceful administrative capacity.

The position of the Order next began to suffer from alterations in the basic political and social structure in the late Victorian age. Though a dedicated imperialist and firm supporter of the Monarchy, Lord Beaconsfield is responsible for an action with far-reaching consequences. On 31 July 1878 he wrote to the Queen, 'With reference to the Military decorations, the war office has always claimed, and exercised, the privilege of recommending to Your Majesty recipients for the Military Division of the Order of the Bath, as the Colonial Office exercised the same privilege with respect to the Order of St Michael and St George. Lord Beaconsfield himself thinks that all applications for honours should be submitted to Your Majesty by the Prime Minister alone; and if Your Majesty, on reflection, approves of such an arrangement, he would carry it into effect. The present occupants of the two offices in question would be favourable to it.' With all Honours channelled through the Prime Minister's office, it obviously became more difficult for the Sovereign to exercise the same precise control over appointments to the Orders that had been customary in the past. The Prince Consort would not have approved, but considering the source of the suggestion, the Queen could hardly do anything else but accept it. The new practice meant that admission to the highest ranks of the Bath would, from time to time, be made with stronger political overtones than had been the case before.

There are examples to illustrate the point. In 1878 the Prime Minister was not satisfied by the trend of events in South Africa. To complicate matters, the local military commander, General Sir Arthur Cunynghame, clashed with his superior, Sir Bartle Frere, Governor of the Cape, who demanded that Sir Arthur be removed forthwith. One of the Prime Minister's secretaries wrote Sir Henry Ponsonby, Private Secretary to the Queen, 'If the Secretary of State for War thinks the General has been rather scurvily treated by the Government, it is open to him to recommend the Queen confer on him the G.C.B., and Lord Beaconsfield will not object to such a step under the circumstances.'[5] Sir Arthur was given his G.C.B., then, to cover up what was regarded in some quarters as his total incompetence. In June of the same year the Rt. Hon. Austen Layard, who had made himself difficult about Crimean awards of the Order, was also admitted to its ranks. Now Ambassador to Turkey, 'he received the G.C.B. as a mark of recognition for his advocacy of Lord Beaconsfield's Imperial views'.[6] In June 1885 Wolseley wrote his wife from Cairo, 'The Government have determined to give some rewards for both the Nile and Suakin columns, and I have been preparing lists. Greaves will be made a K.C.B.—also Buller; but there are some like Evelyn Wood and Graham who are already K.C.B. that cannot be rewarded as they have not earned a G.C.B., although the decoration has just been so prostituted that it is difficult to say that any man has not earned it.'[7]

What can be called only a downward trend in the prestige of the Order was soon shown in another area. It will be remembered that the First Class of the Civil Division had been accepted gladly by Cabinet Ministers on more than one occasion in the not-too-distant past. Now another type of politician was reaching the top in an entirely different political climate. Between Disraeli's Reform Act of 1867 and 1885, the franchise was extended to most urban and agricultural workers. In 1872 the secret ballot was prescribed for all municipal and Parliamentary elections. More and more successful merchants and industrialists, seeking political careers, sprang from the same background as the newly enfranchised voters. It would have been awkward for them to face the electorate as 'Sir William' rather than plain 'Bill'. When W. H. Smith was Secretary of State for several departments in Lord Salisbury's Government in the 1880's, he was in just such a dilemma. If his reaction makes strange reading today, it tells a good deal about the Victorian world in which he moved. On 24 January 1886 the Prime Minister wrote to the Queen, 'Lord Salisbury spoke to Mr Smith with respect to his acceptance of the Grand Cross of the Bath. Mr Smith desires him to lay before Your Majesty his deep and earnest gratitude for this mark of Your Majesty's favour; but, after reflecting, he is of the opinion that for the purpose of serving your Majesty, in his peculiar position with respect to his extraction and the original avocation of his family, it would diminish his usefulness at present if he were to seem to the outside world to be too anxious for a decoration which, until recently at all events, has only been given to men of his social standing for very distinguished services. Lord Salisbury thinks Mr Smith's scruple is exaggerated, but is deserving of respect.'[8]

The Rt Hon Joseph Chamberlain, the Birmingham industrialist and former Mayor of that city, had more personal self-confidence but was equally firm in refusing the G.C.B. In telling the Queen on 16 March 1888 that he respectfully declined the honour, Lord Salisbury added, 'His position towards us as a Radical Unionist places him in peculiar difficulties in that respect. But he expressed a hope that, if Your Majesty approved of his conduct, you would signify it by giving him your portrait signed.'[9] Under the circumstances the substitution of a photograph for the Bath was not as strange as it may sound. The Emperor Francis Joseph always regarded the gift of his portrait as a much higher honour than any of the Austrian Orders, with the exception of the Fleece and the Maria Theresa. Views of this kind, regardless of the reasoning behind them, indicated that the prestige of the Bath was no longer what it had been. By 1899 the G.C.B. was being given to men like Sir Hugh Owen, retiring Permanent Secretary to the Local Government Board. Although Sir Hugh may have been a distinguished official, he can hardly be compared to Ministers who controlled the levers of power in the State. At the end of Queen Victoria's reign the practice of virtually restricting the Bath to civil servants had already begun at the top and continues in our own time.

The distribution of the Second Class of the Civil Division during these years did not at first follow the pattern being established for the Grand Cross. The list contained names like those of Sir Henry Acland, Regius Professor of Medicine at Oxford University, Sir William Jenner, President of the Royal College of Physicians, and Sir Lyon Playfair, who had been Professor of Chemistry in the University of Edinburgh. The K.C.B. was not yet restricted to officials but allowed a much broader social base. Some of the recipients had, or were to receive, the greatly esteemed Prussian Order, 'Pour le Mérite für Wissenschaften und Künste', the precursor of the Order of Merit founded by Edward VII in 1902.

The public reaction to this wider distribution was totally surprising and probably a reflection of other forces at work within the social fabric. The Bath became the subject of a ridicule not unlike that directed at the Order of the British Empire in the years following the first World War. It must be remembered that during the 1870's and early 1880's the Queen had not yet emerged as Imperial Matriarch and suffered from a wide unpopularity. A cacophony of noisy republicanism abroad in the land naturally affected the instruments of the Crown. Those two great and durable artists, William Schwenk Gilbert and Arthur Sullivan, are excellent examples of late Victorian attitudes. For some reason Gilbert connected the Bath with the Navy rather than the Army and directed his barbs accordingly. As Captain Corcoran, the gallant commanding officer of *H.M.S. Pinafore*, stood expectantly on the poopdeck of his ship, the approach of no less a potentate than the First Lord of the Admiralty is heralded with the chorus:

> Over the bright blue sea
> Comes Sir Joseph Porter, K.C.B.
> Wherever he may go
> Bang-bang the loud nine-pounders go!
> Shout o'er the bright blue sea
> For Sir Joseph Porter, K.C.B.

However convenient 'K.C.B.' may have been to rhyme with 'sea', audiences have found Sir Joseph a recognizable character ever since *Pinafore* was first produced in 1878. Gilbert was not one to drop a good thing when he found it because he introduced another Captain Corcoran in *Utopia Limited* as late as 1893 when public opinion had already begun to change. This was Captain Sir Edward, RN who introduces himself with the lines:

> I'm Captain Corcoran, K.C.B.
> I'll teach you how we rule the sea,
>   And terrify the simple Gauls:
> And how the Saxon and the Celt
> Their Europe-shaking blows have dealt
> With Maxim gun and Nordenfelt
>   (Or will when the occasion calls).

The views of the Queen's Private Secretary, Sir Henry Ponsonby, as a K.C.B. finally overwhelmed him, are instructive. Owing to his position, Sir Henry knew a great deal about how the machinery of honours and decorations worked, and he entertained no illusions about human nature. He was rather like a priest attached to the Oracle at Delphi—too familiar with the mysteries to be impressed by the glamour. Still, even when the effect of his environment is taken into consideration, his personal response to the Bath reflects a stronger element of current opinion than he was probably aware of. He had successfully fended off a C.B. in 1872 because he was, 'bitterly opposed to being daubed with that blotch. . . .' When the Queen wished him to have the K.C.B. in 1879, she was so afraid of another refusal that she adopted unusually devious means of approaching the subject. The Marchioness of Ely brought the matter to the attention of the Hon Gerald Wellesley, Dean of Windsor, who was left with the task of persuading Ponsonby. A lively correspondence took place between the two old friends. Referring first to the C.B., Sir Henry told the Dean, 'Biddulph said I was wrong. That as long as I held the position I did I was bound to accept unrepiningly whatever punishment was offered,' and continued, 'Remember your object is to raise me in my office and to make me hold up my head— which I do —you then cover it with abominations and still expect me to be proud of myself!'[10] In the end he gave in and accepted the abominations heaped upon him. When the G.C.B. was offered in 1887, the atmosphere had so far cleared that the Queen felt able to tell him of her intentions directly without fear of rebuff.

The survival of Gilbert and Sullivan's popularity cannot be explained solely by humour and catchy tunes. Gilbert, a major social satirist with a marked ability to put his finger on the pulse of the world in which he lived, signalled a shift in public opinion regarding the Bath in *The Gondoliers*, first produced at the Savoy in December 1889. When the brothers Marco and Giuseppe, find themselves joint kings of Barataria, they describe the nature of their job as follows:

> Rising early in the morning,
>   We proceed to light the fire,
> Then our Majesty adorning
>   In its workaday attire
>   We embark without delay
> On the duties of the day.
>
> *
>
> After luncheon (making merry
> On a bun and glass of sherry)
>   If we've nothing in particular to do
> We may make a Proclamation
> Or receive a deputation—
>   Then we possibly create a Peer or two.
> Then we help a fellow creature on his path
> With the Garter or the Thistle or the Bath. . . .

Even Queen Victoria enjoyed these innocent barbs. Significantly, there is ample evidence that the reference to 'helping a fellow creature on his path' with the Order is precisely one of the functions it was supposed to, and frequently did, perform. The first Lord Hardinge of Penshurst observed in his reminiscences, 'It was on the 28th June 1895, that I experienced one of the most pleasant surprises of my life. On opening a letter on my writing table in the Chancery (of the Paris Embassy), I found it contained an offer from Lord Rosebery (then Prime Minister) of a C.B. couched in charming but simple words. . . . I would like to place here on record my gratitude and indebtedness to Lord Rosebery for having dragged me out of the ruck of the junior branches of the Diplomatic Service by conferring on me such an exceptional distinction as the C.B. at the age of thirty-seven, an irrefutable testimony to my past services. It gave me the forward impetus that I needed. . . .'[11] Lord Hardinge is slightly at fault here for saying that Lord Rosebery conferred the Honour. The Prime Minister only recommended him, but he received his Badge from the hands of Queen Victoria at Osborne. There could be no question about the impetus to his career provided by his first step in the Bath because he rose to become Viceroy of India and Knight of the Garter.

A residue of radicalism in politics, complicated by the Irish question, was still apparent in the late 1880's. The Bath again became a subject of adverse comment in the House. Radical M.P.s were a noisy minority whose only political tactic was to be as obstructionist as possible. They seized upon any issue they thought would attract favourable public attention to themselves. Fiscal questions often gave them the chance to appear as champions of the taxpayer's purse.

Just such an opportunity took place in autumn of 1887 during a debate on Supplies that covered, among other things, certain additional sums for expenses incurred during the recent Golden Jubilee celebrations held to commemorate the fiftieth anniversary of Queen Victoria's accession. The figures included the cost of insignia for the Orders of Knighthood conferred on that occasion. The total came to £4,770. On the evening of 6 September one of the firm supporters of Mr Henry Labouchere, a well known Radical, rose and delivered himself of a number of piquant irrelevancies. He declared, 'My contention is that if noble Lords and others desire to dress themselves up in robes and insignia they should pay for their own enjoyment and not come to the poor taxpayer of this country to pay for their equipment.' Turning to the Order of the Bath, he declared, 'I do not know whether the insignia of the Bath, for instance, is a bath, and whether the repairing of that particular insignia means the repairing of a bath in which these noble Knights and others occasionally wash themselves.' The obvious retort that if he was so ill informed about the subject he hardly had a right to an opinion was not made. Another Member declared that individual items of insignia should not cost more than 10s or 15s apiece. After the usual recess at the end of the year the subject came up again in

March 1888, when the total amount required had risen. One of the Lords of the Treasury observed that, 'The largest expenditure was connected with the Military Order of the Bath, and amounted to upwards of £4,000; that in the Civil Order amounted to £1,900,' adding that certain alterations were being made. He also disclosed that a G.C.B. Collar cost £356 and the Badge £38 10s with the Stars and 'other things' coming to about £20.[12] In reading the record one cannot help feeling that Lord Salisbury's Government was not interested in seriously challenging the Radicals' attack.

The pressure on the statutory limits of membership of the Order was unremitting during these years and resulted in a gradual increase from 1,218 set in 1877 to 1,320 by 1896. These figures were exclusive of appointments made for the Golden Jubilee of 1887, the Diamond Jubilee of 1897 and the South African War, which were to be regarded as additional. The numbers allotted to the different branches of the services still caused difficulties that were 'solved' by borrowing generally from the Navy's portion. When Mr Henry Campbell-Bannerman as Secretary of State for War was proposing an increase in 1886, he suggested that the best way to avoid this practice was to transfer 20 C.B.s from the Navy to the Army allotment.[13] It was at this same time that the Bath may have come very close to acquiring a Fifth Class as Wellington had almost advocated in 1815. Campbell-Bannerman finally came to grips with the old problem of how to reward officers below the rank of Major by some means other than a Brevet promotion. He proposed a new military 'Order'. On 18 May 1886 he wrote Sir Henry Ponsonby, 'It will rather be a decoration than an order. My idea is that it may be a cross or a medal for Distinguished Service in the field—thus carrying into the Commissioned ranks a somewhat similar reward to that which exists in the ranks below. . . . In writing about it before, you mentioned that the Queen hoped that the Civil Service would be included, but perhaps you may be good enough to submit to Her Majesty that the present available honour of the Bath is open to all ranks of the Civil Service; whereas the difficulty we are now desirous to meet arises from the fact that no one under Field rank can receive the C.B. and thus we are reduced to the inconvenient alternative of Brevet Promotion for all junior officers.' This plan was, in fact, the genesis of the D.S.O., an award which, from the looks of things, just escaped having a civil division.[14] It probably came closer to being stillborn because Sir Henry was not at all enthusiastic about the plan. After discussing the form of the decoration with the Duke of Connaught, he objected to a cross being adopted because what was proposed was only an extension of the D.C.M. for commissioned ranks. He also did not understand 'how the actions rewarded will be distinguished from those that earn the Victoria Cross.'[15] He ended by saying that it would almost be better to have a Fifth Class for the Bath. He failed to mention the possibility of a Fourth Class. This last view shows how even at this late date the purpose of the Bath, a reward for senior officers with a record of outstanding service in positions of command responsibility, was being confused with a combat decoration in the mind of one of the Sovereign's most influential advisers. Eventually, the opinions of Campbell-Bannerman and the Duke of Cambridge were accepted, and the D.S.O. created.

Some increases in the membership were inevitable and would have passed even the scrutiny of the Prince Consort. One took place in 1890 when Edward Stanhope, then Secretary of State for War, wished to add 10 Civil C.B.s to be at the disposition of the War Office. He wrote Sir Henry on 10 March to explain his proposal and promptly found himself in a time-consuming controversy. The object of the plan was 'to meet the case of those officials who have rendered great service to the Army, though not in the field'. This seems clear enough today, but it caused a flurry at Windsor. Ponsonby got the idea that Stanhope was suggesting the creation of a special class of the Bath, and a great deal of writing back and forth took place. The Minister rather ruthfully recognized that it had been a mistake to attempt brevity in such a situation. All he wanted was 10 C.B.s to recognize special service to the War Department in a technical civil capacity and found himself accused of proposing inflationary policies. With great care he told the Private Secretary, 'You point out that a good many officials here have been rewarded with the Order of the Bath. It is quite true, but all of them (except one) have obtained it from the Prime Minister after hearing the claims of other Civil Servants in all the public offices each year.' Stanhope was in deep trouble. No explanations he could put forward seemed to help, so in desperation he turned to the Prime Minister for support.

The administration was then headed by Sir Robert Arthur Talbot Gascoyne-Cecil, K.G., ninth Earl and third Marquess of Salisbury. The Cecils, in company with the Cavendishes, Howards, Russells, Stanleys and some others, could regard the history of the country as a series of episodes, often bizarre, in the history of their own families. When Beaconsfield and Salisbury were given the Garter in 1878, the former quipped that it was an achievement for a Disraeli to receive the Order in company with a Cecil. Now Lord Salisbury, huge and inscrutable, ruled Britain and the Empire from Hatfield, resembling nothing so much as a bearded enigmatic Buddha enshrined in a Jacobean temple. It was this formidable man who was called upon to contend with his Sovereign over the question of 10 C.B.s. In the process he made a memorable observation. On 23 March 1890, after telling Ponsonby that there were not too many Bath decorations but too few, he went on, 'Within my recollection the expenditure of the country has increased from fifty millions to nearly ninety; and that expenditure means, in great part, additions to the Civil Service. The rage for distinctions grows; and outside the Civil Service men who have done any good work expect a decoration.'[16] The new 'rage for distinctions' indicated how much attitudes had changed since the days when Sir Robert Peel had proudly told the House that rewarding public service with an Order would not correspond with the simplicity of the English character. Those with tidy minds and an affection for dates may reasonably conclude that the practice, now so widespread, began in 1890 with 10 C.B.s. The process was continued in 1895 and 1896 when the Second and Third Classes of the Civil Division were further increased, partly to allow for additional rewards to the Queen's Household, the Households of other members of the Royal Family, and technical officials of the Admiralty.

If the Queen lost a battle over the question of additional C.B.s she was more successful in rejecting in 1893 a suggestion of Lord Rosebery, her Foreign Secretary. He had recommended for a K.C.B. Sir Thomas Sanderson, the Permanent Under Secretary at the Foreign Office. Using the precedent of Knights of the Thistle and St Patrick relinquishing those Orders upon receiving the Garter, he now urged that Sir Thomas be permitted to resign his K.C.M.G. upon promotion to the Bath. He argued with impeccable logic, 'It is considered invidious that a man who is already a K.C.M.G. should cumulate honours by adding to it the K.C.B. Moreover, the K.C.B. practically swallows up the K.C.M.G., for it is greatly preferred, and, as the insignia are worn similarly, it is scarcely possible to wear both.' The discussion went on for a week, with Rosebery insisting that his proposal, 'would make that available which is useless to the pluralist in Orders. At present he is under the curse of the man who buried his talent in a napkin.'[17] His motives involved more than pure logic because he was looking for an extra place in the St Michael and St George to give away. Actually he was on weak ground because it was not unusual for military officers to hold both distinctions together, and a precedent of the type he advocated would have caused trouble if applied by the War Office and the Admiralty. In any case, Queen Victoria heartily disliked the idea and refused to entertain it. Defeated, Rosebery retired to Scotland for a long weekend.

The last significant event in the long reign to affect the Order was the nomination of Albert Edward, Prince of Wales, as Great Master. During the delicate moves required to persuade the Duke of Cambridge to resign as Commander-in-Chief in 1895, some thought was given again to appointing the old warrior principal Officer of the Bath to ease his disappointment, but nothing came of it. What to bestow on the heir to the throne as a Jubilee Honour in 1897 was a problem because there were no distinctions he did not already have. Giving him the office of Great Master provided a happy solution. The Prince was delighted at finally succeeding his father, and the appointment was marked by a special Statute dated 22 June 1897. On 20 July he revived William IV's pleasant custom and entertained the Knights Grand Cross at dinner in St James's Palace. But the position came too late for him to leave any impression on the affairs of the Bath, even if he had wished to play the Prince Consort's part. The real control over all the Orders of Knighthood was now exercised from the Prime Minister's office, 10 Downing Street, where it has remained with certain exceptions ever since.

CHAPTER VIII

The New Century

When King Edward VII succeeded to the throne in 1901 most of his subjects could remember no Sovereign other than Queen Victoria. Certain doubts were felt by some about the new monarch's fitness to bear the burden of his office. These fears were quickly seen to be uncalled for. The Queen had neglected the ceremonial duties of the Monarchy for forty years. It was necessary for the well being of the institution that they be revived and King Edward set about doing so with enthusiasm. He enjoyed being seen by the public and had a natural talent for ceremonial. He earned a wide popularity which he never lost. One of the King's first acts was to recognize the importance of the Bath by naming his brother Arthur Duke of Connaught, as Great Master on 26 February 1901. The Duke filled the office with distinction for four decades.

During Queen Victoria's reign the custom of automatically giving the Military Division of the Bath to members of the Royal Family, as had been done in 1815 to the sons and a nephew of George III, was allowed to lapse, with the exception of the Prince of Wales in 1865. The Queen's second son, Admiral the Duke of Edinburgh, was not made G.C.B. until 1889 while commanding the Mediterranean Station. The Duke of Connaught had a distinguished military career. He earned his appointments in the Order much as any other soldier, receiving the C.B. in 1882, the K.C.B. in 1890, and the G.C.B. in 1898 when holding the Aldershot Command. During this century the only awards of the Military Division to members of the Sovereign's immediate family were a C.B. to Prince Arthur of Connaught in 1915 (which his father, the Duke, told him he was most fortunate to get), and the G.C.B. to the Marquess of Milford Haven in 1919, and to the Duke of Gloucester upon succeeding his great uncle as Great Master in 1942. In a limited number of cases the Civil Division was given to members of the Royal Family. In 1911, for example, Queen Mary's brothers, the Duke of Teck (Marquess of Cambridge) and Prince Alexander of Teck (Earl of Athlone) were made G.C.B.s at the time of the Coronation of King George V.

Early in the reign the Order lost one of its most devoted servants and a thoroughly remarkable man. Sir Albert Woods had attended to the affairs of the Bath in one capacity or another from the time he was barely of age in the 1830's. In a long and prosperous career he became Garter King of Arms and an official

86

of a great many of the Orders of Chivalry. By 1897 the weight of his years was beginning to tell. Although Sir Henry Weldon, Clarenceaux, acted as Deputy Garter on public occasions, and Farnham Burke took a leading part in preparing the Coronation of King Edward, Sir Albert did the paper work of the several Orders of which he continued to be an official.

An intricate question concerning fees led Balfour as First Lord of the Treasury to appoint a committee to look into the affairs of the Heralds and the Orders of Knighthood. While the Committee sat it became apparent that, considering the problem presented by the succession to Woods' many offices could not, in the course of nature, long be postponed. The old man was going down hill fast. In December, 1903, a private letter disclosed that no less than 485 Patents of Appointment to the Bath, among other papers, had not been sent to the persons entitled to receive them. Then the inevitable happened. Woods finally died in January, 1904. His departure from the scene provided the opportunity to implement a suggestion that it was time the administrative work of the Orders be carried out by a suitably staffed common office. In this way the Central Chancery of the Orders of Knighthood came into being on 1 April 1904, to continue the work old Sir Albert had performed single handedly for a half century, and longer. In due course the Central Chancery has widened its sphere of activities. Today the Secretary pro-tem is also Deputy Secretary of the Bath. This official has now become the actual administrative officer of the Order.

The new Chancery immediately became a more effective keeper of records than Woods had been at his best. It is thanks to these that an element of mystery that once surrounded what must be considered the most historic piece of Bath insignia in existence has been dispelled. In the years after the Second World War, Lloyd's of London was able to add Lord Nelson's Collar to the treasures displayed in their Nelson museum. The validity of the pedigree was naturally of some importance. A reference in the Chancery's files disclosed that in 1904, after the aged Lord Bridport died, the next of kin was able to show that not only had the late peer never received a Collar upon his appointment as G.C.B. in 1891, but he had used the Collar originally given Nelson which, in turn, he had acquired by inheritance.

The vagaries of public taste are frequently easier to observe than explain. Not the least curious of these was the recovery of the Order's historic prestige during King Edward's reign. The carping voices so often raised during the last years of the previous century to complain about Honours, and their cost, were no longer heard. The King had the highest regard for the dignity of all the Orders of which he was Sovereign and his attitude was not long in making itself felt beyond the immediate circle of the Court. When Lord Knollys, His Majesty's Private Secretary, was given the G.C.B. in 1908 Esher commented that little as Knollys probably cared for it, the Bath alone remained 'fairly untarnished'.[1] Lord Esher cultivated a weary philosophical cynicism about most things in life, and like Sir Henry Ponsonby was so close to the source that this tepid approval of the Bath can be construed as a high compliment.

The importance of the Order was again illustrated by a curious incident reported by Lord Hardinge of Penshurst. In 1908 the Foreign Office felt it necessary to support British commercial interests in North Africa by obtaining a substantial loan to strengthen the Bank of Morocco. Sir Edward Grey, Foreign Secretary, approached the well-known financier, Sir Ernest Cassel and asked him if he could arrange to accommodate the Bank with half a million. Sir Ernest agreed to do so with only one condition, that he be made a G.C.B. Grey promised to bring the matter to the attention of the Prime Minister. The loan was made and Cassel was given his G.C.B. Hardinge, then Permanent Under Secretary at the Foreign Office, was not pleased with this manoeuvre of Sir Ernest's which he thought a conspicuous example of bad taste. By pure chance he quickly found himself in a position to even what he regarded as the score against the financier. Shortly afterwards a group in the City, with Sir Ernest's support, decided to found a bank in Turkey. Cassel offered to make Hardinge head of the bank at a salary of £3,000 a year. This would have meant resigning from the Foreign Service and Hardinge refused, but recommended Sir H. Babington Smith for the post, whom he advised to ask for a salary of not less than £10,000 a year. Babington Smith reported back that upon this demand, 'Cassel's face was a picture of astonishment, but within twenty-four hours he was offered the salary he claimed, and accepted the post, . . .' Hardinge commented, 'This little transaction gave me great pleasure as a set off to Cassel's G.C.B.'[2] An incident of the kind, of course, could hardly have happened in Queen Victoria's time, but it is unlikely that in those days a man in Cassel's position would have regarded the G.C.B. as a suitable reward for the service rendered.

Occasionally the insignia of the Bath itself became involved in high Imperial policy during these years. There was an instance in 1908. The new Nepalese Minister to the Court of St James's, a member of that country's hereditary political ruling family, came to London bearing rich gifts for King Edward. It had been determined beforehand to confer a G.C.B. upon him. When the King got wind of the gifts he decided that it would be appropriate to give the envoy from Nepal a diamond G.C.B. Star. Lord Knollys consulted Lord Morley, then Secretary of State for India. Morley was not enthusiastic. He could find no records of a diamond Star having been given on the four previous occasions when the Order had been awarded to an oriental potentate. Even Garrard's had no recollection of having made one for such a purpose. The King stood firm, partly because he liked the idea and partly because the Nepalese Minister had already been informed he was to receive the Star. The Secretary of State gave in without enthusiasm on all points except one. He wrote, 'I assume that the question of payment from the Indian revenues could, under the circumstances arise. It would be very embarrassing to raise this point with the

Indian Council, as you will readily perceive.' In the end everybody was satisfied. The Star was presented and India didn't pay for it. Unfortunately we do not know how much it cost, or who did pay for it.[3]

Before his death in 1910 King Edward established a new precedent that was to have an important effect in the next reign. The Order of St Michael and St George had been growing in stature as an award for distinguished men in, or associated with, the Colonial Empire. George, Prince of Wales was appointed Grand Master in succession to the old Duke of Cambridge in 1904. Further to add to the Order's dignity space was found in St Paul's for a chapel. This was opened on 12 June 1906 by an Installation service for a small number of Knights Grand Cross. The Installation was the first time that the G.C.M.G.s wearing their Mantles and Collars had been convened together with other members of the Order as a corporate body. The innovation was well received and the ceremony proved to be a colourful one. Nevertheless, it threw into high relief the inordinate position of the more senior Order of the Bath which could lay claim to a long history of Installations in the Chapel of Henry VII, and had, by extension, a close association with the Chapel from the time of its building. With this in mind, after the Coronation and Imperial visit to India had been successfully completed in 1911, King George V decided that something must be done to revive the custom of the Bath ceremony.

The immediate difficulty, as we have seen, was one of space. The Stalls within the Chapel could only accommodate the original number of Knights Companions while the body of G.C.B.s had increased to almost one hundred. To resolve this knotty problem, as well as decide exactly what form a revived ceremony should take, the King appointed a Committee of nine members under the Chairmanship of Field Marshal Lord Grenfell, in the Autumn of 1912. The Committee included the Rt Rev H. E. Ryle, D.D., Dean of Westminster, and Sir Douglas Dawson, Registrar and Secretary of the Order. It was immediately obvious that to adapt the Chapel to seat a greater number of Knights Grand Cross would take money. The sum required was estimated at about £3,500. To raise this amount an appeal was launched addressed to the members of the Order. This was the first of several similar appeals the membership was to receive in future years. The results were gratifying. The Committee suggested that the G.C.B.s subscribe from £6 to £10, the K.C.B.s £4, and the C.B.s £2 10s. Altogether 92 G.C.B.s, 292 K.C.B.s and a substantial group of C.B.s responded to raise £4,223. Not all of them stayed within the bounds the Committee thought reasonable. The most generous donation came from Sir Ernest Cassel who, to no one's surprise, gave £100. The Earl of Dudley came next on the list with £50. As a group the Field Marshals and Admirals of the Fleet found 10 Guineas a suitable amount for their rank, but the Generals and Admirals were not so generous. At least 18 of the K.C.B.s subscribed more than their seniors, while among the C.B.s, the name of Rear Admiral David Beatty appeared as the donor of £10. But then he married the daughter of Marshall Field of Chicago, and thanks to this judicious alliance was able to afford the little extras. Not all the members of the Order were so fortunately placed. One of them finally replied rather sharply to Sir Douglas Dawson with a comment that still has a most current ring. He wrote, 'I am sure you will readily understand that the income of a Naval Officer who has no private means, in the present age of high taxation and increased cost of living without increase of salary corresponding thereto, makes it quite impossible for him to indulge in luxuries of any kind, and I therefore much regret that I am unable to comply with your request.'[4] There were probably others who felt the same. Nevertheless, the substantial amount raised was sufficient to rearrange the Stalls in the Chapel to accommodate 46 G.C.B.s and leave a surplus to be invested in 4% Union of South Africa Stock.

With the success of the appeal assured, the King became anxious to see the plans for reviving the Installation service go forward. Perhaps the Committee felt itself on unfamiliar ground. Whatever the reasons, their attention to this aspect of the matter rather noticeably lacked vigour, in spite of the fact that one of the members was Admiral of the Fleet Sir Edward Seymour from whom, as a Naval officer, His Majesty might have expected more enthusiasm to get on with the job. On 18 April 1913, an unsettling inquiry was received by the Dean from the Lord Chamberlain's Office. At the instigation of the Duke of Connaught, Sir Douglas Dawson asked if he could be ready for a Bath function by the end of June. Bishop Ryle replied with feeling the next day. He ventured to say that the Abbey, 'Could not undertake the great ceremony of the revival of the Bath Service at so short a notice as two months.' Everybody was 'knee deep' in engagements so that arranging the rehearsals would be almost impossible. The Clerk of the Works had scheduled repairs to the Chapel for August and September and would find it difficult to change his plans. The banners could not be hung and he himself had planned to go on holiday in May. Pleading for at least six months advance notice, he added, 'May I say that, though all things are possible, the Function in June would be attended with a maximum risk of fiasco and disaster. It would be under a sense of pressure for all taking part in the service, the G.C.B.s, Dean, Choir Organist and everybody concerned.' But the matter was not dropped and the Bishop protested again on 24 April. His Clerk of the Works would be unable to have the Chapel ready. Turning to the Committee he wrote, 'We have not even settled upon the proper uniform to be worn; and the Committee has only once and quite provisionally discussed the Ceremonies to be followed. Nothing has been definitely fixed. Our condition is absolutely inchoate. Our meetings this year have been infrequent, as we knew that the late Autumn was the earliest time we had to prepare for.' Pleading that if the revival was to be carried out, it should be well done, he suggested that it would be better to wait two years. Although Farnham Burke, Norroy King of Arms and newly appointed Genealogist of the Bath thought he could manage the

Banners, Dawson was almost convinced by Bishop Ryle. He forwarded the correspondence to the Duke of Connaught with apologies, although he commented that the Bishop had forgotten 'that certain G.C.B.s have paid £20 for banners to be hung up and it is possible that some of them will not be alive two years hence.'

In trying his best for a postponement the Dean was probably unaware that his views of what could be done, as seen from the Abbey cloisters, were in basic conflict with those of his Sovereign in Buckingham Palace. The King, trained in the Navy, knew perfectly well that the impossible could be done, and well done at that. There was only once concession to the ecclesiastical complaints. Bishop Ryle's insistence that the function could not take place at the end of June was accepted. He was allowed one month's grace. It was scheduled for 22 July. Once this point was decided, the machinery went into high gear, with Dawson at the controls. Sir Douglas who was a most efficient man thought of everything and took the King's pleasure at exactly the right places. Very sensibly he started from the outside and worked inwards. The G.C.B.s were to foregather in the Prince's Chamber, the Palace of Westminster, before proceeding, two by two, in their Mantles and Collars to the Abbey. The Prince's Chamber was, of course, the traditional Chapter Room of the Order. Although the original had disappeared in the great conflagration of 1834, a room with the same title appeared in Barry's Gothic replacement for the old Parliament buildings, and it was only fitting that it should be used, particularly on this occasion. In spite of the notorious fickleness of the English weather, the King was originally against any arrangement for an awning being placed across the road from the House of Lords to the Poet's Corner. Dawson thought it wise to be prepared for the worst and produced the awning used for the Coronation, pointing out on 6 June that in 1911 a gap had been left in the centre of the road as long as possible, 'whereby there was no disturbance of traffic until the last minute.'

The problem of who was to be present at the ceremony was solved by limiting the invitations to members of the Order, their wives and daughters. Only those connected with the Bath in the King's Household were to accompany the Sovereign. This regulation was at first even strictly applied to the Royal Ladies, wives of G.C.B.s, who wished to attend. Apart from the Queen, there were only four, the Duchess of Connaught, the Duchess of Teck (Marchioness of Cambridge), Princess Alexander of Teck (Princess Alice, Countess of Athlone) and Princess Louis of Battenberg (Marchioness of Milford Haven). The King wished them to be inside the Chapel and Dawson had no difficulty in finding a suitable place on one side of the altar. When Queen Victoria's surviving daughters also wished to attend he planned to place them just outside the entrance where they could see in. After a few rehearsals this proved awkward and he decided there was enough room inside to take care of all the Royal Ladies. The King's suite, who were to go in procession with him from the House of Lords, were accommodated in the Choir.

The *Times* approved the instructions issued in advance of the function because the G.C.B. were told they had to wear hats. The *Times* was strongly in favour of hats, and hoped that 'the Knights Grand Cross of the Bath will obey the regulation to the full, as a diversity of headdress does not make for a pleasing combination with the uniformity of Mantles.'[5] Dawson was also concerned with hats. By diligent study of the Statutes he discovered that the Officers of the Order were required to have them. They were to be the same shape as those used by the G.C.B.s but crimson and without plumes. He thought the colour would contrast favourably with the white Mantles. On 7 June he urged Lord Stamfordham, Private Secretary to the King, to let him have His Majesty's views as soon as possible because he was about to order the hats. The *Times* with great prescience also issued a stern warning. 'The Officers of Arms will doubtless see to it that the Mantles themselves are worn in the correct way, as on recent occasions distinguished men have shown a deplorable inability to dress themselves properly in these unaccumstomed garments. If the strength lies in the weakest link, so does much of the effectiveness of so magnificent a pageant as is contemplated depend on the appearance of an incorrectly dressed individual.'[5] It can be imagined that King George V heartily approved this sentiment. He accepted most of Dawson's ideas but knew where to draw the line. The Boys of Westminster School were given places in the Abbey. It was asked if they could cry 'Vivat' when the King passed, as they had done at the Coronation. Sir Douglas had his doubts about the propriety of this gesture and was relieved when his Sovereign gave it a firm negative.

In spite of Bishop Ryle's gloomy forebodings, the revival of the Bath ceremony took place at 11.30 a.m. on 22 July without a hitch. Even the weather cooperated. Altogether 77 G.C.B.s (of whom 46 were Installed), 225 K.C.B.s and 595 C.B.s were present. The outdoor procession from the Lords to the Abbey permitted the citizens of London to enjoy the splendour of the crimson, gold and waving plumes much as they had been accustomed to do in the eighteenth century. Very shrewdly the Committee expressed the view that future services of this kind should not be held annually. In the years after both World Wars it became the practice to schedule an Installation once every three or four years, with a few exceptions. The Sovereign has made it a practice of attending only at intervals, leaving the principal role to be played by the Great Master. After the Great War, as a concession to the omnipresent motor car, the outdoor procession was dropped. The G.C.B.s now robe in the Norman Undercroft and go from there into the Abbey Church, not wearing hats.

Additions to the Statutes made before 1914 were largely confined to a slow increase in the membership brought about by the changing times and an expansion of Imperial responsibilities. In April 1896, the total had been set at 1,315. By June 1909 the figure had reached 1,370, but the increase was confined to the

Second and Third Classes of the Civil Division. Appointments made in connection with the Coronations of 1902 and 1911, as well as the South African War and the Great War, were to be considered additional. The total reached 1,404 on 30 May 1914 because it had been decided that Officers in the Military and Naval Services of the Self-Governing Dominions should be eligible. The position of the Commissariat and Medical Branches of the Armed Forces was also recognized by setting aside a certain number of places for them within the ranks of the Order. Apart from these administrative matters, in 1913 the post of Genealogist was once more revived. There was only one slight change in his position. In Anstis' day, the Genealogist took precedence immediately after the Dean, and was the senior Officer who could be named by the Great Master. Now he was placed after the Registrar and Secretary, and before the Gentleman Usher, in the scheme of precedence established by the Prince Consort's Statutes of January 1859. He was responsible for preparing the Banners, Crests and Stall plates of all newly appointed G.C.B.s which, with Henry VII's Chapel once more in use, were to be affixed as they had been before 1812. Succession to the Stalls was now arranged by seniority within each Division. Inasmuch as accepting a Stall involved a knight in the expense of paying for his own heraldic ornaments, he was permitted to decline to take it up. The Stall could then be offered to the next senior G.C.B. of the appropriate Division.

In an uncanny way the revival of the stately Bath ceremony presaged the end of the civilization that had existed in Europe during the previous century. A year later the outbreak of the Great War set in motion a train of events which subjected the economic and social fabric of Britain to severe strain. The Order, however, was able to meet the pressures put upon it without anything like the upheaval it had suffered in 1815. All appointments made during the hostilities were considered additional to the establishment, as had become the custom when extraordinary circumstances rendered a strict adherence to the statutory limitations virtually impossible. With the mobilization of the Empire on a vast scale, places within the Bath were found for a variety of services by men who were still proud to consider these small islands as the Mother Country. Eventually the war effort became so all-encompassing that the honours available to the Crown were insufficient, and the Order of the British Empire was founded in 1917. It will be remembered that with the creation of the Royal Victorian Order in 1896, the members of the Third Class ranked as Commanders and therefore took precedence before the Third Class of the four senior Orders whose members were called Companions. If this practice continued the new C.B.E. would be senior to the C.B. King George V decided a time for change had come.

On 1 June, 1917, the Companions of the Bath, Star of India, St Michael and St George, and Indian Empire were given back their original precedence. In addition, from this date it was decreed that their Badges were no longer to be worn on the breast, but round the neck. This change met with universal approval. The former method of displaying the Badges was a curious inheritance of French custom dating from the reign of Louis XIV. When the Order of St Louis was founded in 1693, the Knights were directed to wear their crosses *à la boutonnière*. The French practice was adopted by the Austrian Order of Maria Theresa in 1757, the Russian St George in 1769, and copied by the Bath in 1815. The modification of men's clothing styles in the nineteenth century changed the location of the buttonholes but left the decorations in the same position pinned to the coat. The third class Badges of British Orders had never looked well, worn in this way. When they were moved to the neck only the Civil C.B. suffered because its rather small size made it less conspicuous than the importance of the Order justified.

CHAPTER IX

Modern Times

In spite of the flexibility with which the Prince Consort's foresight had endowed the Bath, the Order did not emerge from the Great War quite what it had been in 1914. Unlike so much else in the country, an improvement became visible in its affairs. The history of the institution had been noticeably affected by the strong personalities of a number of distinguished men from Anstis on down. When there was no real controlling hand at the helm, whether that of a Great Master or a concerned Secretary of State, prestige declined, as had been the case toward the end of the Victorian era. In short, like any other organization, be it a government department or a business enterprise, the Bath required some form of executive management of its own.

After the Prince Consort's death there was no governing hand at the helm, and practically no helm for that matter. Although the Duke of Connaught was now Great Master, the position of a Prince was much more restricted than it had been in his father's time. Post war conventions allowed him great dignity but gave him little authority he could actually exercise on his own. This was rather hard on a man who had a successful military career. Nevertheless, the Order now found itself with an executive that still continues to function, quietly successful in the high flying age of the 1970's. In true British fashion it evolved unexpectedly from a body created to deal with finance.

On 14 March 1914, a committee of Officers, composed of the Registrar and Secretary, the Genealogist and the Gentleman Usher, presided over by the Dean, met to regularize the administration of the Bath Chapel Fund, as the surplus left after the costs of refurbishing Henry VII's Chapel and the Installation of 1913 had been paid, was called. The Committee decided to retain the services of a solicitor to draw up a document by which the Great Master gave the necessary powers to administer the Fund to the Registrar and Secretary, Sir Douglas Dawson. On 15 October 1915 control was transferred to three trustees, Bishop Ryle, Dawson and Farnham Burke. In this way the Bath Chapel Committee came into existence. All Officers for the time being are members, with the Dean of Westminster and the Bath acting as Chairman. To anticipate slightly, when the post of Deputy Secretary was established in 1925 it was held by the Registrar of the Central Chancery of the Orders of Knighthood. He was chosen to act as Secretary of the Bath Committee. The primary function of the Committee is, of course, to supervise the expenditure of the small income accruing from the Fund. It may come as a surprise to some readers that there are expenses—of a generally foreseeable nature—that must be provided for, although the members of the Order are certainly reminded that this is the case upon their appointment, and when one of the special appeals on behalf of the Fund is launched to strengthen the capital position. The most recent of these took place in 1968. One of the Committee's principal interests is the care and upkeep of the fabric of the Chapel. The ancient building is constantly subject to the wear and tear of the London atmosphere and traffic. Quite rightly the Committee feels that the Order should share the burden of maintaining the Chapel with the often hard-pressed Dean and Chapter of Westminster. The costs of the Installations, now generally held every four years, must also be provided for from the Fund, as well as certain other small expenses connected with maintenance of the Banners and Stall-Plates which contribute so much to the splendour of the Chapel's interior.[1]

With the Chapel Committee in existence as a viable body, meeting at least once a year under the Chairmanship of the senior Officer, it became only natural to consider other matters requiring a decision. These were many and varied. A few examples will be given here and others will be dealt with in the course of the narrative. In 1915 it was decided that whenever three or more vacant Stalls had been accepted by G.C.B.s their achievements should be put up, irrespective of the actual date of an Installation. In 1919 the old custom of re-assigning the Stalls by seniority and re-arranging all the Banners accordingly, as had been the traditional practice, was abandoned and the vacant Stalls were in future assigned as they occurred, without reference to the seniority of the prospective holders. At the Installation of 1920 the custom of seating the senior K.C.B.s in the Choir was adopted. The unprovided-for contingency also arose from time to time, as usual taking all concerned by surprise. For example, Rufus Daniel Isaacs, Earl and later first Marquess of Reading, accepted a Stall in 1924, only to discover during the rehearsal for the approaching Installation ceremony that he was debarred by his Faith from taking the oath and could not attend. The Committee mulled over this problem for the next three years and then came to grips with it by concluding that a general Warrant of Dispensation might provide the solution. Finally, in 1928 the Reading case was dealt with by a Warrant under the Sovereign's Sign Manual, and the Genealogist directed to prepare it.

About the middle of Queen Victoria's reign a Treasury foray, aimed at the Order in the interest of economy, resulted in dropping the practice of furnishing newly appointed G.C.B.s with Mantles at public expense and the Knights were left to provide their own, if they so wished. With the general rise in the cost of living after the War this became increasingly difficult, and the Committee decided the G.C.B.s might be urged to bequeath their Mantles to the Order for the use of their successors. The Great Master and the Knights took kindly to the suggestion. In 1929 it was decided that Mantles acquired in this way should be marked with the names of the donors so that they could be used by members of the same family who might be appointed in the future—a pleasantly thoughtful touch. Over the years sufficient Mantles were accumulated to permit all the G.C.B.s who wish to attend an Installation to be properly equipped. The supply is housed in the Central Chancery for safe keeping. While there was other business of perhaps more importance dealt with, these examples serve to show that the Committee formed to administer finance quickly took over the general direction of the Order's affairs with much of the executive control once exercised by John Duke of Montagu, the Duke of Sussex and the Prince Consort. For perhaps the first time in the history of the institution the Officers now had serious responsibilities commensurate with their dignity. Harris Nicolas would have approved.

Useful as the Officers sitting in Committee had become, they were still not up to the massive piece of work now long overdue. The various changes in the basic constitution of the Order were all carried out by means of additional Statutes. Keeping track of the new provisions was the responsibility of the Central Chancery of the Orders of Knighthood, and quite a burden it had become. Finally, Major Sir George Crichton, Registrar and Secretary, was moved to take steps. On 4 February 1924 he wrote with marked understatement to Sir Douglas Dawson, State Chamberlain and intimate friend of the King:

> The Statutes of the Order of the Bath have now got into a somewhat cumbersome state, and the work entailed in drawing up additional Statutes of the Order has become rather unnecessarily complicated.
>
> The former Statutes of the Order were abrogated by Queen Victoria on 31 January 1859, from which date the present Statutes began to take effect. Since that date there have been 16 additional Statutes in Queen Victoria's reign, 6 in King Edward's and 19 in King George's.
>
> I would suggest that it now might be possible to revise the Statutes into one complete new version, eliminating those that have become superfluous, making certain necessary alterations in nomenclature of Naval and Air Force Ranks, and thus simplifying work on them in the future, and also saving considerably on the cost of reprinting.
>
> If you concur in this suggestion will you please submit for the Sovereign's Commands, on receipt of which I could communicate with the Prime Minister and the representatives of the Fighting Services and obtain their suggestions as to any further alterations.[2]

By the end of the month Dawson replied giving the King's approval in principle. On 7 March letters were addressed to the Prime Minister and the heads of the Service Ministries, informing these gentlemen of His Majesty's decision and requesting their views. Mr Ramsay MacDonald promptly and wisely turned the problem over to Sir Warren Fisher, Permanent Secretary of the Treasury and Head of the Civil Service. To deal with it Sir Warren decided to convene a conference in the Treasury Chambers composed of the Permanent civilian heads and the Service Secretaries, with himself as Chairman. Sir Douglas Dawson was also included and Major Henry Stockley of the Central Chancery was appointed Secretary. In advancing this proposal Crichton also provided a further illustration of the *ad hoc* way in which the Order had been handled during the previous sixty-five years. Dawson summed up the matter when he wrote Fisher on 19 March, 'since 1859, measures seem to have been taken to meet some specific requirement of the moment without regard to the Statutes as a whole, and it is this piecemeal practise which has brought about the inequalities and anomalies to which you so rightly call attention.'

To follow the labours of Fisher's conference in any great detail is hardly necessary for the purposes of this work. Nevertheless certain facts emerged from the discussions that illuminate the position of the Order. The object of the operation was to examine the establishment as it stood and adapt it to the changes brought about by the War. The quotas for the Military were still based on the prewar strength of the armed forces, while the civil quota did not take the expansion of the Civil Service into account. During the War the Fighting Services worked on the principle that every appointment was additional to the establishment, while the Civil Service only resorted to 'Additionals' when every vacancy in the statutory number was filled. As a result most of the eligible officers had been decorated, while a large margin of places was left in the establishment. On the civil side there was no margin and many men who deserved recognition had little hope of receiving it. Altogether a total of 1,087 additional members had been admitted during the war. A formal request for information was drawn up and sent to the appropriate authorities. The Army gave the most interesting and certainly the most succinctly presented reply. There were 10,280 officers, both active and retired, of the grade of Major and above, technically eligible for the C.B. under the Statutes. Of these 1,071 had received it and none were Majors. According to the Departmental rule that no appointments should be made under the rank of Colonel, there were 576 places and 576 C.B.s on the active and retired lists.

The Civil Service was interpreted to mean all non political persons in the direct service of the Crown. Although there were no statutory criteria for eligibility, it had been the custom to make the C.B. available to Assistant Secretaries or Counsellors in the Departments of State and to officers of equivalent rank in the professional, scientific and other posts. Officers in this area numbered 800, of whom 150 were decorated with the C.B. Inasmuch as the Bath was given to a number of persons outside the Crown service, the Civil allocation for those in Crown employment was correspondingly reduced. Quite obviously the balance was tipped against men who were not in the armed services. The inquiry also produced another interesting statistic. In the 1890's a special allotment of 10 K.C.B.s and 6 C.B.s had been made available for the Royal Household. By 1925 there were only 2 K.C.B.s and 3 C.B.s in the Household. This marked reduction was easily explained by the use of the Royal Victorian Order in place of the Bath to reward those who directly served the King.

After subjecting a considerable amount of illuminating statistics to a careful analysis Sir Warren, fully supported by his colleagues, concluded his labours in the Spring of 1925. Recognizing that it was impossible to reach any permanent settlement of the question of the allocation of quotas, they recommended that the position be reviewed every five years. The total number of places in the Order was not increased but more appointments were made available to the Navy and Royal Air Force at the Army's expense. The Civil Division was consolidated as one unit. The King decided that, in the future, any appointments the Sovereign wished to make within his Household, up to the old limit, were to be considered supernumerary to the establishment. On 25 May 1925, the Lord Chamberlain was able to submit a draft of the new Statutes to the Great Master for his approval. He took occasion to mention that the actual work of drawing them up had been done by Garter King of Arms and Major Henry Stockley. He recommended that the latter be made Deputy Secretary of the Bath, pointing out that this position was included in Article XXXI. While the Duke of Connaught agreed, the King questioned the need of an additional Officer of the Order. His doubts received no encouragement from Sir Henry Ponsonby, Keeper of the Privy Purse, who told him rather bluntly that, inasmuch as the Fisher Committee had come to the conclusion that the post was needed, there must be some good reason for it. Dawson, a bit more helpful, added that the additional ceremonial work connected with the Order required the extra Officer. Stockley got his appointment and retained it until his retirement in 1951. It is an interesting reflection on the complexities of life in the twentieth century that the last revision of the Statutes in 1859 was carried out by two men—Prince Albert and Albert Woods. By 1925 a similar piece of work required the joint efforts of the Head of the Civil Service associated with a large committee of military and civilian officials.

If the decade of the 'Twenties' was not entirely an easy one on the social and economic fronts, the affairs of the Order proceeded along their placid traditional path. The first ceremony after the War was held on 18 May 1920, when 22 members were installed in the presence of the Sovereign and the Great Master. The arrangements were organized by the Bath Chapel Committee, and the clerical work carried out by the staff at the Central Chancery. Robing took place in the Norman Undercroft. The procession then went from the Chapter House through the cloisters up the centre of the Nave into the Choir where the first part of the Service was held. It returned from the Chapel through the Choir again and by way of the north aisle of the Nave back to the Cloisters, thus establishing a pattern of movement that was to be used in subsequent years with few changes. The King did not attend the next Installation in 1924 but was present at the following one held in 1928. On this occasion the procession left the Abbey by way of the Great West Door, thus giving the public a wider glimpse of scarlet and gold splendour.

Permission was given the well-known artist, Mr Frank O. Salisbury, to be in the Chapel for the purpose of making the necessary sketches for a picture of the Sovereign's offering at the altar. When the painting, a massive work in which all the personalities were shown virtually life size, was finished the next year the artist generously presented it to the Order. The picture was accepted by the Great Master on behalf of the King, who commanded that it be hung in the East corridor of the first floor of Buckingham Palace, where it remains to this day. Among other curiosities of the period was the permission granted Sir Basil Zaharoff, an Honorary Civil G.C.B. of a somewhat indeterminate national status, to wear the robes and Collar and to assume the distinctive appellation of Knighthood. There was also an interesting straw in the wind that, like similar omens of great import, attracted no one's attention. In 1920 an inquiry was put forward by the Treasury about the possibility of admitting ladies to the Order. After careful consideration, the appropriate authorities decided, in view of the Statutes then in force, the suggestion was not practicable.

Any narrative dealing with the history of the Bath inevitably tends to be heavily weighted with references to the G.C.B.s, for what should be perfectly obvious reasons. Nevertheless, the high position of the Order in its two lower classes should not be overlooked. In fact it is one of the particular distinctions of the British Honours System that, normal human error, weakness and plain bad luck notwithstanding, appointments to all grades of the Orders have the happy faculty of being equally important for the persons receiving them. To put it another way, a Companionship has the same relative value as a Grand Cross for the appropriate recipient. The story of Lord Hardinge's C.B., referred to in an earlier Chapter, is example. There must be many similar instances, now hard to trace because natural reticence prevented them from being recorded. The biographer of the late Lord Ismay provides another later case very much in point. On retirement in 1930 from a successful tour of duty on the Committee of Imperial Defence, the then Lieutenant Colonel Ismay was awarded a Civil C.B. and a C.I.E. in the same Gazette, an event that caused no little astonishment, not to say perturbation. 'This example of co-ordination between government departments created something like a crisis, as not only had no one before in history been gazetted in the same honours list to two comparable honours, but, as an honour is theoretically in the gift of the Sovereign, once given it cannot be revoked. No one knew what to do. It is believed that a Cabinet meeting was held. Finally it was agreed that Ismay should write a letter saying he realized that a mistake had been made, and might he keep the Bath, which was the senior order.'[3] It is significant that a 'crisis' of this kind could still bring a C.B. to the level of Cabinet discussion. When General Sir Hastings Ismay was given the Military G.C.B. in 1946 on the Prime Minister's nomination, he joined the small group of distinguished men who have held both Divisions at the same time.

The Order's concern for the fabric of the Chapel was sharply focussed in 1933 when the Dean reported to the Bath Committee that a fall of stone showed the roof required extensive repairs, which, if carried out properly, would take at least two years. At the same time the Genealogist said the Stalls themselves needed cleaning and maintenance for their preservation. The Committee also accepted the Dean's suggestion that the Altar table was seriously in need of attention. Accordingly, the Chapel was closed and dismantled to permit the work to be carried out. An Altar Appeal Fund was launched and received wide support from both the members and the public. The object of the operation was to reproduce the original altar designed by Pietro Torregiani and completed in 1526. He was the Italian artist who had created the bronze screen surrounding the Founder's tomb. The final result was enriched by the generous gift from Viscount Lee of Fareham of a painting to form the background of the Altar by Bartolomeo Vivarini, a contemporary of Torregiani's. Lord Lee will also be remembered as the donor of Chequers to the Nation for the use of the Prime Minister, and of a splendid collection of English Silver to Hart House in Toronto. He and his American wife were devoted antiquarians all their long lives. Inasmuch as the cost of the restoration was not entirely met by the Appeal, the Bath Chapel fund was called upon to help make good the deficit.

On 3 July 1935 the Duke of Connaught presided over the ceremony of re-opening the Chapel, the dedication of the new Altar, and the Installation of 21 G.C.B.s. Unfortunately, it was not possible to follow the precedent of 1928 when the procession had passed outside along the north front of the Abbey, where the public had a most effective view of the Knights, a light breeze stirring the mantles and plumes of their hats on a brilliant sunlit morning. The next day the *Times* observed editorially, 'St George's Chapel, where the banners of the Knights (of the Garter) hang proud and solemn above their stalls in the choir, is a very noble and beautiful building. But some there are who would claim that King Henry VII Chapel is an even more beautiful setting for the pageantry of Knighthood, especially now that, like St George's, it has been restored and cleaned so that the lovely light for which it is famous is able to fall with the clearest beauty on the banners and stall plates of the Knights, and upon the Knights Grand Cross themselves as they take part in their peculiar ceremony of installation, a ceremony consecrated and majestic beyond parallel.'[4]

In 1936 additions to the Statutes reflected two changes in the internal arrangements of the Order. The number of Civil G.C.B.s and K.C.B.s was increased by one and five places, respectively, while the Military Division was correspondingly reduced, leaving the total membership unchanged. At the same time the qualifications were modified to include the award of the Military C.B. for 'good and efficient service' and not necessarily for mention in despatches alone. The following year the Officers took another matter of interest under consideration. The suggestion was advanced that the names of all the K.B.s and G.C.B.s appointed from the time of the Order's foundation in 1725 should be recorded on the west wall of the Abbey. There was an excellent historic precedent for the suggestion in St George's Hall in the Kremlin, where the names of the Knights of the Military Order of St George appear engraved and gilded on the marble walls of the vast and magnificent chamber. By 1938 when the tally of 954 names was complete it was found that there was insufficient room to inscribe them all. As an alternative the decision was then made to prepare a suitable book listing not only the names of the Knights, but also those of the Great Masters and Officers, to be kept in the Chapel. On 23 February 1939 the Genealogist was able to report that a total of 1,030 names written on 55 pages of vellum, with 10 blank pages for additions and 22 pages of index, was ready and had cost £34 11s 2d, a remarkably small sum by later standards. It was to be 'bound in a similar manner to the prayerbooks used in the Chapel,' that is to say, in crimson morocco, gold tooled on the spine, with an impression of the Badge of a K.B. on the front and back covers. Whether the binding was ever carried out is not known, because the Bath Book and all the working papers associated with it was destroyed when the Dean's residence was severely damaged by enemy action on the night of 10 and 11 May, 1941.

With the outbreak of the second World War in 1939 all discussion of the internal affairs of the Bath was naturally put aside for the duration. The Chapel was dismantled and the banners, intricate carvings and other glories removed and placed in safe storage. The only occurrence of note during these years was the death of the Duke of Connaught in 1942. Born in 1850, he was godson of the Great Duke of Wellington and the last but one of Queen Victoria's children, truly an amazing historical survival, and a worthy Great Master of the Order. He was succeeded in this last office by Henry, Duke of Gloucester, the Sovereign's brother. His Royal Highness, in the person of his wife, has a close connection with the early history of the Order. The Duchess, formerly Lady Alice Montagu-Douglas-Scott, daughter of the seventh Duke of Buccleuch, is a direct descendant of John Duke of Montagu, the first Great Master.

In the same year King George VI commanded that an additional Statute be prepared, allowing the appropriate Minister of State for any Dominion to forward submissions for appointment to the Order directly to the Sovereign. This personal gesture was a small indication of the King's deep consciousness of his high position as head of the British Commonwealth of Nations. When the Bath Committee met again on 7 February 1946 they were encouraged to hear from Mr Bishop, Clerk of the Works at the Abbey, that the Chapel had suffered no serious structural damage, but that the replacement of Torregiani's Bronze screen around the tomb of Henry VII and the Stalls would take about two years. In the event, other priorities and a shortage of skilled labour prevented the rehabilitation from being completed until 1951. As soon as the Chapel was nearly ready the King informed the officers that he wished an Installation service to take place on 24 May. At the same time the Great Master was to be installed, and His Majesty further explained that he was anxious to have his own sword dedicated on the Altar as part of the service. Although all the Officers were new, the ceremony was conducted without a hitch and made the deepest impression on all those fortunate enough to be present.

The condition and allotment of Stalls now became a matter of some recurring difficulty. When the preparations were under way for the revival of the Installation service in 1913 the cost of actually increasing the number was found to be prohibitive. Places for 46 Banners and Plates were provided without an actual Stall for each being available, although it was possible to arrange suitable seating up to that number. Late in 1951 the Bath Committee decided that the number of G.C.B.s who, in the future, would be given the option of occupying a Stall, be gradually reduced to 34, the number that had existed from the beginning, by the process of offering one for every two vacancies. This suggestion was eventually approved by the Sovereign, although King George VI had not been entirely happy about it. Regardless of the seating arrangements, however, the proportional distribution of those allotted to the Military and Civil Divisions had never been easy to decide, partly because both World Wars had resulted in the additional appointment of a larger than normal number of senior officers who had made distinctive contributions to victory. On the assumption that the number of Stalls would, in reasonable probability, be reduced, 22 were assigned to the Military and 12 to the Civil Division.

So the matter rested until May 1964 when concern was expressed about the Stalls available for the Military members, many of whom had been waiting since 1949, while their opposite numbers in the Civil Division, appointed as late as 1960, were already in possession. After a discussion suggestions were advanced that all vacancies be offered to the Military members until the balance had been redressed, and that thereafter Stalls be given according to strict seniority, regardless of the Division to which the Knight belonged. Sir Ivan De la Bere undertook to approach Sir Laurence Helsby, then Head of the Civil Service, for his views. Sir Laurence's response was illuminating. He pointed out that there were very few Civil G.C.B.s, for whom the standard of appointment was high. Of the 27 allowed by the Statutes, there were only 16, leaving 11 vacancies.

The Civil members also tended to be older upon appointment and therefore had less time to wait. Very cogently he added that the difficulty existed because of the large number of additional Military Knights made during the Second World War. After considering this reply the Officers concluded that, under the circumstances, the system then obtaining could not be altered.

Attention was once more drawn to the problem in 1969. In that year the degree of imbalance between both divisions attracted the attention of Major General Peter Gillett, the present (1972) Deputy Secretary of the Bath. He was forcibly struck by the wide discrepancy between the time a Military G.C.B. had to wait before being offered a Stall compared with the members of the Civil Division. General Gillett discovered it could take almost twenty years before the turn of some military members came, while a Civil G.C.B. was often given the opportunity to accept one within three years after appointment. He was directed by the Officers of the Order to look into the matter and report his recommendations. That there is more to this than meets the eye will be immediately apparent when it is realized that, under the prevailing custom, there was no way of recording the names of the Knights Grand Cross in the Abbey or Chapel until they had taken the oath and their Plates been erected. After considering various possibilities the Officers decided there were certain immediately feasible steps to be adopted. The allotment between the Military and Civil Divisions was changed to a ratio of 26 to 8. When reassessing the allocation of Stalls only 'Quota' appointments were used to arrive at these figures, 'Additional' appointments were not taken into consideration. But, depending on seniority, a Stall can be allotted to either a 'Quota' or an 'Additional' G.C.B.

Correcting the imbalance in the assignment of Stalls did nothing to meet the problem of recording the names of those Knights who for one reason or another did not accept a Stall or were never offered one. The solution to this problem was found in a book listing the Knights of the Order, similar to the one which, it will be remembered, was completed in 1938 only to be lost without a trace during the war. The disappearance of the book was bad enough, but the destruction of the preparatory work was even a greater tragedy. After considering the question of expense it was decided that the new Bath Book could only begin with the G.C.B.s appointed in the reign of Edward VII. Extra Pages of vellum have been planned to permit it to contain names of future appointments. The basic costs are being met by a generous donor who has agreed to present the book to the Order. In one way it is strange that a volume of this kind was not thought of before, because just such a record is maintained by the Order of the Garter and is held by the Dean of Windsor, Register of that Order. When completed during 1972 the Bath Book will be kept in the Chapel of Henry VII.

In the present reign the Order has acquired two swords, one of intimate Royal interest for display and the other for ceremonial use. In 1953 Dr Alan C. Don, Dean of Westminster and of the Order, reported to the Officers that he had

suggested that the personal naval sword offered by King George VI at the ceremony held in 1951 be presented to the Abbey. Her Majesty the Queen and
Queen Elizabeth the Queen Mother graciously agreed to this request. By May
1955 a suitable case had been prepared in which to display the sword within the
Chapel of Henry VII. On 7 July of that year Queen Elizabeth formally trans-
ferred the weapon to Dr Don, and a small private service was held to commemorate the gift, attended by the Duke of Gloucester as Great Master, the
Officers and their wives. Three years later Sir Ivan De la Bere, the Deputy
Secretary, was informed that the late Air Chief Marshal Sir Charles Longcroft,
Gentleman Usher of the Scarlet Rod and Register and Secretary from 1932 to
1954, had left a legacy to, 'The Trustees of the Chapel Committee of the Most
Honourable Order of the Bath'. The Trustees decided to use the sum to commemorate Sir Charles's long and devoted service. After consideration of the best
means to achieve this end, the idea of a specially bound bible was hit upon.
While the thought had much to recommend it, it was quickly discovered that
the Order indeed already possessed such a bible, presented by Bishop Ryle at the
time of the re-inauguration of the Chapel in 1913.

Sir Ivan finally concluded that the purchase of a ceremonial sword for use by
the senior G.C.B.s at the Installation service would in every way make a suitable
memorial. The suggestion met general approval and Messrs. Wilkinson were
commissioned to prepare the design that was eventually adopted. They produced a handsome weapon with a plain cross hilt, pommel and scabbard mounts
of silver-gilt, the grip of white fishskin bound with gold wire. The hand-forged
blade bears a suitable inscription and is engraved with the Star of the Military
G.C.B. on one side and the Civil G.C.B. on the other. The Badges of both
Divisions appear on opposite sides of the hilt. Silver-gilt rings on the crimson
velvet scabbard permit the sword to be worn from slings if necessary. It was
ordered in March 1959, promised for January 1960, but not finally ready until
the end of May, thanks to delays of a nature now sufficiently familiar to require
no comment. When ready it was presented for the Sovereign's inspection and
met with Her Majesty's full approval. It was used for the first time at the service
held in October of that year, and now plays an important part in all Bath
ceremonies.

During these same years two other mementos of Royal Interest also passed
into custody of the Dean and the Order. In February Princess Alice, Countess of
Athlone, requested that the late Earl's Banner be allowed to remain hanging in
the Chapel. This was rendered possible because Lord Athlone's Stall was one of
those without a real seat beneath it. In any case the Officers were more than
pleased to be able to agree to the wish of a great Lady, one of the last survivors
of those who had witnessed the opening of the Chapel in 1913. The following
year the Marquess of Cambridge presented the Order with the Mantle and hat
worn by his father, the second Duke of Teck and first Marquess. In this way the

Order acquired objects closely associated with the two brothers of Queen Mary who had received their G.C.B.s as Coronation Honours in 1911.

Early in 1963 the Chapel Committee was called upon to consider the first of three requests based on the medieval origins of the Knighthood of the Bath so dear to Anstis. The Chaplain of the Tower forwarded a memorandum pointing out that in former days, on the eve of the Coronation and on other occasions of State, the Knights of the Bath had kept their vigils in the Chapel of St John the Baptist, within the White Tower. He inquired if this connection with the Chapel and the Order could not in some way be revived. While sympathetic to the idea, the Officers felt that it presented too many potential complications. Regretfully the Dean wrote on 21 March, 'The G.C.B.s who are Installed are almost invariably men of considerable seniority in age and the Installation is a sufficiently elaborate ceremony to tax their strength, while at the same time it involves the Bath Committee in many hours of organization and rehearsal. The Committee feels that the connection between the Order and the Tower should be kept in memory, but that it would not be wise to add any ceremonial connection at the time of the Installation of the Knights of the Bath.'

A further suggestion, made the following year, that some form of Bath Service be held in the Chapel of St John, was also vetoed because of the 47 steps that would have to be climbed up to it, and its small size. At the same time the idea that Banners of deceased Knights be displayed there was considered inadvisable on several grounds. Quite rightly Sir Anthony Wagner, Garter King of Arms and Genealogist of the Bath, emphasized that there was no real connection between the Chapel of St John and the Order as it now exists. In 1966, however, the Constable of the Tower advanced a request that received favourable consideration. He proposed that the Altar be provided with a cloth of the traditional crimson, carrying a representation of the Badge used by the Knights before the Order's foundation. This was agreed to, with the proviso that the preparation of the device be supervised by the Genealogist to insure that it would be correct in all respects. The handsome Altar cloth now adds a welcome touch of colour to the otherwise starkly Norman Chapel. It displays the type of Badge worn by the last Knights of the Bath created at the Coronation of King Charles II in 1661.

As the 900th Anniversary of the Abbey's founding approached in 1965, the Dean, Dr Eric S. Abbott, was naturally deeply engaged in plans for a series of events to commemorate the occasion. As senior officer of the Bath and Chairman of the Chapel Fund Committee, Dr Abbott felt that the Order's connection with the Abbey should be as widely recognized as possible. His interest was to have far reaching effects. The Officers, wearing their robes, chains and Badges, took part in the inaugural ceremony held on 28 December. But the Dean believed that something must be done to remind the members of the Order that the Abbey and the Chapel of Henry VII were, in effect, their headquarters, to be used more generally than they had been in the past. Like all such germinal ideas, the development was slow and the way not clear. A first tentative step was taken in the Autumn of 1966, also as part of the Anniversary. On 18 October their Royal Highnesses the Duke and Duchess of Gloucester, the Officers, G.C.B.s and their wives attended a short Service in the Chapel. Afterwards they were entertained at supper in the Great Hall of Westminster School as guests of the Dean and Chapter.

Dr Abbott next received strong support from Major General Peter Gillett, who had succeeded Major General Sir Cyril Colquhoun as Secretary of the Central Chancery in 1968. It was the Dean who advanced the plan of holding a Bath 'at home' for all members of the Order and their wives who wished to attend. The first of these took place during the summer of 1969. A special guided tour of the Abbey ending in the Chapel of Henry VII was followed by a social gathering in the Cloisters and College gardens. Similar 'at homes' were held in 1970 and 1971. They have served the useful function of bringing the members of every grade together within the fraternity of the Bath.

While social gatherings serve their purpose, the primary religious use of the Chapel by members of the Order on occasions other than the quadrennial Installations required careful thought. The building is not only part of the Abbey, but a Chapel Royal, and hence open to the general public. The fees paid by visitors also provide an important part of the revenue needed for its upkeep. So, although the Chapel is closely tied to the Order by the bonds of history and tradition, there are absolute limits to the personal use to which it can be put by the members. As long ago as 1934 the Sovereign and Great Master approved the granting of certain privileges to the G.C.B.s. They were allowed to have their children married, grandchildren baptised and their own memorial services held there. In 1969, the Dean and Chapter felt able to allow the K.C.B.s and C.B.s use of the Chapel for six marriages and six baptisms each year.

Throughout this narrative one of the principal threads has been the way in which the Bath did, or did not, accommodate itself to changing times. The Prince Consort has been given due credit for providing a flexible framework that permitted adaptation to the changing pressures to which it was bound to be subjected over the years. But when full recognition has been granted to the talents of that remarkable man, it remains doubtful if even he could have anticipated what, by all counts, must be considered the most startling development in the Order's history. On 30 September 1970, it was announced from Buckingham Palace that the Sovereign had approved the admission of ladies to all classes of the Bath from 1 January 1971. In a way the surprise this announcement created is a form of recognition of the peculiar position the Order holds in the public estimation, at least when the public is moved to consider it at all. The granting of Honours to women is certainly not a new development. Their admission to the Order of the British Empire upon its foundation in 1917, and later to the Royal Victorian Order and the Order of St Michael and St George, was accepted with general nods of approval. An extension of the same privilege to the Bath caused comment and even a few smiles. It is just possible to suspect that this response was an automatic reaction to the disappearance of one of the last purely male preserves. But the long military tradition of the institution must not be overlooked and undoubtedly it helped create an element of astonishment. When the matter is given a moderate amount of thought there is less reason for surprise than perhaps at first appeared.

Foreigners, who by definition are always scientifically logical thinkers, are continually puzzled by the British evolutionary habits of thought. When something is needed it is first produced and then, however improbably, made to work. The characteristic was neatly expressed by the Great Duke of Wellington when he compared the campaigns of his opponents to a fine leather harness and his own to a harness of rope. When their's broke they were in trouble. When his broke he tied a knot and went on with the business in hand. It can be said that there never was any policy of excluding women from the Order any more than there was a long range plan to admit them. When the idea was first broached in 1920 it was dropped because the time had not yet come. Since the last war, however, the whole position has changed. The opposite sex has very rightly gained a practical equality with their male counterparts, as the reader will quite readily recognize. This has been particularly true in the professions and in the government service. Their success in this latter field of endeavour unexpectedly created a problem in the area of honours and awards. For a long time only the Order of the British Empire was available to meet the need. Curious inequalities resulted. Either a lady was over-recompensed with a D.B.E. or under-rewarded with a C.B.E. A C.B. in between would have been helpful in many cases. When the problem became particularly acute in the Foreign Service the Order of St Michael and St George was opened to women. Those in the civil and military employ of the Crown remained in the same unfortunate position. But their position was less uncomfortable than that of the authorities responsible for the distribution of Honours, who naturally take a sound professional view of their job and wish to carry on with a minimum of fuss.

In 1968 an idea emerged from the depths of the appropriate department of the Treasury. Why not admit women to the Bath, it was asked? As soon as the question had been proposed only one answer was possible. There was no reason at all. In fact, the idea was an excellent one. The Ministry of Defense and the Treasury were in favour. The next step was to ascertain the views of the Officers of the Order. They expressed themselves with caution and undertook to canvass some of the senior G.C.B.s for an opinion. To no one's surprise several of these distinguished gentlemen registered a singular lack of enthusiasm. An objection was raised that had not been thought of before. How could a lady take the great oath? There could be no difficulty about honouring God and the Queen, but the Knights of the Bath were also required to swear to 'Defend Maidens, Widows and Orphans in their Rights.' The prospect of a Dame Grand Cross undertaking the last duty alarmed the senior members. When the matter was subjected to further deliberation it became apparent that these fears were likely to be groundless for several reasons. A Minute was prepared for the Committee on Honours, Decorations and Medals for their consideration. Not only the Committee, but the Services were also in favour of opening the Order to women, as was the Prime Minister, The Rt Hon Edward Heath M.P. When the proposal was laid before the Queen, Her Majesty was able to give her approval. The first appointments of two Military and two Civil C.B.s took place in 1971. In bringing this story of the Bath to a close it is a pleasure to be able to express the opinion that the latest development in a long history can only contribute to the health and strength of the Order in the future.

Now that this brief survey of the history of the institution has been completed we can see in retrospect how successful Anstis was in associating it with the medieval practice of the old Knighthood of the Bath. He built on such a substantial antiquarian foundation that many later observers have often confused the Order with a body of Knights created at the Coronation of King Henry IV in 1399. During the early part of the nineteenth century a great deal of criticism was directed at the provisions of the original Statutes in the name of modern efficiency. It was a question of throwing out the old because the new was, by definition, better. This attitude is not unfamiliar today. In 1834 when Harris Nicolas' projected reforms seemed likely to be adopted the aged George Beltz, Lancaster Herald and historian of the Garter, warned Lord Stanley that the rites and ceremonies of the Bath Knighthood as they had been carried out for almost seven centuries kept alive the memory of usages which from their high antiquity had become venerable. To remove them from the Statutes would deprive the Order of a measure of its ancient dignity. In the long run the old man's fears turned out to be groundless. Thanks to Anstis the Order, although founded as late as 1725, has a perfectly genuine claim to an historic connection with the medieval world. In this sense it can rank with the Garter as the most venerable Honour available for distribution by the Crown in our day. The members included within its ranks belong to a Society that can trace a lineage at least as far back as the fourteenth century. They themselves are part of a national tradition further enhanced by the close association the Order has long had with the Chapel of Henry VII, an architectural glory that is the common heritage of the English speaking world. To cherish and help preserve this building is a privilege of which they have every right to feel proud.

CHAPTER X

The Robes and Insignia in the Eighteenth Century

In providing the Order with suitable ornaments Anstis was able to draw on the ancient Bath records, and to use the insignia which had evolved over the years for the Garter as models. Of the various vestments given the medieval Knights the crimson Mantle lined and edged with white was the final one to be assumed before they received the accolade. This robe had one distinctive peculiarity. A white silk lace of two strands was attached to the left shoulder. In accordance with chivalric tradition it was to be worn in this manner until the new Knight had performed some gallant feat of arms, after which it could be taken off either by a lady of his choice or by a Prince. Eventually the white lace came to be regarded as a species of badge only associated with those Knights who, in the words of the fifteenth century chronicler Upton, had been created 'by the Bath.' When a Knight had won his spurs the custom evolved of having the strands braided together rather than removing them.[1] The crimson robe, adopted as the Mantle of the Bath in 1725, continues to be used today by the G.C.B.s. In the beginning a pair of white gloves was suspended from the lace, but this addition was dropped after 1815. According to the original Statutes, the 'Ensign', or Star in embroidery, was also attached on the left, and the garment was closed by cordons with crimson tassels in gold net at their ends. The rest of the original uniform conformed more or less to the clothing styles of 1725. It consisted of a shirt, breeches, and doublet (or waistcoat) of white, a surcoat of crimson silk, a white belt to suspend a plain cross-hilted sword, and white kid boots. The hat was a splendid creation of white silk with a standing plume of white ostrich feathers.

Nothing was said about a wig being part of the proper equipment for a K.B. until the Chapter held on 21 March 1803. Then it was considered a requirement and described, 'The Wigs, or Hair, as the Knights of the Garter (flowing).' The Chapter was held to prepare for the Installation on 19 May, and several interesting particulars emerged from the proceedings. Three days before the ceremony the full details of just what each Knight should wear were agreed upon. The Mantles were to be furnished by the Lord Chamberlain's Office. Bath King of Arms had to pay the Lord Chamberlain £5 7s 0d for Warrants authorizing him to receive them and a further £5 11s 6d when they were handed over. But the rest of the costume had to be bought by each Knight for himself. William Webb, the Robemaker, submitted his bill on 16 May. He undertook to supply each Knight with the following:

> A white rich Sattin Doublet & Breeches trimmed with
> pink Sattin according to the Order of the Bath, with
> kid boots trimmed with rich crimson Sattin; Do. Gloves
> trimmed with Sattin ribbon & silver fringe; flowing
> curls; jewel piece Shoulder Knott; Do. Rosettes Knee;
> Do. Boots; Do. Hair Do. & c.   £29 17s 0d
> To a green Baize Robe Case   5s 0d
> _____
>   £30 2s 0d

On 21 February, Sarah Townsend & Son had already informed the distinguished gentlemen that their 'fine white Ostrich Installation Plume of feathers' and a case to contain it would cost them a further £27 6s 0d. But they relented on 22 April and reduced the price to 20 Guineas, 'as she now had plenty of feathers.' With no fewer than 22 Knights-elect to be Installed, Mr Webb and Mrs Townsend were no doubt pleased at the pretty piece of business that came their way.[2] The total cost to the Knights of £51 2s 0d was probably borne with equanimity inasmuch as the Crown had paid the rest of the fees for them.

The formal dress of a G.C.B. worn at the Coronation of George IV in 1821 varied considerably from that specified in the Statutes. The underdress was composed of a jacket and trunk hose *à la Henri Quatre*, a ruff that could not have been very comfortable, a red sash, and red-heeled white boots turned at the top with crimson. There was a similar costume for the K.C.B.s with the notable difference that their short knee-length Mantle was worn off the left shoulder and, of course, carried the Star of their grade. The hats were also changed to black velvet at this time. There is a splendid example of the complete habit of a G.C.B. used in 1821 to be seen in the National Army Museum, Chelsea. The Knights never appeared again arrayed in such finery. As the various Chapters convened during the reigns of King William IV and Queen Victoria, G.C.B. Mantles and Collars alone were worn over full dress uniform or Court dress. The K.C.B.s wore only their Stars and Badges. After the death of the Prince Consort in 1861 the custom of convening the Knights to assist at an Investiture was virtually abandoned. In practice the Mantles were seldom, if ever, seen until the Coronation of King Edward VII, and after the Installations were once more revived in 1913. Now they are provided on the day of Installation from a supply held by the Central Chancery of the Orders of Knighthood.

Those associated with the Order in any capacity, or who took part in the Installations, were also provided with a distinctive dress. The two Esquires Governors and the Young Esquire assigned each Companion were appointed only at the time of an Installation, and none was made after 1812. In the Statutes of 1847 the positions were not revived. They wore doublets and breeches of crimson silk Mantua, and stockings and shoes of the same colour, purchased by themselves. The Lord Chamberlain supplied them with a black hat, sword belt, and a surcoat of white silk Mantua lined with crimson bearing a blue shield with three embroidered crowns. Not a robe, this garment resembled an Oxford undergraduate's gown with a hood at the back. The Officers were not arrayed much differently than they are today with due respect to the changes in the style of men's clothing. The Dean originally wore the Mantle of a Knight. After 1815 his Mantle carried the 'original Star of the Order', now that of a Civil G.C.B. He was accompanied by the Prebendaries of Westminster who assisted him in the performance of Divine Service. These gentlemen were attired in a Mantle of white, lined with crimson and fastened at the throat by cordons like the Knights. The same blue shield used by the Esquires appeared on the left shoulder. All the other Officers wore similar Mantles, with surcoats like those of the Esquires underneath. Surcoats are now no longer used. Inasmuch as the Great Master has always been a member of the Order, his Mantle resembled that of a K.B. or G.C.B. The Duke of Sussex used the Civil Star, but all the other occupants of the office after 1815 have belonged to the Military Division. The Sovereign's Mantle differs from the others in that it is long enough to require being carried by a Page. The Star of the Military G.C.B. on the shoulder, of chipped silver, gold and enamel, made for Queen Victoria, is the only one of its kind.

Reference has been made earlier to Anstis having to produce his Order for an impatient Walpole in a great hurry. The story of the insignia provides further evidence that this indeed must have been done. The Statutes were dated 23 May and issued on 25 May 1725. In their original form the Collar is barely mentioned and not described. On 1 June, four 'Articles and Explanations' were added to be 'deemed Part and Parcel of the Statutes'. The first of these specified that the Collar should be of gold, weighing thirty ounces Troy, and composed of 'several Imperial Crowns of Gold, tied or linked with Gold Knots enamelled White, representing the White Laces mentioned in the Ancient Ceremonials of Conferring the Knighthood of the Bath'.[3] The introduction of the laces was one of Anstis' most imaginative touches and, at the same time, shows how closely he was following his model. The lace is the Bath equivalent of the investment Garter and probably almost as old a symbol. In this sense it can be considered the first element in the Order's insignia. The Jewel House was responsible for providing insignia much as the Central Chancery now does. With the Installation scheduled for 17 June one wonders what the officer in charge thought of so abruptly being required to come up with a quantity of Collars with nothing better to go on than their being composed of several crowns and knots. There was a confusion behind the scenes and a frantic rush to have everything ready on time. No drawing or any other representation of this type of Collar has yet come to light, and it is different from the one finally adopted. Nevertheless there is no question about it having existed, though in a slightly modified form. In the official account of the Installation, quoted by Nicolas in his Appendix B, we read that the Great Master wore, 'the Collar of Gold, composed of several Imperial Crowns, tied, or linked, with Knots of gold, representing the white laces mentioned in the ancient Ceremonials of conferring the Knighthood of the Bath'.

On 15 June with only two days to spare, the Collars were all delivered and signed for by the Knights' representatives. The King's was collected by Mr Mahomet, one of the Turkish servants George I acquired during the wars on the Continent and brought with him from Hanover. The weight of each varied from about 31 oz. 11 dwt. to over 31 oz. 14 dwt., as against the 30 oz. specified in the Statutes, because the Badge was included. The Collar of young Prince William weighed only 20 oz. The total number came to 38, including the Sovereign's, Prince William's and the Great Master's. The receipts were for the Great Master's records. On the same day the Duke of Montagu had to sign one of his own for the Master of the Jewel House. It reads, 'Received thirty-four (eight crossed out) Collars of gold belonging to the Knights of the Most Honourable Order of the Bath to be returned into the office after Installation, in order to be enamelled and finished.' In short, the first important ceremony of the Order was held with the members wearing plain unfinished gold chains.[4] Why Montagu signed for 34 when 38 were issued remains obscure.

With the great day over, there was an opportunity to give the Collar more careful thought. The original design must have looked too simple and lacking in style. It is true that the two devices employed matched the Gartered roses and love knots in the Garter Collar, but the effect was not nearly so fine. The solution to the difficulty was felicitous. Another 'Explanation' came forth from 'Our Court at Hanover', dated 16 November. It had been decided, 'That each of the said Collars shall be composed of Nine Imperial Crowns of Gold, and of Eight gold roses and Thistles, issuing from a Gold Sceptre, enamelled in their proper colours, tied or linked together with Seventeen Gold Knots, enamelled White.'[5] The design made sense because the rose and thistle emblems were already part of the Badge. The Master of the Jewel House at last had specific details with which to work. When finished, the new Collars measured over 5 feet 8 inches in length and $1\frac{1}{8}$ inches width. So they remain today with very little change. Until 1815 the Badges were attached to one of the white enamel laces.

Sir Joseph Banks, the Order's original scientist, is credited in 1802 for having advanced the idea that a shamrock be added to the other national flora in view of the Union with Ireland two years before. Sir Joseph's submission to Deputy Bath King of Arms also contained the suggestion that the presence of the three would greatly augment the meaning of the Motto. He was certainly right on this point because the Sovereign had recently divested himself of the empty title of King of France. It is much easier to accept TRIA JUNCTA IN UNO as representing the

Kingdoms of England, Scotland and Ireland.[6] Nevertheless it was many years before the shamrock was actually added. The design of the crowns will probably always remain a mystery. They are certainly heraldicly Imperial in that the arches are raised rather than depressed in the centre, but they bear little resemblance to most of the historic English crowns and none at all to those of the House of Hanover. Certainly a fleur-de-lys has never been used on the top of a British crown, and four arches in place of the conventional two have always been an uncommon device except for some of the Tudor diadems. On occasion it has been called a 'Prince Consort's Crown'. It is true that the design of the Prince's crown used for heraldic purposes bore a remarkable resemblance to those of the Collar. What is overlooked is that he was Great Master of the Bath.

Some of the Collars still in use are certainly very old, but whether any of them date back to 1725 can never be known. It was not the custom to hallmark Bath insignia before 1800, and consequently dating an early specimen is reduced to the lack of a hallmark. Some of the eighteenth-century K.B. Collars do, however, exist. Sir Charles Grey, later the first Earl Grey, received his as a personal gift from King George III in 1783. It is now in private hands ane does not carry a hallmark. Several others in possession of the present G.C.B.s carry early hallmarks and do not contain a shamrock. Several new ones have been required in this century. The Treasury has strongly objected to the expense of having them manufactured of 30 ounces of 22 carat gold. As a result, very handsome ones have been turned out in silver gilt.

From the purely human point of view the original Knights of the Bath suffered from a great disability. Once the impressive rituals of their creation were completed, they were left with no outward symbol to wear that would set them apart from an ordinary Knight Bachelor. When insignia of any kind could hardly be said to exist, such a lack made no great difference. By the beginning of the sixteenth century, the position had changed. The full complement of Garter ornaments had finally been established. The Lesser George, then worn around the neck, was in constant evidence. It is easy to understand why the Knights of the Bath would long for a similar device of their own. In February 1625, a month after the Coronation of Charles I, the Earl Marshal decreed by command of the King that all the Knights of the Bath should continually wear a Badge around their necks.[7] There are some grounds for thinking that such a device already existed in the reign of James I. Although the Earl Marshal did not describe it, the one adopted in 1625 is better documented. There is a Vandyke portrait of Sir Thomas Wharton, now in the Hermitage, that gives a clear indication of what it was like. Wharton was one of those who received the Bath in 1625. Following the custom then being adopted by the Order of the Garter, he is shown wearing a crimson ribbon over his right shoulder tied high under his left arm. Attached to it is a round openwork enamelled gold medal with three crowns in the centre contrived from branches and green leaves. The surrounding motto is only sketched in. A remarkably similar piece was shown in the Heraldic Exhibition at Burlington House in 1894. The centre consisted of a tree with the branches and leaves interlaced to form three imperial crowns in green enamel; four white enamelled quatrefoils were arranged two and two on either side; and the whole surrounded by a circular red enamelled border bearing the motto TRIA IVNCTA IN VNO in gold with a pendant pearl beneath.[8] There can be little doubt that this Badge was the type used during the reign of Charles I. Unfortunately, its present whereabouts is not known.

The Knights created at the Coronation of King Charles II in 1661 were actually invested with a Badge by the King when they received the accolade. Inasmuch as the Regalia had been destroyed by the Commonwealth, it all had to be made again. In addition to the Regalia, Sir Robert Vyner, the Court Goldsmith, supplied Garter insignia and 75 Badges of the Bath.[9] A few of these have survived. Of the four known to the author, two are at Windsor and two in private collections. Three of the four are, for all practical purposes, exactly alike when due allowance is made for slight variations inherent in handwork. They are of gold, enamelled green. In the centre a gold sceptre supports three crowns of leaves, a larger above and two smaller below, with a gold rose to the right and left of the tops of the lower crowns. The whole is enclosed by an oval border carrying the motto TRIA JVNCTA IN VNO in gold, interspersed with rosettes and stops, a gold arabesque above, and a pendant pearl beneath. The oval measures $1\frac{1}{2}$ inches in width and $1\frac{3}{4}$ inches in length or $2\frac{3}{4}$ inches when the arabesque and pearl are taken into consideration. The weight of one of these is 11 dwts. 21 grains (18.5 grams), and it may be assumed that the others weigh about the same. The fourth specimen at Windsor is slightly smaller but heavier, with the roses enamelled white. Inasmuch as the last is the only known example of the variety, it would seem likely that the other three may be considered to have been standard for the creation of 1661.

Of the two Badges at Windsor, the lighter is catalogued as having been worn by Sir Edward Walpole, who received the Bath at the Coronation of Charles II, and later by his grandson, Sir Robert Walpole, upon the foundation of the Order.[10] Nicolas reproduces a woodcut taken from a drawing of the Walpole Badge in the College of Arms, and gives its weight as 18 dwts. 22 grains. Neither the illustration nor the weight bears any resemblance to the specimen at Windsor. A Badge very similar to the Nicolas woodcut exists, however, although much smaller. This piece weighs only 10 dwts. The workmanship makes a seventeenth-century origin unlikely. We shall probably never know whether it was copied from the Nicolas illustration or is the original from which his design, or that of the College of Arms, was taken.

It is easy to see that the Badge of the Knighthood of the Bath provided the model for the device adopted in 1725 as the Badge of the Order and continued today as that of the Civil Division. Beyond this general conclusion very little is known about what the early eighteenth-century examples looked like. It is doubtful that any have survived. The evidence provided by portraits is not conclusive, or even helpful, and the Statutes are exasperatingly vague. In Article XII it is described simply as, 'being Three Imperial Crowns, Or, which shall be placed within the ancient Motto of the Order.'[12] Nevertheless, there is some information available to tell us a few things the Statutes do not disclose. Montagu was a good man of business and a very active Great Master. On 12 May 1725, he directed a Warrant to the Master of the Jewel House, countersigned by Walpole, requesting 39 Badges to be worn 'to a red Ribbon by the Knights Companions of the Most Honourable Order of the Bath that are shortly to be elected.' There was no time to waste because the first Investiture took place just under six weeks later. These pieces were, 'to be made of gold according to Draught and Size herewith exhibited.' Unfortunately, the drawing in question is not in the Public Record Office. The Warrant then goes on to say, 'Whereas there were forty other Badges or Jewels of gold made for the said Knights of a different fashion from what has since been thought proper to be made use of, and the same being of no Service, These are to authorize and direct you to melt down the said Badges,' as part payment for the £750 the new ones were to cost.[13] This document hides as much as it discloses. There were two different varieties of insignia made for the new Order, one of which was destroyed almost immediately, while the pattern for the one adopted has disappeared. We are left knowing almost less about the subject than when the investigation started.

If the form remains a mystery, the records do disclose a detail of considerable interest. It would be a logical assumption, based on current practice, that there was such a thing as a Badge of the Bath established at this time. Like many other logical assumptions, this one is incorrect. The receipts signed on 15 June by the Knights' representatives were for Collars and Badges, each weighing together slightly over 31 oz. 11 dwts. The difference of about 1 oz. 11 dwts. above the prescribed weight of the Collar can be accounted for by the Collar Badge. The weight of the 'jewel of gold appendant to a red ribbon' listed on the same receipt was only 10 dwts.[14] From the very beginning, then, there were two Badges of the Bath rather than one. This custom was followed throughout the century and until 1847 for the Civil Division. The insignia of the Military Division will be discussed later. The size of each remained fairly constant and varies only a few pennyweights one way or the other. It wasn't until later that the price of these ornaments began to be listed in documents. Although departing from the period, it might be interesting to learn how much was paid in 1804 for Sir John Moore's because his insignia can be seen in the National Army Museum. Moore's Collar cost £190, with gold at 85s the ounce, £40 for manufacture and 24s duty; the Collar Badge came to £13 5s 6d; the Sash Badge, £5 15s 6d; two yards of ribbon 7s; and a morocco case, £2 5s. The total amounts to £212 13s, considerably less than would be the cost for the same quality today.

In spite of not knowing exactly what the first insignia looked like, one may reach a fairly close estimate. The oldest surviving Collar Jewel dates from the reign of King George II and has a close resemblance to the representations of the Badges that appear stamped on the covers of a 1725 edition of the Book of Common Prayer bound for use in the Chapel. The tantalizing thought that the piece may be even earlier must await further evidence. The arches of the top crown are almost depressed, and the stems of the rose and thistle curve against the sceptre to reach the frame at the bottom. The weight is 1 oz. 11 dwts. 21 grains (49·57 grams) of 18 carat gold. By the 1780's the pattern had been modified. The crowns have now become more sharply arched, and the rose and thistle spring directly from the sceptre. Although slightly larger in diameter, the piece weighs about the same. The Badges of Lord Nelson and the Peninsular Generals were almost identical in appearance, with the arabesques at the top extended. The size is the same, but the weight has been reduced by a few grains. The only K.B. Sash Badge extant belongs to Sir Galbraith Lowry Cole. So far, no earlier ones have come to light. No shamrocks were added to these Badges. Those of the Civil Division after 1815 introduced other variations and will be dealt with later.

The Star is called 'the Ensign' in the Statutes and consisted of three gold imperial crowns surrounded by the motto in gold on red resting on a glory of wavy rays issuing from the centre. It was embroidered in gold and silver thread, worn on the Mantle and 'constantly' by the Knights on their 'upper vestment'. The portrait evidence for the Stars is ample because they were the most visible part of the insignia. The earliest were broad, but by the time of the Napoleonic Wars, they became narrower, measuring $4\frac{1}{4}$ in. × 5 in. Lord Nelson's at Greenwich are considerably smaller because he was a small man. In the beginning they were not supplied to the Knights, although by 1800 two were generally given at the Investiture. The commandment to wear them constantly was taken seriously. Soon showing the effect of normal deterioration, the embroidered specimens had to be replaced. Between October 1803 and August 1805, for example, Lord Nelson purchased five from Barrett & Corney at between £1 and a Guinea each.[15] These bits of embroidery were treated more as clothing, or uniform equipment, than insignia. They wore out and were thrown away. Practically speaking, there were no 'official issue' Stars in the modern meaning of the term for any of the British Orders until well into the reign of Queen Victoria.

The wearing of Stars worked in gold, silver, and enamel bought from any of several prominent London jewellers became fashionable only after 1800. Finely jewelled examples were made occasionally for Royal use, or for presentation purposes. Only Nabobs could be counted on for an exception to the prevailing rule. The 'Universal Museum' reported on 4 June 1762 that, 'The Star and Badge of the Order of the Bath, which Lord Clive carries over with him to the

East Indies, are said to be as magnificent as any ever yet made. There are, it seems, but two others like them in this Kingdom, one belonging to His Majesty, the other to the Earl of Northumberland, the present Lieutenant of Ireland. In the centre of the Star is a very large brilliant of considerable value encompassed with the three crowns, which are set with yellow diamonds; the letters of the motto (Tria Juncta In Uno) are formed also of diamonds, and placed on a kind of crimson enamel ground. Thirty-two large diamonds compose the exterior ring, and the rays issuing from it are made up of diamonds of different sizes which gradually lessen until they die away (as it were) and come to a point'[16] Lord Clive sporting this eye-catching object in India must have appeared a most suitable representative of the Honourable Company's power and Britain's prestige. A very attractive diamond Star not quite so heavily weighted down with large gems was given to Sir John Moore by the Officers of his Staff. It still survives. Lord Clive's has not. A fascinating note is added by the second Lord Esher. Commanded to dine at Windsor in January 1909, at the King's request he wore a diamond Star given him by his aunt, Miss Adele Gurwood. Obviously pleased at the attention the piece attracted, he wrote, 'No one had ever seen so fine a one. There is only one other real diamond Star of the Bath which anyone had ever heard of, and that belonged to Sir John Moore.'[17]

The privately purchased metal Stars were supplied by a number of jewellers. They conform to no standard pattern and show a wide deviation in their details from the one specified in the Statutes. Only very infrequently do they seem to have had the prescribed wavy rays from the centre. The eight principal points were hinged to permit them to conform to body contours and either drilled or provided with loops so they could be sewn on the coat. The one illustrated has plain engraved rays, dates from about 1800 and is $4\frac{1}{2}$ in. by 5 in. in size. Often the centres were enamelled like Sir John Moore's in the National Army Museum. But the second of the K.B. Stars illustrated is in a class by itself. It was made for the Prince Regent by Rundell, Bridge and Rundell, and measures $4\frac{1}{4}$ in. by $4\frac{3}{4}$ in. In their accounts submitted on 14 July 1813, the piece is described as 'an elegant diamond cut silver Star of the Bath, with waved rays from the centre, and diamond motto and crowns, . . . and the centre paved inside with Brilliants.' It cost the Regent £95.[18]

Stars were not the only items of insignia the Companions provided for themselves. Many of the Knights of the Garter found that the gold Lesser George was too plain an ornament for them, and bought their own set with stones and decorated with coloured enamels. The Knights of the Bath were in a more difficult situation. Their investment Badge, generally measuring only $1\frac{1}{4}$ in. by $1\frac{1}{2}$ in., was almost too small to be seen. It might do very well under conditions of active service. In London and at Court a man with so tiny a bauble felt almost undecorated. Few K.B.s were magnates with the wealth and dignity of a Garter Knight. They took two steps to improve the situation. The simplest was to transfer the seldom worn Collar Badge to the Sash. A portrait by Reynolds sold by Park Bernet in 1968 shows Sir William Fawcett, made K.B. in 1786, using his Collar Jewel in just this fashion. There seem to have been few purchases of expensively jewelled Badges, like Lord Clive's. His was, 'adorned with many brilliants beautifully disposed', around, 'a very large and fine agate with the crowns and other ensigns of the Order cut in *alto relievo*, and the letters of the motto most beautifully enamelled upon gold.'[16] It was more common to use a stone or Wedgwood cameo in an ornate gold and enamelled frame, as Lord Nelson did. This historic Badge disappeared in the great theft of Nelson relics from the Painted Hall at Greenwich in 1901 and has not been seen since. Some of the Peninsular Generals had fine pieces in carved gold and red enamel, like Sir George Murray's, now preserved with his other insignia in the Adjutant's office of the Scots Guards, Wellington Barracks. If the portraits at Greenwich can be taken as a guide, Naval officers tended to wear their investment Badges most of the time. They were not in London very often.

A handsome set of insignia was assigned to the Officers, with the exception of the Great Master and the Dean. The former had to wait just over one hundred years before assuming a Badge of his own. The Dean's was not specified until the Statutes of 1847. He was given one fairly early in the proceedings, nevertheless, and it continued to be used by his successors as a matter of custom. On 13 October 1726, Samuel Bradford, Lord Bishop of Rochester and the first Dean of the Bath, was issued a gold chain weighing just over $6\frac{1}{2}$ oz. with a Knight's investment Badge attached. On 4 November he was given a Collar Badge. When Bishop Willcocks succeeded in 1731, on Bradford's death, he was supplied with a similar chain with the Collar Badge attached and, 'one lesser gold Badge to wear with the Ribbon'.[19]

As might be expected from the looseness of the Statutes in dealing with the insignia, the other Officers' Badges finally emerged looking somewhat different from the specifications. The reasons may be partly, if not wholly, explained by the additional heraldic rank granted most of them in 1726. None of the originals was described as being surrounded by the motto, and only that of the King of Arms was to be surmounted by an Imperial crown. In 1726 these two missing elements were properly added to other Officers' insignia. All were oval. In the eighteenth century the circle and motto were in plain gold and the crown and centre enamelled. Later the motto appeared on a background of red enamel. In summary, the following devices were used until 1847:

	Obverse	*Reverse*
Genealogist	Three gold crowns with the cypher GG in the centre on a blue ground	The White Horse of Hanover and the motto NEC ASPERA TERRENT, as Blanc Coursier Herald

King of Arms	The Arms of the Order impaled with those of the Sovereign on a shield within an ornamental frame	The Arms of Luneberg as Gloucester Herald
The Registrar	Three gold crowns with a book in the centre on a blue ground	The same until the office was combined with that of Secretary
The Secretary	Three gold crowns with pens in the centre on a blue ground	The same until the office was combined with that of Registrar
The Usher	Three gold crowns on a blue ground	Two Lions of Brunswick on a reddish ground, as Brunswick Herald
The Messenger	Three crowns of gold with a greyhound in the centre	The Same. Originally this Badge was to be a simple gold crown

The King of Arms also carries a silver rod two feet long surmounted by a four-sided shield containing the Arms of the Order impaled with the Sovereign's and the Arms of the Order alone, all surmounted by a crown. The Usher carries a red enamelled rod, 44 inches long surmounted by a scroll bearing the motto, with three imperial crowns above.

Pieces resembling these Badges were ready by 15 June 1725 for the Installation. The Genealogist's and King of Arms' were not yet enamelled, but the others were. The King of Arms' rod was plain silver with a gilt crown on top. The Usher's is described as, 'one rod with Brass furniture, gilt', from which it can be assumed that it was not yet red. It took more than a year before matters were put right. By August 1726 the Officers had, 'Six Badges that had been new made and enamelled, wh. One rod enamelled red, part gold and part silver gilt for the Usher of the said Order.'[20] These pieces did not continue to be used throughout the century. The Lord Chamberlain's Accounts show that new ones were purchased for the Officers from time to time. Apparently the families were allowed to retain them.

Exactly what happened to the Bath insignia during the eighteenth century after the death of each Knight is still open to question. The additional Statute of 2 June 1725, declared that the Collars were not to be alienated 'for any cause whatever; but the Executors or Administrators, of every deceased Companion, shall return the same within Three Months to the Great Master of the Order.'[21] No further provisions were made for their disposition after the Duke of Montagu's death in 1749, even though no successor was appointed. According to an undated memorandum prepared in the reign of George IV, they were kept by the families.[22] It is also possible that along with the investment Badge they were turned over to whoever was executing the office of Genealogist. In short, the insignia became a form of perquisite. This state of affairs may raise eyebrows today but was not at all unusual for the times. The Chancellor of the Garter received the Collars of that Order for years and sold them for his own profit. Something of the kind appears to have happened with the Bath insignia. There are two pieces of evidence for this assumption. The Lord Chamberlain's Accounts show that a new set of ornaments was purchased whenever a Knight was appointed. The prices of the metal and workmanship, and the amount of tax for every piece are meticulously listed for each Knight in his name. In 1785, for example, a complete set cost £174 9s 6d. In 1787 we find an entry, 'Paid for a Gold Collar of the Bath, a do. Badge, a small do.' with the total cost, including repairs and a new case, coming to only £136 4s 10d. The lower figure can be explained by the fact that they were 'second hand' and therefore did not include the workmanship charges for new pieces.[23]

By 1812 the wars were popularizing the idea of economy in state expenditure. The alert Nayler, who knew as much as Anstis about catching the smallest puff in his well trimmed sails, attracted favourable attention to himself by suggesting that the original requirement for the return of the Bath Collar and Badges be enforced. Accordingly, on 8 May 1812, there was another addition to the Statutes. All the Knights were strictly enjoined to make proper arrangements for their executors to send back the insignia within three months of their decease. In default of a Great Master, the Genealogist was empowered to receive them for eventual transmission to the Secretary of State for the Home Department. The amendment also made a particular point of explaining that, after Montagu's death, they had been allowed to remain in private hands. If nothing else, this was a useful screen. Inasmuch as Nayler drew the Statute, it can also be presumed that, whatever had been happening to the Collars, by 1812 they were no longer one of the Genealogist's perquisites.

CHAPTER XI

The Robes and Insignia after 1815

Upon the reorganization of the Order no change was made in the Collar, but additional Badges were obviously required for the K.C.B.s and C.B.s. As usual, the Royal Warrant, published in *The London Gazette* of 3 January 1815, made only a passing reference to the insignia. Article VI made clear that the members of the First Class, 'shall henceforth bear upon the Ensign or Star, and likewise upon the Badge of the Order, the addition of a wreath of laurel encircling the motto, and issuing from an escrol inscribed, ICH DIEN.'[1] These additions to the old K.B. insignia never appear to have been made. Nevertheless the representation of just such a Badge without the ICH DIEN was included among the insignia of the various Orders used to decorate the borders of a Royal Worcester porcelain dinner service made for William IV, examples of which are still at Windsor. Having taken due care of the G.C.B.s, the Warrant disclosed nothing about what the two lower classes might expect, apart from a shadowy reference to their wearing the Star and Badges assigned to them. It can only be concluded that the authorities were as vague about the whole matter themselves as the Warrant sounds. We simply do not yet know who was responsible for the designs eventually adopted. Certainly the well-known taste of the Prince Regent must have played a part. A laurelled version of a K.B. Jewel would not have looked well suspended around an officer's neck.

The Regent was well acquainted with the various versions of the cross used for such purposes on the Continent. The Chancery of the Netherlands' Orders in the Hague possesses beautifully hand-illuminated drawings of the patterns which finally emerged from councils in high places. What was adopted were, of course, the same insignia as are still used today for the Military Division. The Badge is a true Maltese cross with eight points tipped with small gold balls. There are four lions of England facing left in each angle, an acanthus leaf on the top arm for the suspension ring, and a slightly modified version of the old K.B. design in the centre, surrounded by a laurel wreath tied with a blue ribbon carrying the words, ICH DIEN, the Prince of Wales' motto. The shamrock was introduced below the rose in the central design. The reverse is exactly the same except that the lions are seen from the rear. This similarity has been a source of confusion to members of the Order, museum curators and others. The tendency is to pick up a Badge, turn it over, and lay it down again. As a result it is too frequently worn, or displayed, with the lions' backsides being given undue prominence.

The G.C.B.s were equipped with two Badges, as the K.B.s had been, but the sizes were reversed. The Collar Badge was smaller. It measured $2\frac{7}{8}$ in. square, weighed 3 oz. and cost £41 6s 0d. The Sash Badge measured $3\frac{3}{4}$ in. square, weighed 3 oz. 19 dwts., with slight variations, and cost £48. There were 58 of each type made. The total paid for them, including red morocco cases and a supply of sashes, amounted to £6,103 1s 1d. From the fact that individual cases were made for this particular lot of Collar Badges, it may be inferred that the chains themselves were given individual containers of their own. In the future, the Collars with Badge appendant were cased together. Now that they were no longer suspended from one of the white enamelled laces but from one of the crowns, 47 Collars were modified accordingly, at a cost of £11 15s.[2] The size of the various pieces has never been specified in the Statutes of any of the British Orders, and the custom of illustrating these documents with photographs is of recent standing. Consequently the quality of the design and the execution of the insignia have always depended on the manufacturing jeweller, who in turn was a man of his times. Fortunately, the goldsmith's art in Britain during these years achieved a standard of excellence seldom surpassed anywhere. The new Bath Badges were very well made. The G.C.B.s come in two major varieties with broad and narrow arms. The Collar pieces all fall into this second group. The expense looks formidable. Actually the Order was being administered with an economy to which it had not hitherto been accustomed. The regulations requiring the return of the insignia upon promotion or decease were being strictly enforced, and the annual outlay for new pieces was reduced to a minimum. The Lord Chamberlain's Accounts reflect very few purchases during the remainder of George III's reign or in that of George IV. After 1830 the veterans began to drop off rapidly, and a surplus of stock resulted.

The first great revision of the Statutes in 1847 contents itself with saying that the K.C.B. and C.B. Badges will be the same as the preceding class but smaller. The original K.C.B. Badges also came in two varieties like those of the First Class. They measure slightly over 2 in. square and came equipped with a large suspension ring decorated with oak leaves. Though handsome, the ring is now a little awkward because of the current styles of uniform and evening dress. The piece was originally designed to be worn outside the uniform collar from a broad $3\frac{3}{4}$ in. crimson ribbon joined at the ends with a gold clip. The Badge then rested low on the chest, a very effective way of displaying it. The C.B.s had a greater variety of execution because even before 1830 the supply had to be replaced from time to time. They were worn on the breast from a two-inch ribbon with a gold buckle that was to appear in the centre and under no circumstances used to attach the decoration to the uniform. They measured $1\frac{3}{4}$ in. square, except for the rather clumsy broad-armed variety made between 1825 and 1827. The K.C.B. Badge was priced at £28 5s 0d and the embroidered Star £1 13s 0d. The Companion's Badge cost £27 6s 6d, or about £10 more than a Lesser George of the Garter. Additional C.B. Badges were required after nomination of East India Company and other officers in 1825, and for foreign officers after the Battle of Navarino in 1827. At the suggestion of the Duke of Clarence, then Acting Great Master, several jewellers were asked for quotations. By this manoeuvre the cost was reduced to fifteen Guineas each, but quality had been sacrificed. With the sanction of the Duke of Wellington and the Lords of the Treasury, some of the Collars of deceased Grand Crosses which had been returned to stock were melted down and the gold used to manufacture the new insignia, 'thus securing a great saving to the public purse.'[3] The saving was illusory because within a decade there was a serious shortage of Collars.

The Badges of the Officers of Arms and Secretary to the Knights Commanders and Companions were also distinctive. The former carried the same pattern as the Genealogist but impaled with a white horse of Hanover, and the latter was similar to the Secretary's but had only one pen. Both were surrounded by laurel wreaths and surmounted by Bath crowns. Nayler was appointed first Officer of Arms Attendant on the Knights Commanders and may have been responsible for a curious innovation. The embroidered Stars given the first K.C.B.s were, like those of the First Class, supplied by the Lord Chamberlain. By devious means not entirely clear Nayler because responsible for furnishing the K.C.B. Stars 'at his own expence'. William Woods, who succeeded to the office in 1831, finally complained about this practice in 1834 because the cost now fell on his shoulders. He 'respectfully submitted' that the Lord Chamberlain relieve him of the burden. Anyone familiar with Sir George Nayler's methods will find it difficult to believe that he did not make a profit on the business, but never let poor Woods in on the secret.[4]

No sooner had the new insignia been approved than the Prince Regent introduced an interesting innovation. He commanded that the Badges of those G.C.B.s who were also Knights of the Garter be surmounted by a crown. The group was small and select. The only persons who qualified were himself, the Royal Dukes of York, Kent, Clarence, Cumberland, Cambridge and Gloucester, and, of course, Field Marshal, the Duke of Wellington. It is probable that he intended this regulation to be a permanent one. The nature of both Orders was such that only very rarely would they be conferred upon the same person and this may have been the reason why the custom lapsed. Crowned insignia were provided for only two other G.C.B.s—Prince Leopold, upon his marriage with Princess Charlotte in 1816, and the Marquess of Hastings in 1819. There was more to it than at first meets the eye. The Gartered G.C.B.s were supplied with no fewer than four different Badges, one for the Sash, one for the Collar, another to wear around the neck, similar to the K.C.B. and a still smaller one, 1 in.

square, to use in the buttonhole of evening or civil dress. All carried the crowns.

As might be expected, there is some doubt about what type of crowns were first used. The Lord Chamberlain was billed for 8 complete sets costing £1,474 14s. The accounts submitted for payment do not mention the crowns and thus make a solution of the mystery more difficult. But the same set of accounts also lists the costs of the regular insignia for ordinary G.C.B.s, with the Sash Badges described as the same as those made for the Royal Family but without the crowns. There is, then, no doubt about the addition having been made in accordance with the Regent's wishes.[2] When Prince Leopold's insignia was prepared in 1816, a little more light is thrown on the subject. His Badges are described as having an Imperial crown.[5] A portrait of the Duke of Kent in the Queen's collection at Windsor shows him wearing a neck Badge from a rather elongated version of the Bath crown.[6] A Badge of this type survives today. It seems logical to conclude that the original crown was Imperial in form and executed in plain gold if it were not for two other pieces of evidence.

The Crown Jewellers, Messrs. Rundell, Bridge and Rundell, in their quarterly bill to the Lord Chamberlain, dated 5 July 1817, have the following entry: 'Remaking Crowns to the Gold enamelled Badges prepared for Their Royal Highnesses the Dukes of Kent, Cumberland and Cambridge to drawing received, surmounted by the English Crown and afterwards altered to Imperial Crown.'[7] If this description can be understood at all, it can only mean that the first type was an 'English Crown' which was later replaced by the Bath crown just noticed. The change in 1817 involves a third variety. Only three of the original group were mentioned and one may safely assume that the others did not have their Badges altered. King George IV's Sash Badge in the Royal collection is equipped with a rather small and unimpressive enamelled version of a conventional heraldic English crown. The neck Badges of the Duke of Wellington and William IV have also survived, the former in the Apsley House Museum and the latter in the possession of a descendant. Both pieces have crowns resembling the King's. We are left with the conundrum presented by the Duke of Cambridge's unaltered Badge mentioned above. Rundell and Bridge did not specify how many of his Badges were altered in 1817. It is suggested, therefore, that he did not have the complete set changed. He was absent from London at his post as Viceroy of Hanover so that it seems logical that he reserved one Badge for use, and it is this one that has survived. The question of what type of crown replaced the second variety on the Royal Duke's Badges in 1817 still remains.

The insignia supplied Lord Hastings in 1819 were provided with crowns, 'overset with Rubies, Sapphires and Emeralds'. That attached to the neck Badge was set with 'oriental stones'.[8] It is this piece that exists in the Royal collection today and has been used in the past as the Soveriegn's Badge of the Order of the Bath. It seems likely that the third alteration on the insignia of the Royal Dukes may have resulted in similar devices. The last person to receive a crowned Badge upon his appointment as G.C.B. was Prince Albert. The second Duke of Cambridge received the Bath in 1855 and the second Lord Londonderry succeeded to the Duke of Wellington's Garter in 1852. Although both were G.C.B.s neither was provided with crowned Badges. The Prince Regent's attempt to introduce an additional type of insignia not contemplated by the existing regulations did not succeed. In retrospect, the wisdom of the effort seems dubious because it had the effect of setting one small group apart from the other members of the same grade when all should have been equal within the Order.

The Stars designed for the Military Knights of the First and Second Class bore little resemblance to those formerly used. The G.C.B. emblem was almost triangular in profile and composed of flaming silver rays. A gold Maltese cross was placed upon it with three crowns on a silver ground in the centre surrounded by the motto, the whole encircled by a laurel wreath tied with a blue ribbon as on the Badge. The central crowns were Royal, a shape that had no traditional connection with the Bath. Although the anachronism was noticed, no steps were taken to modify them. On Investiture the G.C.B.s were handed two of these Stars rather cheaply embroidered, and no longer intended to be worn. By 1815 the practice of having them attached to virtually every outer garment had long been given up. They were seen only when formal dress was required. The decorations were manufactured in gold, silver and enamels, and privately purchased from London jewellers. From January to June 1815, they were much larger than they subsequently became because the style of dress dictated that they be worn high on the left breast about where war medals are now. After Waterloo the size was reduced until they became slightly smaller than the modern type. The original wreaths were flat although they became convex in the next reign and after. The larger pieces measured $4\frac{5}{16}$ in. by $4\frac{1}{4}$ in., while the small versions were $3\frac{11}{16}$ in. by $3\frac{3}{8}$ in. Examples made up to early Victorian times changed very little.

The centres of K.C.B. Stars took the form of the First Class but without the gold Maltese cross. More variety is found among these pieces than is usual with the G.C.B. Stars. They ranged $2\frac{7}{8}$ in. to $3\frac{1}{4}$ in. square. One type has the crowns placed in a triangular fashion. In the first examples all the individual rays were of equal length. In the reign of George IV they were arranged one long and one short, as they are now. To understand how these Ensigns were regarded by the members one must abandon all modern fixed ideas about medals and other insignia received at the hands of the Sovereign. If a man could buy one, he could buy more than one and often did. Sir Thomas Brisbane had three K.C.B. Stars, each differing from the other. Field Marshal Lord Combermere, the 'Lion d'or' of Peninsular days, and the Marquess of Londonderry treated themselves to G.C.B. Stars set with diamonds. When Lord Londonderry was visiting Paris in 1823 the Star was stolen, much to his annoyance, although he could well afford as many as he liked.[9] Some were set with paste and looked very well in the evening under candlelight. George IV favoured Stars with diamond centres for his own more casual use. The men of those days paid as much attention to their Stars as their descendants now devote to wrist watches.

In the midst of the new military finery the small remaining number of Civil G.C.B.s were left with their old K.B. insignia. The question of whether the decorations changed when Civil G.C.B.s as such began to be appointed is worth a brief examination. Those K.B.s in the naval and military service were required to turn in their Collars for alteration, and it may be presumed, therefore, that there must have been an ample supply of oval Badges in the hands of the Genealogist for the use of any new Civil Knights. On 1 April 1815, Richard Le Poer Trench, second Earl of Clancarty in Ireland and Ambassador to the Netherlands, received the first Civil appointment. A new Collar and Badge had to be made for him at a cost of £259 4s. Although the Badge weighed 1 oz. 10 dwts., like the others used on the Collars, it was described separately as being for Investment.[10] If this was not a clerical error, the implication is that the large Collar type Badges were now to be worn on the Sash. Whether this was the intention in Lord Clancarty's case will probably never be known. His Bath insignia have survived. The Badge weighs 1 oz. 9·6 dwts. Although it is not hallmarked, the weight is close enough to justify the thought that it could be the piece mentioned in the Crown Jeweller's accounts, if one assumes that the one attached to the Collar came from the surplus just mentioned.

Regardless of what happened in this particular situation, the pattern soon reverted to what it had always been. In 1819, Sir William A'Court, later Lord Heytesbury, who received the Bath that year was also given a new suite of ornaments. They included, 'A small gold Investment Badge for the Ribbon of a Civil Knight,' weighing the usual 11 dwts. and costing 8 Guineas.[11] In effect, the Civil G.C.B.s continued to be given the same decorations that all K.B.s had once received, and they treated them in the same way. A portrait of Lord Palmerston by Partridge, now loaned to the House of Commons by Lord Mountbatten, shows a large gold Badge on the Sash. But it must be recognized that they did not necessarily look exactly like those of the earlier century. This was particularly true of the Stars the Knights supplied for themselves. The Clancarty specimens are a mixed group characteristic of a period of rapid change. They measure $3\frac{7}{8}$ in. by $4\frac{1}{4}$ in., 4 in. by $4\frac{1}{8}$ in. and $3\frac{3}{8}$ in. square, respectively. By the 1820's, possibly as a result of some pressure from the King, they had settled down to a modernized version of the old K.B. type. It should be noted that the specimen illustrated has the correct wavy rays from the centre. More important, the profile is entirely different from those of the Military Division. The dimensions are $3\frac{5}{8}$ in. by $3\frac{3}{4}$ in.

The manufacturers and the purveyors of insignia were generally not the same, a detail not always understood. The Crown Jeweller acted as a middleman between the maker and the Lord Chamberlain who paid the bills. The maker's symbol in the hallmark stamps cannot always be read today. A few of the Bath Collars were marked as early as 1804. Beginning with the goldsmith's year 1814/15 all the insignia carried the official marks down to about 1900. After that year the military pieces were no longer stamped but the Civil Badges still are. The date letter, an integral part of the hallmark, enables anyone interested to read the year in which each piece was made. Most of the first military insignia carry the initials *IE* in a cartouche for John Edwards, a working jeweller in London. Some of the C.B.s are stamped with *IN* whose name is not known. In the 1850's and 1860's the initials *WN* and then *WC* were used by the makers. By 1860, however, Garrard & Company held the Crown Appointment and began to make all the Bath insignia except the Stars, which they did not begin to produce until 1865. Until 1860 the metal was 'old standard gold', or 22 carats fineness, after which 18 carat gold was used. For many years the Stars were engraved with the names of the firms that sold them but were not hallmarked. The great majority of the original pieces were purchased at the Ludgate Hill shop of Rundell, Bridge and Rundell, *'Jewellers to Their Majesties/ His Royal Highness the/ PRINCE REGENT/ And the Royal Family'*. Rundell & Bridge had the Warrant and were much patronized by George IV as Regent and as King. It was fashionable to follow where he led. Over the years the inscription changed and enables the Stars to be dated with reasonable accuracy.[12] The one quoted above indicates that the piece was produced between 1815 and 1820. From 1820 to 1830 Rundell's were jewellers 'To the King' after which they became jewellers to 'Their Majesties', King William IV and Queen Adelaide. In due course we find Garrard's describing themselves as jewellers to the Queen and then the Queen and Prince Albert. The less useful expression, 'Jewellers to the Crown' was adopted from about 1861 to 1865 when the practice ceased.

Why it lapsed may probably be explained by Victorian attitudes. In 1854 when Prince Albert directed that a silver Star instead of the usual embroidered one be given to Field Marshal Omar Pasha, commander of the Turkish forces in the Crimea, it was returned to Albert Woods by the Duke of Newcastle, Secretary for War and the Colonies. Woods was informed, 'that the Duke cannot allow the same to be transmitted to Turkey in its present state not until such name and words are removed as are engraved on the back. His Grace conceives that no words should be engraved upon any decoration or upon any part of the same unless explicitly ordered by the Grand Master.'[13] When His Grace was transferred to other spheres of activity more suitable for those talents he had, the matter was dropped. The fact that his opinions finally prevailed can be taken as a sign of the times. Information disclosed by the engraved backplates of the Stars and hallmark dates on other pieces may strike some readers as being of little practical value. The contrary is actually the case. Owners of ancestral family decorations and collectors who possess Bath insignia would do well to see that the traditional pedigrees are not faulted out by information the awards themselves can disclose if a minimum of intelligent attention is paid to them.

Makers of insignia have played an important if unsung role in the history of the Order of the Bath for a reason that casts an interesting reflection on the habits of some early members of the Military Division. Until it was decided in 1859 that insignia could be kept by the families, the regulation that all the Badges had to be returned was strictly enforced. The meticulous William and Albert Woods in succession were in charge of the operation. The G.C.B. Badges were returned by the heirs to the Sovereign in audience and then sent to the Woods, who received the Collar and lesser insignia directly from the heirs or their representatives. After seeing that necessary repairs were made the Woods turned them over to the Lord Chamberlain for eventual re-issue. The book still exists in which a record of the incomings and outgoings from 1835 to 1843 was kept.

It is perfectly understandable that some of the decorations would have suffered through use. Badges were worn more often than they are today and subjected to normal damage through no immediate fault of the possessors. Young Harry Smith supplies an example of what could happen. On the cold night of 23 October 1818, he was returning home with his wife after a triumphant day that began with a review of the troops by the Allied Sovereigns and ended with a Ball at which Juana had been presented to Alexander I by the Duke. The Smiths kept to the centre of the road because troops of all kinds were marching on either side. Suddenly Juana Smith noticed that her husband had lost his C.B. Badge. Not very confidently he turned back for a look. When he was just about to give up, 'a great flat footed dickey dragoon horse, having set his hollow foot upon it, tossed it under my horse's nose out of the dust . . . bruised by horse's foot in which shape I wore it for twenty-nine years.'[14]

The Woods could take a damaged piece of this kind in their stride. What they would too often get caused mounting exasperation. The C.B.s lacked the swivel and the buckle. The K.C.B.s were turned in without the gold ribbon clasp, or the large gold ring. It was not only monotonous but expensive. The Crown had to pay the costs. For example, Garrard's submitted a bill for, 'Repairing, re-enamelling, and re-casing & doing up as new 8 Commander's Badges of the Bath. One gold oak ring to be made, 3 gold snaps, 8 new cases and ribbons. £39.'[15] These must have been in a shocking state. The last straw was finally laid in 1840. On 19 June William Woods recorded that he had received 'of Lieut. Genl. Lord Keane the K.C.B. Badge lately worn by him. Imperfect.' It took him almost a month to make up his mind and trace the gallant Peer. On 14 July 1840 he was able to enter the triumphant note, 'Delivered to Lord Keane his Badge of a K.C.B. to be made perfect & returned to me.'[15] He had at last caught up with one delinquent. According to the Woods' evidence much of the Bath insignia during these years was in a totally unwearable condition. It is strange that the members treated their decorations in such a cavalier fashion.

During the forty-four years following 1815 the return of insignia was more complicated in practice than on paper. Until the 1840's the Officers were allowed to keep theirs with the exception of hapless Dr Thomas Turton, Dean of Westminster from 1842 to 1845. After his translation to the See of Ely the Lords Commissioners of the Treasury directed that his chain and Badges be made available for the use of the Crown.[16] Illogically, Their Lordships paid no attention to Dr Turton's colleagues, at least before 1845. William Henry Stephenson, appointed Messenger in that year, paid a commutation of £45 in lieu of returning his Badge when he vacated the office.[17] There was a curious incident in 1852. On 29 April Albert Woods received back Sir George Bonham's Civil C.B. Badge sent to Garrard's for re-finishing because it turned out to be silver gilt. Bonham had had it made in 1848 to save his gold one and 'must have returned it in error'. The Lord Chamberlain instructed Woods to get the other from Sir George and inform Garrard's they must not accept a commission of the kind again in the future.[18] Undoubtedly a few pieces must have escaped Woods' grasp but not many. Naturally there were exceptions. He received a letter from Albert Grey on 17 March 1853 informing him it was the Queen's desire, 'the Duke of Wellington should be allowed to retain the insignia of the Order of the Bath worn by his late Illustrious Father but that it is to be clearly understood that this is to be considered as an exceptional case & it is not to be drawn into a precedent.'[19] The second Duke had already lunched with the Queen and Prince Albert at Osborne earlier in the year and delivered up his father's Lesser George and Bath Investment Badge. We can thank Queen Victoria, and the seventh Duke of Wellington, for being able to see today the Great Duke's Collar with crowned Badge appendant, and crowned neck Badge, in the Apsley House Museum.

The general undercurrent of official interest in reorganizing the Order mentioned in an earlier chapter produced one suggestion from the busy pen of Sir Nicholas Harris Nicolas. He, of course, was a fountain of complaints and never had approved of the insignia adopted in 1815. In an exhaustive proposed new draft of the Statutes submitted in 1834, he suggested that the Badges envisaged in the original Royal Warrant be adopted, with the Civil Badge being similar to those of the Military Division except that the centre be surrounded by an oak wreath. This idea died a quiet death. There was no change in the form of the Civil G.C.B. except in the general style of execution. When Prince Albert ordered six new ones in 1859, the variety finally appeared that was to last until 1900 with no variation apart from the use of 18 carat gold in 1860 and silver gilt in 1887. After 1900 the type still in use was introduced.

Prince Albert had an exceptionally orderly mind. It is not surprising that the designs of the Civil K.C.B. and C.B. in 1847 were based on the already established insignia. The Star had the same profile as that of the Military Division but without the laurel wreath. The Badges, oddly enough, were not just smaller versions of the G.C.B., but more oval and not exactly of the same pattern. They were used with only a slight modification until 1900 when the Badges of the three grades were all made alike, apart from the size. In June 1847 the Lord Chamberlain was directed by the Great Master to have 25 K.C.B. and 50 C.B. Badges prepared. This supply lasted until 16 August 1851, when the Lord Chamberlain's office let Woods know that the last K.C.B. had been issued 7 August. Woods promptly wrote the Great Master the same day and the Prince noted in the margin of the letter, '10 K.C.B. and 20 C.B.'.[20] The Stars were embroidered as was still the custom. But the practice of giving a silver Star on special occasions was not unusual and foreshadowed the improvement to come. An exchange between Prince Albert and Woods on this subject gives an interesting example of the Civil Service mind at work. On 10 August 1847, anticipating the appointment of Count Albert Mensdorff-Pouilly, the Queen's cousin, as a Civil K.C.B., Colonel Phipps wrote Woods from Osborne asking him on Prince Albert's behalf to have a silver Star made for Count Mensdorff, and to charge it to H.R.H.'s account. He added, 'Of course, I mean the Star such as is usually worn, and not the paper Star supplied by the Lord Chamberlain's Office.' This was not good enough for Woods, who could never resist a pedantic question. Two days later he was told somewhat acidly, 'It was the wish of the Queen that the silver Star should be sent in addition to, and not in place of, the embroidered Star issued from the Lord Chamberlain's office.'[21]

The new Statutes also modified the insignia worn by the Officers of the Order. In effect, the Officers lost the additional heraldic titles bestowed on them in 1726 and consequently the Badges of the Genealogist, King of Arms, and Messenger no longer carried the devices of Blanc Coursier, Gloucester, and Brunswick Heralds. The King of Arms' Badge had already been changed in 1837 because the Royal Arms no longer showed the Hanoverian escutcheon in the centre as they had from 1714 to Queen Victoria's accession. For the first time the Great Master was assigned a Badge although the Duke of Montagu is shown wearing a large K.B. jewel around his neck in a portrait now on display in the National Army Museum. The device adopted was simply the crowned K.C.B. neck Badge, one of the pieces the Regent had created for those G.C.B.s who were Knights of the Garter. The Duke of Sussex was the only one of the Acting Great Masters who assumed a Badge representing his office. He used a Civil Badge enamelled in the proper colours surmounted by a large enamelled Bath crown. From portrait evidence it was solid in construction and in general presentation resembled those of the other Officers. No drawing of it has yet been discovered and the Badge itself may no longer exist. While Prince Albert had been given George IV's diamond neck Badge by the Queen in 1840 he had crowns added to his own Collar Badge and to an 1815 K.C.B. The same Collar is used by the present Sovereign of the Order when Her Majesty attends a Bath

Installation. The Prince's neck Badge has been used by his successors in office, and is still used by the present Great Master.

Another small administrative difficulty was also settled by these Statutes. The problem of Knights who held appointments in both Divisions of the Order at the same time had been a vexing one, as we have seen. On 25 May 1847, Woods referred a letter to Prince Albert from Lieutenant General, the Earl of Westmorland, who had been awarded a Civil G.C.B. for his diplomatic services in Berlin, requesting that he be allowed to keep his Military K.C.B. At the same time he pointed out that the case was taken care of by the provisions in Article XXIII. This inquiry brought the matter to a head. The Prince replied on 29 May that Lord Westmorland could wear his Badge but not the Star. The same decision was applicable to Lord Hardinge and Sir Howard Douglas. In June the Lord Chamberlain was instructed to return the K.C.B. Badge of which he had been deprived, to Sir Howard.[22]

During the first century of its existence no one worried very much about the costs of the Order of the Bath. As the Civil Service became more professional and the country as a whole became engrossed with the pleasures to be derived from the pursuit of business and profits, a change took place. The Lords Commissioners of the Treasury began to take a great interest in the Order, and have not yet relaxed their grip. Sometimes the results were bizarre. In 1838 Sir Richard Jenkins of the East India Company's service, just appointed a Civil Knight, followed the usual practice and asked the Lord Chamberlain for the issue of a Mantle and Collar. Because none were available, the matter was referred to the Treasury. The Secretary to Their Lordships replied on 12 June 1839, 'The Lords Commissioners of H.M. Treasury having had under consideration your letter of the 30 ult. with the application therein enclosed, from Sir Richard Jenkins soliciting H.M.'s authority for wearing the Collar and Mantle of a G.C.B., as if he had been installed, I have it in command to request you to state to the Marquess of Normanby that My Lords are not prepared to meet the expense which would arise from the general relaxation of the Statutes and regulations of that Order as related to the ceremony of Installation, but there can be no objection on the part of the Board to his Lordship recommending a relaxation in the case of Sir R. Jenkins, or any other party, on condition that they provide the Collar at their own expense.'[23]

It is interesting to imagine the reply this little bit of arrogant interference in the affairs of the Order would have received had Prince Albert been Great Master at the time. On the other hand, no one could object to the Treasury minute of 27 April 1843, addressed to the Lord Chamberlain in which they approved the expenditure of £1,153 for new insignia and repairs, even though it was not without a sting. The document closed with the admonition, 'I am at the same time to state to your Lordship that My Lords consider that as the number of Commanders of the Bath is limited, and as the Badges have been provided for the whole original number, and these Badges are, or ought to be regularly returned into store on the death or promotion of each officer, there can be no necessity for making any provision for the purchase of new Badges for this class of the Order of the Bath.' But Their Lordships' interest in these matters resulted in a startling situation elsewhere. On 31 January 1844, Woods informed Prince Albert that since the previous 1 July, 52 C.B.s had been gazetted and none of them had received their insignia. He had only 14 damaged Badges in stock and plaintively asked if he could be authorized to have these repaired and 17 new ones made. This was carrying penny pinching a bit far.[24]

A pattern of this kind might have been expected to continue unabated. What actually occurred in the next decade was an unexpected interruption in the Treasury's drive for economy. The Crimean War opened the ranks of the Bath to officers of foreign countries allied with Britain for the first time since Waterloo. The presentation of silver Stars to foreigners had already been adopted in special cases, as we have seen. In 1855 when Napoleon III and Victor Emmanuel II received the Garter, they were given metal Stars. General Sir William Codrington describing an Investiture held in the Crimea wrote, 'The French, I am glad to see, had their real Stars given them; it looked a little awkward to see our own officers getting the spangled affair at the same time put into their hands. We made the best of it, though I must say it looked like a little economy for a great nation at the time.'[25] This practice conflicted with the Statutes of 1847 which described the Stars as silver rather than embroidered. The country was at last becoming conscious of being a great nation. Finally, the logical step was taken and the first silver Stars were issued at the Crown's expense on 9 July 1858.[26]

The next step was to be more costly. In 1856 the decision had already been taken to dispense with the requirement in Article XXIII of the 1847 Statutes that the insignia of officers of the French Army and Navy appointed Honorary members of the Order be returned, with the exception of the Collars. On 16 August 1858, the Secretary of State for War informed the Prince Consort of the Government's opinion that the time had arrived when the provision of Article XXIII should be dispensed with for all existing and future members of the Order. As Great Master, the Prince was asked to submit this proposal to the Queen and to investigate and inform the Lord Chamberlain of the costs this change would entail.

Only the insignia held by members who had been promoted were to be returned.[27] In his reply on 23 October the Prince showed that the total cost of all Badges in use by ordinary members was £16,072 1s 0d. A further schedule attached to the letter breaks down the expenses projected against a five year period. Inasmuch as this schedule shows the cost of each of the decorations, a factor that was to become important thirty years later, it is introduced here in full.

ORDER OF THE BATH

Statement showing the expense that would have been incurred during the years 1853, 1854, 1855, 1856, and 1857, had Silver Stars been provided and had the Insignia of the Order been retained in the families of the deceased Members, instead of being returned for the use of Her Majesty's Government. This is exclusive of Collars.

For Knights Grand Cross

	£	s	d		£	s	d	£	s	d
26 Military Badges at	40	0	0	—	1,040	0	0			
26 Military Silver Stars at	17	10	0	—	455	0	0			
6 Civil Badges at	16	10	0	—	99	0	0			
6 Civil Silver Stars at	17	1	0	—	102	0	0			
								1,696	0	0

For Knights Commanders

	£	s	d		£	s	d	£	s	d
87 Military Badges at	28	0	0	—	2,436	0	0			
87 Military Silver Stars at	14	10	0	—	1,261	10	0			
22 Civil Badges at	13	0	0	—	286	0	0			
22 Civil Silver Stars at	11	11	0	—	254	2	0			
								4,237	12	0

For Companions

	£	s	d		£	s	d	£	s	d
382 Military Badges at	17	0	0	—	6,494	0	0			
28 Civil Badges at	9	9	0	—	264	12	0			
								6,758	12	0
				TOTAL				£12,692	4	0

Annual expenditure on an average of 5 years

	£	s	d
For Knights Grand Cross	339	4	0
For Knights Commanders	847	10	4
For Companions	1,351	14	5
Yearly average	£2,538	8	9

28

A revised set of Statutes was accordingly issued on 31 January 1859, in which the old Article 23 specifying that the insignia should be returned was dropped with the exception of the Collars and the decorations of members promoted within the Order. The same regulations still apply.

This abrupt reversal of what had been an old established practice had several effects worth noting. All the old insignia could now remain in the hands of the families of the deceased members. In the case of the G.C.B.s and K.C.B.s most of the decorations dated back to 1815. After the stock of 17 K.C.B. Badges in stock on 1 January 1859 had been exhausted new ones would have to be made. At the same time there were 12 Collars, 27 Collar Badges and 32 Investiture Badges for the G.C.B. Military Division on hand to leave a surplus of 15 Collar Badges. When the first Badges began to be manufactured about 1865, the distinction between those worn on the Collar and those used for Investiture was dropped. As a result, it is evident that some of the former Collar Badges were used for Investiture. At present the position is best described as mixed. Some of the Collars still retain the original 1815 decorations, some are provided with 1815 Investiture Badges, and the remainder have the more modern type made either in gold or silver gilt. In a very few cases this is also true of the Collars given to the Civil G.C.B.s, although there were very few old Badges in stock on 1 January 1859.[29]

There is another aspect to the change of great potential importance to museum curators, collectors and families with inherited groups of decorations. Before January 1859, for all practical purposes, all Bath insignia were returned on the death of the Order's members. This means that a group of decorations that falls anywhere between 1815 and 1859 should not contain a Badge of the Bath. The author has seen interesting combinations in recent years that are simply not possible. For example, a group awarded to an officer who died in 1858 was sold complete with a K.C.B. and a C.B., although he had never held the Third Class of the Order. The very fine group that had belonged to General Sir Thomas Brisbane, G.C.B., stolen some years ago from the premises of a London dealer, contained an 1815 K.C.B. Badge despite there cords showing that he had returned the piece to Sir William Woods on 30 May 1837 after his promotion to the First Class. There are also cases where Bath insignia of Victorian vintage have been attached to medal groups of Peninsular officers. One particularly illuminating example, later corrected, occurred recently where the medals of an obviously Civil K.C.B. offered for sale had had the decorations of a Military K.C.B. added to them purely from an unconcerned ignorance. No doubt there is the odd exception where insignia might have escaped the vigilance of officials of the Order, but it is safer to assume that none did, particularly if the presence of a fine Badge adds to the interest, and the cost, of a group of decorations.

After 1860 Garrard's gradually took over the manufacturing of all the insignia of the British Orders. The general appearance of the Bath pieces became substantially similar to what it is today. Strangely enough, the firm does not seem to have been subjected to any control from the Lord Chamberlain or Albert Woods who had become a species of Universal Secretary to most of the Orders. The decorations became what Garrard's thought they ought to be and the Crown paid what Garrard's thought it ought to pay. The results were satisfactory. The quality of the pieces was excellent. Nevertheless, the firm introduced one regrettable innovation of its own. The Stars of the old K.B. and of the early Civil G.C.B. were different from the triangular profile and flaming rays adopted for the Military Division. About 1865 the firm began to produce Civil G.C.B. Stars with exactly the same shape as the Military ones, the only difference lying in the centre devices. This was at variance with the tradition that the Civil Stars should be composed of wavy rays from the centre. No doubt this change may have seemed logical, but it was not in accord with the provisions of the Statutes and deprived the Civil Knights of an attractive and particularly distinctive piece of insignia.

The Statutes of 1847 had fixed the widths of the K.C.B. and C.B. ribbons at 3 in. and 2 in. respectively. In fact, many of the Military Badges continued to be worn from $3\frac{3}{4}$ in. ribbons until the supply of gold clasps of this size used to secure both ends gave out. A decade later the ribbons were further reduced to 2 in. for the Second Class and $1\frac{1}{2}$ in. for the Third Class at Prince Albert's suggestion. On July 20, 1857 General Grey wrote Woods on the Prince's behalf, 'H.R.H. thinks that the C.B. riband as well as that of the K.C.B. may be advantageously narrowed—particularly that of the former now that there are so many war medals worn with it—the breadth of the former C.B. Riband wd. be wide enough for the K.C.B. H.R.H. wd. wish you to send patterns of the narrower Ribands accordingly'.[30] This small change was finally introduced into the Statutes of 1859 and the measurements have remained the same ever since.

The whole question of the costs of the Queen's Golden Jubilee, mentioned in an earlier chapter, had already attracted watchdogs in the Treasury who, before the event in June 1887, were objecting to some of the more ceremonial parts of the expenditure. This had led to the appointment of a Committee to see if the price of the Indian Orders could not be reduced in response to the Treasury's campaign to force the adoption of cheaper insignia. Nothing much was accomplished with the Indian awards, although a slightly better bargain was forced on Garrard's. The minor political uproar simply strengthened the Treasury's hand exactly at the juncture when it needed the help. The radicals were left with the impression that they had gained a point whereas it was really the civil servants who won the battle. In 1887 the insignia of the Bath and St Michael and St George began to be manufactured in silver gilt rather than 18 carat gold. Here it should be noted that Bath decorations exist in gold and gilt, each carrying the hallmark date for 1887 and 1888.   There was only a small reduction in the overall expense because most of the cost by this time was charged to the workmanship and no Collars were required. The results were not entirely happy. The gilt soon wore off the centre of the Badges and they began to look shabby. The Stars required cleaning from time to time, as all silver will, and the gilt easily rubbed off the crosses on those of the Military G.C.B. An earlier generation would have regarded this bit of niggardliness as a very strange economy. The reaction of Lord Palmerston or Sir Robert Cecil, first Earl of Salisbury, can be imagined. The position was partially improved fifteen years later. In 1902 the centres of both pieces of insignia were once more made in gold without anyone raising the slightest objection. The bodies of the Badges, however, remained silver gilt. Oddly enough, the workmanship of G.C.B. insignia is better today than it was during the reigns of Edward VII and George V.

The C.B. Badges for both divisions continued to be suspended from a hinged split ring secured by a knurled nut attached to the bar through which the ribbon was threaded until 1915. In that year manufacturing insignia became a problem because so many men were called to the fighting services or engaged in other vital war work. To speed up the production the split ring was abandoned and the Badges of the C.B. and C.M.G. were attached directly to the suspension bar by a simple bent ring. They continued to be made this way until 2 June 1917, when the King commanded that the Badges of the Third Class of the senior Orders should be worn at the neck. From 1896 until 1917 the C.B. was considered junior to a C.V.O., which had been designed for neck suspension from the beginning. Although the regulation had much to recommend it, no change in the size of the decorations took place. As a result the Civil Badge, designed to be displayed on the breast, looks rather inconspicuous below a white tie. The C.B.s in stock were officially altered by the addition of a small connecting link between the top of the acanthus leaf or arabesque and the suspension ring mounted at right angles to the plane of the Badge. Many of them were also contained in the original long narrow cases, the interior arrangements of which necessarily had been modified. Inasmuch as the regulation was retroactive, the Treasury agreed, within certain limits, to bear the cost of altering insignia already issued to the existing members. The work could not be handled by Garrard's alone, with the result that there are a good many variations in the suspension devices.

The great work of consolidating the Statutes in 1925 had led Major Henry Stockley into unexpected by-paths. To his surprise he discovered the same faults in the insignia Nicolas had noted in the previous century. In spite of Sir Joseph Banks providing a sketch in 1801, and the provisions of the Statutes of 1847 and 1859, no shamrocks had been added to the Collars as they had to the Badges. No specifications had been drawn for the Stars of the Military Division until the Statutes of 1847, when the crowns at the centre were referred to as Imperial. In fact, the crowns used for the Military Stars had been Royal in form from the beginning and remained that way after 1847. After discussing both these points with the Duke of Connaught, new designs were prepared for the Collars and Stars which met with the King's approval. 'The Treasury agreed to ten Collars being altered annually, until the present stock has been corrected, so that all Knights Grand Cross created in the future will be issued with the correct Collars.'[31] His Majesty also directed that the Crowns on the Military Stars should, in the future, be imperial to conform to those used on the Civil Stars, as they had been on the Stars of the K.B.s during the latter part of the eighteenth century. The existing Military Stars were, however, to be issued until the stock became exhausted.

Just how far the work on the modification of the Collars proceeded is not known. By 1938, however, the Crown Jewellers submitted a disquieting report that some of the gold ones had become so much deteriorated by age that it was impossible to repair them without supplying many entirely new pieces. They suggested that they should examine each Collar returned upon the decease of a G.C.B. and give their opinion whether it could be remade using parts of others, or melted down and the bullion value credited against the supply of new silver gilt Collars. The Treasury approved this course but in the upheaval caused by war breaking out in 1939 it is not clear to what extent it was ever carried out.

The admission of ladies to the ranks of the Bath in 1970 has naturally required some adjustment in the size and method of wearing of insignia. Here the precedents already established for the Orders of St Michael and St George and the British Empire have been closely followed. The Sash for the Grand Cross of both divisions has been reduced to $2\frac{1}{4}$ in. in breadth. In the Military Division the Badge of the G.C.B. has been made $2\frac{5}{8}$ in. square and the Star measures $3\frac{1}{4}$ in. by $3\frac{1}{8}$ in. The Star of the D.C.B. is $2\frac{5}{8}$ in. square and the Badge is $2\frac{1}{4}$ in. square but is fitted with an ingenious device that enables it to be suspended from the neck when uniform is worn or from a bow on the left shoulder in ordinary evening dress. The way the traditional large ring decorated with oak leaves has been modified to appear on this bow is well done. The D.C.B. ribbon is $1\frac{3}{4}$ in. in breadth. The C.B. Badge is also fitted so that it may be used with either type of dress and is the same size as those used by the gentlemen. The Stars of the Civil G.C.B. and D.C.B. are the same size as those of the Military Division and the size of the Badges remains unchanged. The Collar, of course, has also been made smaller. Although composed of the same number of pieces, it is only $\frac{3}{4}$ in. in depth and 50 in. long. Queen Victoria had a small Bath Collar made for her own use when she presided over the formal Investitures that were such a feature of the reign before the Prince Consort's death in 1861. Her Majesty the Queen, however, prefers to wear the Prince's full size Collar whenever she is present at an Installation.

NOTES

CHAPTER I: *Mr Walpole and Mr Anstis*

1 *Statutes of the Most Honourable Order of the Bath.* London, 1812. p 111.
2 Nicolas, Sir Nicholas Harris. *History of the Orders of Knighthood of the British Empire.* London, 1842. Volume III. *History of the Most Honourable Order of the Bath.* p 39.
3 Beattie, John M. *The English Court in the Reign of George I.* Cambridge, 1967. p 218.
4 Wagner, Sir Anthony. *Heralds of England.* H.M.S.O. London, 1967. The author is indebted to Sir Anthony Wagner's splendid book for many of the details about John Anstis' career.
5 Wagner, p 357.
6 Anstis, John. *Observations Introductory to an Historical Essay Upon the Knighthood of the Bath.* London, 1725. pp 1, 2.
7 Nicolas, p 12.
8 Anstis. Appendix. pp 47, 48, 51.
9 Ashmole, Elias. *The Institution, Laws & Ceremonies of the Most Noble Order of the Garter.* London, 1672. p 15.
10 Ashmole, p 15.
11 Anstis. p 70.
12 Anstis, pp 71, 72.
13 Wagner, p 357.
14 Anstis, pp 38, 39.
15 Anstis, p 48; Appendix. p 51.
16 Anstis, p 87.

CHAPTER II: *Mr Anstis' New Order*

1 Nicolas, p 32. Footnote 3.
2 Anstis. Appendix LXXXIV, p 34.
3 Nicolas, pp 237, 238. Footnote 7.
4 Anstis, p 42.
5 Statutes. Articles 7, 8. pp 9–24.
6 Nicolas, p 38.
7 Statutes. Articles 19, 20. p 43.
8 Nicolas, pp 226, 227.
9 Nicolas, p 234.
10 Beattie, p 51.
11 Statutes. Article 6. p 8.
12 *War Office Bath Record Books.* In 1971 a group of six record books apparently originally in the office of the former Secretary of State for War and the Colonies was turned over to the Central Chancery of the Orders of Knighthood. They cover the period 1825–1851. Five are numbered and bound and contain papers in date sequence. The sixth is not numbered and contains papers for the period from 1825 to the late

1840's. Citations from these volumes will take the form of *W.O.B.*, or *W.O.B.* (*misc.*). *W.O.B.* (*misc.*) No page number. Letter from Sir N. H. Nicolas to R. W. Hay, Permanent Under Secretary of State for War and the Colonies, 16 December 1832.

13 Nicolas, pp 238–247.
14 Leake, Stephen Martin. *Mss. in the College of Arms.* SML 64. p 233.
15 Pine, John. *The Procession and Ceremonies Observed at the Time of the Installation of the Knights Companions of the Most Honourable Military Order of the Bath upon Thursday, 17 June 1725, etc.* London, 1730. Plates XIX, XX.

CHAPTER III: *The Order in the Eighteenth Century*

1 Ernst-Browning, William. *Memoirs of Philip Dormer, 4th Earl of Chesterfield.* London, 1893. pp 32, 33.
2 Ernst-Browning, p. 32.
3 Leake, SML. Vol. III. pp 12, 13.
4 Nicolas, pp 85, 88, 91, 92.
5 Forrester, C. S. *Lord Hornblower.* Boston, 1946. pp 3–5.
6 Wagner, pp 433–436, 445, 446.
7 Nicolas. Appendix H. pp XCVII, XCIX.
8 Nicolas, Sir Nicholas Harris. *The Letters and Despatches of Vice Admiral Lord Viscount Nelson.* London, 1845. Vol. II, p 348.
9 Nicolas, Nelson. p 351.
10 Nicolas, Nelson. pp 400, 401, 467.
11 Larpent, Sir George. *The Private Journal of F. Seymour Larpent.* 2nd Edition. London, 1853. p 90.
12 Nicolas, pp 116–118.
13 Nicolas, p 111.
14 Davies, Godfrey. *Wellington and His Army.* Oxford, 1954. p 120.
15 Brett-James, Anthony. *General Graham, Lord Lynedoch.* London, 1959, p 222.
16 Nicolas, pp 121–123.

CHAPTER IV: The Great *Upheaval of 1815*

1 W.O.B. (misc.) Letter from Sir G. Nayler to R. W. Hay, Permanent Under Secretary for War and the Colonies, 4 February 1829.
2 *The London Gazette, Number 16972.* Supplement. Tuesday, 3 January 1815.
3 Gazette. p 1 *et seq.* for all quotations.
4 Gazette. Art XVII.
5 Quoted in Nicolas, p 271.
6 *Dictionary of National Biography.* Vol. III. Campbell, Sir James, p 815.
7 Private Archive. Admiralty letter to Rear Admiral Sir Pultney Malcolm, K.C.B. dated 3 January 1815.

8 Private Acrhive. Prince Regent's letter to Lord Bathurst, 7 December 1819.
9 W.O.B. (misc.) Letter from Sir G. Nayler to R. W. Hay, 4 February 1829.
10 W.O.B. (misc.) Letter from Sir G. Nayler to R. W. Hay, 20 November 1829; Nicolas, pp 140–142.
11 W.O.B. (misc.) Letter from Sir W. Woods to R. W. Hay, 13 June 1834; Nicolas, pp 138–140, 144; W.O.B. (misc.)
12 W.O.B. (misc.) Letter of Dean Ireland to Sir Herbert Taylor, 23 May 1832.
13 Nicolas, pp 133–137.

CHAPTER V: *Transition and Attempts at Reform*

1 Nicolas, p 146.
2 Nicolas, pp 151–154, 164, 165.
3 W.O.B. Vol. I. Letter from Sir W. Woods to R. W. Hay, 13 June 1834; Royal Archives L. 8. Letter from the Duke of Wellington to R. W. Hay, 23 November 1839.
4 W.O.B. Vol. III. Admiralty letter to Lord Glenelg, 27, 30 July 1835.
5 W.O.B. Vol. III. Document 1030. Letter from the Duke of Sussex to Lord John Russell, 23 June 1840.
6 W.O.B. Vol. I. Letter from Sir W. Woods to R. W. Hay, 13 June 1834.
7 W.O.B. Vol. III. Correspondence between the Duke of Sussex and Lord John Russell dated 23 July, 7 August and 16 August 1841.
8 W.O.B. (misc.) Letter from Sir G. Nayler to R. W. Hay, 29 July 1830.
9 W.O.B. (misc.) Letter from Sir W. Woods to Prince Albert. 25 June 1843; W.O.B. Vol. II. Letter from the Lord Chamberlain to Sir W. Woods, 20 August 1834.
10 W.O.B. Vol. II. Letter from Lord Uxbridge to the Duke of Sussex, 1 June 1840; letter from Lord J. Russell to the Duke of Sussex, 15 June 1840; letter from the Duke of Sussex to Lord Uxbridge, 8 July 1840.
11 W.O.B. Vol. I. The material dealing with Sir N. H. Nicolas' proposals regarding the Bath are based on his memorandum of 16 December 1832, sent to R. W. Hay; subsequent correspondence with Hay during 1833 and 1834; and the record of his shattering interview with Sir Herbert Taylor on 10 May 1834. The latter document also gives the full story of his troubles with the King in connection with the Chancellorship of St Michael and St George. The details of Lord Stanley's resolution about reforming the Bath, presented to the House on 17 April 1834, and the subsequent debate on the matter will be found in Nicolas, pp 168–181.
12 Nicolas, p 170.
13 Nicolas, p 177.
14 Nicolas, p 176.
15 W.O.B. Vol. I. Letter from Sir N. H. Nicolas to R. W. Hay dated 23 April 1834.
16 Nicolas, p 181.

CHAPTER VI: *Prince Albert Takes Charge*

1 Creston, Dormer. *The Youthful Queen Victoria*. New York, 1952. p 238.
2 Queen Victoria, *Diary*.
3 W.O.B. Vol. III. Document 1030. Letter from the Duke of Sussex to Lord John Russell, 23 June 1840.
4 W.O.B. Vol. I. Letter from Sir W. Woods to R. W. Hay 13 June 1834.
5 W.O.B. Vol. III. Correspondence between the Duke of Sussex and Lord John Russell dated 23 July, 7 August and 16 August 1841.
6 W.O.B. (misc.) Letter from Sir G. Nayler to R. W. Hay, 29 July 1830.
7 W.O.B. (misc.) Letter from Sir W. Woods to Prince Albert. 25 June 1843; W.O.B. Vol. II. Letter from the Lord Chamberlain to Sir W. Woods, 20 August 1834.
8 W.O.B. Vol. II. Letter from Lord Uxbridge to the Duke of Sussex, 1 June 1840; letter from Lord J. Russell to the Duke of Sussex, 15 June 1840; letter from the Duke of Sussex to Lord Uxbridge, 8 July 1840.
9 W.O.B. (misc.) Correspondence between the Duke of Sussex and Lord Stanley, 1842–1843.
10 W.O.B. (misc.) Letters exchanged between Lord Stanley and Prince Albert dated 13 June and 3 July 1843; 23 July 1845; draft Statutes prepared by Albert Woods.
11 *Royal Archives*. The following section is based on the correspondence relating to the Order of the Bath addressed by Lord Grey and Sir Robert Peel to Prince Albert from September 1846 to May 1847 filed under RA E35/10–35 and RA Add. B2 for letters of Prince Albert during the same period.
12 W.O.B. Vol. III. Letters exchanged by Sir H. Douglas with the Duke of Sussex and by the Duke and Lord Stanley, dated 1, 3 and 11 October 1841.
13 Letters Patent and Statutes of the Order of the Bath. Supplement to *The London Gazette*, 25 May 1847, No. 20737, pp 1947–1957.
14 W.O.B. Vol. III. Letter from Lord Grey to Prince Albert, dated 21 May 1847.
15 W.O.B. Vol. IV. Letters from Albert Woods to India, Lord Grey and the Prince dated from June 1849 to January 1850.
16 RA Add. B2/154. Letter from Lord Grey to the Queen, 26 February 1851.
17 The Queen to Lord Grey. RA Add. B2/155.
18 Benson, A. C. and Esher, Viscount (Editor's). *Letters of Queen Victoria*. 1st Series. London, 1907. Vol. III, p 269. Letter to Lord Panmure, 9 November 1856. Later citations from the full series will be restricted to the date under the heading *Victoria*, except in those cases where the date is used in the text when no citation will be given.
19 *Hansard's Parliamentary Debates*. 1856. Vol. CXL 29 February 1856. Column 1624.
20 Private Archive. War Office letter from Lord Panmure to Prince Albert, No. 0172/462 dated 26 December 1857.
21 RA N23/6–81. Correspondence between Prince Consort and Sir Charles Wood, April 1860.
22 RA B18/140. Letter from Lord Palmerston to Lord John Russell, 15 October 1860.

CHAPTER VII: *The Late Victorian Age*

1   RA B19/60. Letter from Sir Charles Phipps to the Queen, 6 January 1862.
2   RA E14/4. Letter from the Duke of Cambridge to Sir Charles Phipps, 7 January 1862.
3   Confidential, "Memorandom on the Order of the Bath". Private Office, Admiralty, April, 1896. pp. 12-18.
4   Maurice, Sir F. and Arthur, Sir G. *The Life of Lord Wolseley*. New York, 1922. p 73.
5   Ponsonby, Arthur. *Henry Ponsonby, Queen Victoria's Private Secretary*. New York, 1943. p 330.
6   *Dictionary of National Biography*. Layard, Austen. Vol. 22, p 950.
7   Arthur, Sir George. *The Letters of Lord and Lady Wolseley*, 1870–1911. New York, 1922. p 219.
8   Buckle, G. E. (Editor). *The Letters of Queen Victoria*, 3rd Series. London, 1930. Volume I. pp 17, 18.
9   Buckle, G. E. Op. cit. pp 393, 394.
10 Ponsonby, pp 66, 67.
11 Penshurst, Lord Hardinge of. *Old Diplomacy*. London, 1947. pp 56, 57.
12 Hansard. 6 September 1887. Columns 1474–1842; 1 March 1888, Columns 1875–78.
13 RA B37/62. Letter from H. Campbell-Bannerman to the Queen, 11 May 1886.
14 RA R54/27. Letter from H. Campbell-Bannerman to Sir H. Ponsonby, 16 May 1886.
15 RA R54/38. Letter from Sir H. Ponsonby to the Queen, 9 July 1886.
16 RA L715/54, 58, 64. Letters from Mr E. Stanhope and Lord Salisbury to Sir H. Ponsonby, dated 10, 17 and 23 March 1890.
17 RA B46/93, 96, 98. Letters from Lord Rosebery to the Queen and Sir H. Ponsonby dated 1, 4 and 8 December 1893.

CHAPTER VIII: *The New Century*

1   Brett, M. V. (Editor). *Journal and Letters of Reginald, Viscount Esher*, Vol. 2, 1907–1910. p 326.
2   Hardinge of Penshurst. p 165.
3   RA W5/43, 44. Letters dated 14 July and 17 July 1908.
4   Paragraph from a letter in the Archives of the Central Chancery. Further quotations dealing with the revival of the Bath Installation come from the same source and will be mentioned by date without a specific footnote.
5   *The Times*, London, 27 June 1913.

CHAPTER IX: *Modern Times*

1 *Bath Chapel Committee Minutes, and Annual Reports, Central Chancery of the Orders of Knighthood, 1914–1971.* The details of the administration of the Order from 1914 to 1971 are substantially based on these two fundamental documents. Both the *Minutes* and *Reports* have been kept partly in manuscript and partly in typescript in a series of bound notebooks. The dates supplied in the text are intended to serve the same purpose as the page numbers generally furnished when more formal printed sources are cited.

2 *Central Chancery of the Orders of Knighthood.* Revision of Statutes File, 1920–1925.

3 Wingate, Sir Ronald. *Lord Ismay—A Biography.* Hutchinson & Co., Ltd. London, 1970. pp 22, 23.

4 *The Times*, London, 4 July 1935.

CHAPTER X: *The Robes and Insignia in the Eighteenth Century*

1 Anstis, pp 49, 51, 75, 76.

2 *Bath Chapter Minutes*, 1803. This information was taken from a document purchased by the author in London in 1965. It appears to have been kept by someone associated with the Chapter held in 1803 and even includes samples of the silk used for the various garments.

3 Statutes, pp 45, 46.

4 *Lord Chamberlain's Department Papers. Public Record Office.* LC 9/44. pp 275, 278, 279.

5 Statutes, p 44.

6 Nicolas, p 193.

7 Nicolas, p 37.

8 Antiquaries, Society of. *Illustrated Catalogue of the Heraldic Exhibition, Burlington House, 1894.* London. p 16, Number 40 and Plate IX, Number 5.

9 Twining, Lord. *A History of the Crown Jewels of Europe.* London, 1960. p. 151.

10 Windsor Castle. *Catalogue of Gems and Jewels.* #33.

11 Nicolas, p 38.

12 Statutes, p 28.

13 L.C. 2/109. p 355.

14 L.C. 9/44. p 275.

15 Bosanquet, Captain H. T. A. *The Naval Officer's Sword.* H.M.S.O. 1955. pp 238–240.

16 *British Museum Banks Papers.* Additional Mss. 6325, F. 44, p 15.

17 Brett, M. V. (Editor). *Journals and Letters of Reginald Viscount Esher.* London, 1934. Vol. 2, pp 366, 367.

18 L.C. 10/10, p 44.

19 L.C. 9/44, p 279.

20   L.C. 9/44, pp 278, 279.
21   Statutes, pp 45, 46.
22   W.O.B. (misc.) No page number.
23   L.C. 9/350. 25 October 1785; 25 October 1787.

CHAPTER XI: *The Robes and Insignia after 1815*

1   Gazette, Art. 6, p 7.
2   L.C.C. 10/10, p 106.
3   W.O.B. (misc.) Letter from Sir W. Woods to R. W. Hay, 13 June 1834.
4   W.O.B. (misc.) An unnumbered sheet slipped in the pages.
5   L.C.C. 10/10, p 170, D 11.
6   Millar, Oliver. *The Georgian Pictures in the Collection of Her Majesty the Queen.* London, 1969. No. 742. Plate 251.
7   L.C.C. 10/10, p 170.
8   L.C.C. 10/10, p 218.
9   Londonderry, Edith Marchioness of. *Frances Anne.* London, 1958. p 123.
10 L.C.C. 10/10, p 104.
11 L.C.C. 10/10, p 174.
12 Bosanquet, pp 144–213 of this useful book give all the important details about London Sword Cutlers, many of whom became Jewellers. The pattern of changing names and business addresses provides an invaluable guide for dating Stars.
13 W.O.B. Vol. V. 1851–1855.
14 Moore, Smith G. C. (Editor). *The Autobiography of Lieutenant General Sir Harry Smith, Baronet of Aliwal on the Sutlej, G.C.B.* London, 1901. Vol. I, p 311.
15 Bath Book, p 60.
16 W.O.B. (misc.) July 1845.
17 W.O.B. Vol. V., p 170.
18 W.O.B. Vol. V, p 239.
19 W.O.B. Vol. V, p 241.
20 W.O.B. (misc.) and Vol. V, p 1.
21 W.O.B. (misc.)
22 W.O.B. (misc.) 25, 29 May and 5, 10 June 1847.
23 W.O.B. Vol. III.
24 W.O.B. (misc.)
25 Risk, J. C. *British Orders and Decorations.*
26 This is recorded somewhat obscurely in a ca. 1860 copy of the Statutes now in the Central Chancery.
27 Private Archive. August 16, 1858.
28 Private Archive. October 23, 1858.
29 Private Archive. January 1, 1859.
30 Private Archive. July 20, 1857.
31 Central Chancery. Revision of Statutes File, 1920–1925.

BIBLIOGRAPHY

I Manuscript Sources

Central Chancery of the Orders of Knighthood. Bath Chapter Minutes, 1914–1971; Annual Reports, 1904–1971; Revision of Statutes File, 1920–1925.

L.C. Public Record Office. Lord Chamberlain's Department. Jewel Office delivery and account books. Series L.C. 1/47, 59, 67; 2/109; 9/44; 10/10.

Private Archive. This consists of a number of official documents dealing with the Order of the Bath acquired by purchase over a period of years. The papers do not appear to be duplicated in any of the official archives.

RA and RA Add. Royal Archives, Windsor Castle. Letters relating to the Order of the Bath from the B, E, L, N, R and Victoria Additional Manuscripts series.

S.M.L. Leake, Stephen Martin. A Manuscript by Leake preserved in the College of Arms.

W.O.B. War Office Bath Record Books. In 1970 a group of six record books apparently originally in the office of the former Secretary of State for War and the Colonies was turned over to the Central Chancery of the Orders of Knighthood. They cover the period 1825–1851. Five are numbered and bound and contain papers in date sequence. The sixth is not numbered and contains papers from 1825 to the late 1840's. Citations from these books will be preceded by W.O.B. and W.O.B. (Misc).

II Printed Sources

ANSTIS, John. *Observations Introductory to an Historical Essay Upon the Knighthood of the Bath.* London, 1725.

ANTIQUARIES, Society of. *Illustrated Catalogue of the Heraldic Exhibition, Burlington House, 1894.* London, 1896.

ARTHUR, Sir George. *The Letters of Lord and Lady Wolseley, 1870–1911.* New York, 1922.

ASHMOLE, Elias. *The Institution, Laws & Ceremonies of the Most Noble Order of the Garter*. London, 1672.

BEATTIE, Dr J. M. *The English Court in the Reign of George I*. Cambridge, 1967.

BENSON, A. C., Esher, Viscount and G. E. Buckle. *The Letters of Queen Victoria*. 1st, 2nd & 3rd series. John Murray. London, 1907, 1926, 1930.

BOSANQUET, Captain H. T. A. *The Naval Officer's Sword*. H.M.S.O. London, 1955.

BRETT, M. V. (Editor). *Journals and Letters of Reginald, Viscount Esher*. 4 volumes. Ivor Nicholson & Watson. London, 1934.

BRETT-JAMES, Anthony. *General Graham, Lord Lynedoch*. MacMillan & Co., Ltd. London, 1959.

CRESTON, Dormer. *The Youthful Queen Victoria*. G. P. Putnam's Sons. New York, 1952.

DAVIES, Godfrey. *Wellington and His Army*. Oxford, 1954.

ERNST-BROWNING, William. *Memoirs of Philip Dormer Stanhope, 4th Earl of Chesterfield*. London, 1893.

FORESTER, C. S. *Lord Hornblower*. Little, Brown & Co. Boston, 1946.

Hansard's Parliamentary Debates. 1856 and 1887.

LARPENT, Sir George. *The Private Journal of F. Seymour Larpent*. 2nd. Edition. London, 1853.

The London Gazette. Number 16972 Supplement. January 3, 1815. Number 20737 Supplement. May 25, 1847.

LONDONDERRY, Edith Marchioness of. *Frances Anne*. MacMillan & Co., Ltd. London, 1958.

MAURICE, Sir F. and ARTHUR, Sir G. *The Life of Lord Wolseley*. New York, 1922.

MILLAR, Oliver. *The Georgian Pictures in the Collection of Her Majesty The Queen*. Phaidon Press. 2 volumes. London, 1969.

MOORE, Smith G. C. (Editor). *The Autobiography of Sir Harry Smith, Baronet of Aliwal on the Sutlej, G.C.B.* London, 1901.

NICOLAS, Sir N. Harris. *History of the Orders of Knighthood of the British Empire*. 4 volumes. London, 1842.

NICOLAS, Sir N. Harris. *The Letters and Despatches of Vice Admiral Lord Viscount Nelson*. 7 volumes. London, 1845.

PENSHURST, Lord Hardinge of. *Old Diplomacy*. John Murray. London, 1947.

PINE, John. *The Procession and Ceremonies Observed at the Time of the Installation of the Knights Companions of the Most Honourable Military Order of the Bath Upon Thursday, June 17, 1725*. London, 1730.

PONSONBY, Arthur. *Henry Ponsonby, Queen Victoria's Private Secretary*. The MacMillan Co. New York, 1943.

RISK, J. C. *British Orders and Decorations*. New York, 1945.

Statutes of the Most Honourable Order of the Bath. London, 1812.

STEPHEN, Sir L. and LEE, Sir S. (Editors). *Dictionary of National Biography*. XXII volumes. Oxford University Press, 1950.

'THE TIMES.' London. June 27, 1913; July 4, 1935.

TWINING, Lord. *A History of the Crown Jewels of Europe*. Batsford. London, 1960.

WAGNER, Sir Anthony. *Heralds of England*. H.M.S.O. London, 1967.

Windsor Castle. *Catalogue of Gems and Jewels*.

WINGATE, Sir Ronald. *Lord Ismay—A Biography*. Hutchinson & Co., Ltd. London, 1970.

PLATES

PLATE I

John Anstis, Garter King of Arms
who originated the Order in 1725.

PLATE II

John Duke of Montagu, K.G.
The First Great Master of the Order, 1725–1749.

John Duke *of* Montague K.G.
Mas.^r Genl of the Ordinance
Ob 1749

PLATE III

Prince Frederick Augustus, Bishop of Osnabruck
and later Duke of York, as a boy in 1770,
wearing the full Habit of a Knight Companion.

FREDERICK II SON OF
GEORGE THE III
KING OF GREAT BRITAIN
BISHOP OF OSNABRUG
AGED VII YEARS SIX MONTHS
FEB. MDCCLXX
R. MORTON pix

PLATE IV

Sir Albert Woods, G.C.V.O., K.C.B., K.C.M.G.
Registrar and Secretary of the Order, 1859–1904.

PLATE V

Early Badges of the Knighthood and the Order of the Bath

1 One of the Badges made for the Knights created at the Coronation of Charles II in 1661. Gold, green enamel and a pendant pearl.

2 A Sash Badge of a Knight of the Bath similar to that illustrated by Sir Harris Nicolas. Gold and white enamel with a plain reverse.

3 A Collar Badge of the Order, ca 1750. Gold.

All the pieces are unmarked.

PLATE VI

The Insignia of a Knight Companion

1 A Collar Badge, ca 1780. Gold.

2 A Collar Badge, ca 1797–1814. Gold.

3 A Star, ca 1800–1805. Silver, gold and red enamel with hinged rays.

All the pieces are unmarked.

PLATE VII

George IV's Star of a Knight Companion, 1813

The Star is silver, gold and red enamel, with the centre set
with brilliants and small diamonds. The reverse is engraved.

Rundell, Bridge and Rundell
Jewellers
TO THEIR MAJESTIES
His Royal Highness the
PRINCE REGENT
and the Royal Family

PLATE VIII

Lord Nelson's Collar of the Bath in possession of Lloyds

The Collar is in gold and coloured enamels. The plain
gold Badge resembles that illustrated as No. 2 on Plate VI.
Neither pieces is marked.

PLATE IX

The Insignia of the Officers of the Bath

1 Bath King of Arms. Gold and coloured enamels.

2 The Registrar and Secretary. Gold and coloured enamels.

3 The Genealogist. Gold and coloured enamels.

4 The Gentleman Usher and Scarlet Rod. Gold and coloured enamels.

All the pieces are unmarked.

1

2

3

4

PLATE X

The Collar of a G.C.B., with Badge Appendant, worn by Frederick III,
German Emperor and King of Prussia

1 The elements of the hallmark on the Collar include a lower case 'e' for 1820, the maker's initials 'JJE' and the lion passant for the 22 carat fineness of the metal.

2 The Collar Badge. The elements of the hallmark carry the upper case 'T' for 1814, the maker's mark 'IN', and the lion passant for the 22 carat fineness of the metal.

1

2

PLATE XI

The Crowned Sash Badge of a G.C.B. worn by George IV

The elements of the hallmark carry the upper case 'T' for 1814, the maker's mark 'IE', and the lion passant for the 22 carat fineness of the metal. This is the 'broad armed' type of G.C.B. Badge.

PLATE XII

The Sovereign's Badge of the Bath

The elements of the hallmark are not visible. This is the 'narrow armed' type of the K.C.B. Badge with the Crown added. It originally belonged to Francis Rawdon, 1st Marquess of Hastings.

PLATE XIII

The first G.C.B. Stars

1 A large Star of the type worn before June, 1815. The reverse carries the name of Rundell, Bridge and Rundell in the style described on Plate VII, and the Cambridge family 'No. 1'. This figure indicates it was the first of the Stars that belonged to Adolphus Frederick Duke of Cambridge, the youngest son of George III.

2 A small Star of the type worn after Waterloo. The reverse is engraved as above with the exception of the Cambridge family number.

1

2

PLATE XIV

Late Georgian Insignia of a G.C.B.

1 The Sash Badge. The elements of the hallmark include a lower case 'h' for 1823, the makers initials 'IE' for John Edwards, and a lion passant to indicate the 22 carat fineness of the metal.

2 The Star, ca 1830–1837. Silver, gold and coloured enamels.

The reverse is engraved:

HAMLET
Goldsmith and Jeweller
TO THEIR MAJESTIES
& ROYAL FAMILY
Princes St., Leicester Squ.
LONDON

1

2

PLATE XV

The first Insignia of a K.C.B.

1 The Badge, with the original ring. The elements of the hallmark include an upper case 'T' for 1814 and the lion passant for the 22 carat fineness of the metal. This is the 'broad armed' type, of K.C.B. Badge.

2 The reverse of the Star is engraved with the name of Rundell, Bridge and Rundell in the style described on Plate VII.

1

2

PLATE XVI

Early C.B. Insignia

1 A George III C.B. Badge. The elements of the hallmark include a lower case 'a' for 1816, the maker's initials 'IN', and a lion passant for the 22 carat fineness of the metal.

2 A William IV C.B. Badge. The elements of the hallmark include lower case 's' for 1833. The specimen is one of the less expensive variety first ordered by William IV as Duke of Clarence in 1827.

1   2

PLATE XVII

Mid Victorian Military G.C.B. Stars

1 A G.C.B. Star, ca 1850–1855. Silver, gold and coloured enamel. The reverse carried the maker's mark 'WN' and is engraved

R & S Garrard & Co.
Goldsmiths, Jewellers &c
To the Queen
his Royal Highness Prince Albert
and all the Royal Family
Panton Street, London

2 A presentation G.C.B. Star, ca 1856–1860. Silver, gold, coloured enamel, small diamonds and emeralds. The reverse carried the maker's mark 'WN' and is engraved

WIDDOWSON & VEALE
Goldsmiths
73 Strand
LONDON

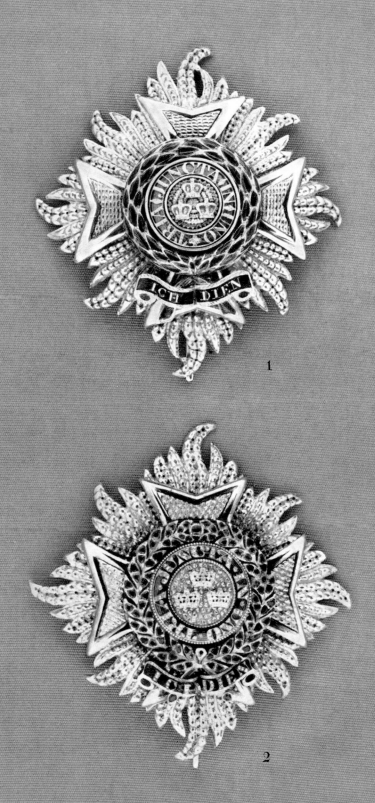

1

2

PLATE XVIII

Late Victorian Insignia of a Military G.C.B.

1 A G.C.B. Star in silver, gold and coloured enamels. There are no marks but the style of execution indicated that the piece was made by Garrards.

2 The Sash Badge. The elements of the hallmark include an upper case 'B' for 1877, the maker's initials 'RG' for Garrard & Co. and the figure '18' to indicate the fineness of the metal.

1

2

PLATE XIX

Late Victorian Insignia of a Military K.C.B.

1 The Badge. The elements of the hallmark include the lower case Gothic 'g' for 1862 and the figure 18 for the fineness of the metal.

2 The Star is silver, gold and coloured enamels. The reverse is engraved.

R & S Garrard & Co.
Goldsmith & Jewellers
to the Crown
23, Haymarket
London

1

2

PLATE XX

The Insignia of a Military D.C.B.

1 The Badge in silver gilt and enamel.

2 The Star in silver, gold and coloured enamel.

1

2

PLATE XXI

The Insignia of the 2nd Earl of Clancarty, the first Civil G.C.B.

1 The Star in silver, gold and red enamel, with the motto in diamonds. The
reverse is not fitted with a pin and is engraved

HAMLET

JEWELLER

to their Royal Highnesses Princesses Augusta, Elizabeth

Mary & Sophia

Princes Street, Leicester Square

————— London —————

Belonged to

The 2nd Earl of Clancarty

1767–1837

Appointed G.C.B. 1st April, 1815

Lord Clancarty also possessed 2 additional small Stars.

2 The Badge, resembling that of a K.B. is unmarked.

1

2

PLATE XXII

The Insignia of a Civil G.C.B., 1820–1830

1 The Star in silver, gold and red enamel. The reverse is engraved.

Rundell, Bridge & Rundell
Jewellers
To His Majesty
and
the Royal Family

This particularly fine piece is typical of the Stars made during the reign of George IV.

2 The Investiture Sash Badge. The elements of the hallmark include a lower case 'm' for 1827, the maker's initials 'JJE', and the lion passant for the 22 carat fineness of the metal.

1

2

PLATE XXIII

Early Victorian Civil G.C.B. Insignia

1 The Star in silver, gold, red and white enamel, ca 1855. The reverse carries the maker's initials 'WN'. Heraldically it was perfectly correct to substitute white enamel for silver in the centre.

2 The Investiture Sash Badge. The elements of the hallmark include an upper case Gothic 'C' for 1838, and the lion passant for the 22 carat fineness of the metal.

3 A large Sash Badge, ca 1845–1850. Gold. There are no marks.

1
2   3

PLATE XXIV

The Insignia of a Mid Victorian Civil G.C.B. worn by the 2nd Lord Lyons,
Minister to Washington during the American Civil War

1 The Star in silver, gold and red enamel. The reverse is engraved with the name of Garrard and Co. in the form used during the 1840's, although the piece is the type issued ca 1859–1864. It also carries the name.

Earl Lyons, *G.C.B., G.C.M.G.*

2 The investment Sash Badge. The elements of the hallmark include a lower case Gothic 'e' for 1860, the maker's initials 'RG' for Garrard & Co., and the figure '18' for the fineness of the metal.

1

2

PLATE XXV

The first Insignia of the Civil K.C.B., worn by Sir Benjamin Hawes

1 The Badge, has the original investment ribbon 3 inches in width, and gold suspension clasp. The elements of the hallmark include an upper case Gothic 'M' for 1847, the maker's initials 'RG' for Garrard & Co., and the figure '18' for the fineness of the metal.

2 The embroidered investment Star.

Both pieces are contained in the original Garrard case with Hawes' name written on the silk lining in an old hand.

1

2

PLATE XXVI

Early Civil K.C.B. Stars

1 The earliest type of Civil K.C.B. Star, ca 1847–1850. Silver, gold and red enamel. The Knights were required to purchase metal Stars at their own expense. The reverse is engraved with the name of Widdowson & Veale and carries the maker's initials 'WN'.

2 A foreign made Civil K.C.B. Star, ca 1847–1850. Silver and gold with red and white enamel. The use of Royal in place of Imperial crowns in the centre is incorrect. The reverse is engraved.

Andrews
St. Petersburg.

1

2

PLATE XXVII

Civil C.B. Badges

1 The first Civil C.B. The elements of the hallmark include an upper case
Gothic 'M' for 1847, the maker's initials 'RG' for Garrard & Co., and the
figure '18' for the fineness of the metal.

2 The last C.B. issued for breast wear. Now made in silver gilt, the elements
of the hallmark include a lower case Gothic 'a' for 1916 and the maker's
initials 'SG' for Garrard & Co.

1   2

PLATE XXVIII

The Collar of a Dame Grand Cross

The Collar, in a reduced size, is in silver gilt
and coloured enamels. The Badge has not been
reduced and the reverse side is shown.

INDEX